TERRORISM
IN THE
TWENTY-FIRST
CENTURY

TERRORISM
IN THE
TWENTY-FIRST
CENTURY

Cindy C. Combs

University of North Carolina—Charlotte

Prentice Hall, Upper Saddle River, New Jersey 07458

Library of Congress Cataloging-in-Publication Data

COMBS, CINDY C. [date]
    Terrorism in the twenty-first century / Cindy C. Combs.
    p. cm.
    Includes index.
    ISBN 0-13-490731-0
    1. Terrorism. 2. Terrorism—Forecasting. I. Title.
HV6431.C6472   1997
303.6'25'0112—dc20   96-28270

Editorial director: *Charlyce Jones Owen*
Editor in chief: *Nancy Roberts*
Marketing manager: *Chaunfayta Hightower*
Acquisitions editor: *Michael Bickerstaff*
Editorial/production supervision
  and interior design: *Edie Riker*
Cover design: *Wendy Alling Judy*
Cover photo illustration: *top, AP/Wide World Photos; bottom, Gamma-Liaison, Inc.*
Buyer: *Bob Anderson*
Editorial assistant: *Anita Castro*

This book was set in 10/12 Stone Informal by East End Publishing Services
and was printed and bound by Courier Companies, Inc. The cover
was printed by Phoenix Color Corp.

© 1997 by Prentice-Hall, Inc.
Simon & Schuster / A Viacom Company
Upper Saddle River, New Jersey 07458

Printed in the United States of America

10 9 8 7 6 5 4 3 2 1

ISBN   0-13-490731-0

Prentice-Hall International (UK) Limited, *London*
Prentice-Hall of Australia Pty. Limited, *Sydney*
Prentice-Hall Canada Inc., *Toronto*
Prentice-Hall Hispanoamericana, S.A., *Mexico*
Prentice-Hall of India Private Limited, *New Delhi*
Prentice-Hall of Japan, Inc., *Tokyo*
Simon & Schuster Asia Pte. Ltd., *Singapore*
Editora Prentice-Hall do Brasil, Ltda., *Rio de Janeiro*

CONTENTS

Part Two: Who Are the Terrorists?

CHAPTER SEVEN
How Do They Operate?

Part Three: Responses to Terrorism

CHAPTER EIGHT
Legal Perspectives on Terrorism

CHAPTER NINE
Counterterrorism: The Use of Special Forces

CHAPTER TEN
Terrorism, Intelligence, and the Law

CHAPTER ELEVEN
Security Measures: A Frail Defense   202

Part Four: Conclusions

CHAPTER TWELVE
Future Trends   219

Index   235

PREFACE

Conceived, organized, and written while teaching an undergraduate course in Political Violence, this book addresses the increasingly vital need to understand the phenomenon called "terrorism," which continues to threaten the peace and stability of a post-Cold War world. I began this project because I could not find a book that made clear to students as well as to instructors, not only what terrorism *is* and has been, but also what it may be like as we approach a new century. I searched without success for a text that dealt not only with the reality of terrorist attacks of increasing lethality, but also with an assessment of the laws and special forces that nations within the international community have created to meet this challenge.

It was important, from my perspective, that the book be easy for both students and professors to use, organized clearly and concisely, and presented without prejudice. For the latter reasons, the concept of "terrorism" is examined with emphasis on a legal, operational definition applicable to terrorist *acts*, rather than to the individuals, groups, or states who carry out such acts. This makes the term much less likely to be perjoratively applied, since if the term is applied in the legally correct fashion, it can be done objectively rather than subjectively. It also facilitates the use of the book by a wider audience, since each individual, group, and state can be evaluated in terms of the nature of the actions taken.

In order to make the book "user friendly" for students, I have organized it to catch the interest of, and to build knowledge about, the reality of international terrorism. It begins with a chronology of a few recent terrorist events, making the reader aware of the dimensions of the problem. This is followed by a brief look at terrorism in historical perspective, with emphasis given to understanding the cyclical nature of these acts of violence. Evaluation sections at the end of each chapter challenge readers to apply their understanding to current issues and events. This is particularly useful, since the world has witnessed several "new" terrorist events, whose historic roots contribute significantly to an understanding of this phenomenon.

In addition to building an interest in the study of terrorism, I have tried to highlight criteria by which the types of modern terrorists can be studied. Applying such criteria to individuals, groups, and states makes it possible to differentiate, to some degree, between such terms as "crusaders" and "criminals," between state-sponsored and state-tolerated terrorism, and between "separatist" and "nationalist" groups. Familiarity with operationalized terms makes it easier to apply such terms without prejudice, and more significantly, to evaluate the response options for each type.

The text is organized in a style intended to be quite comfortable for course use in a regular or a seminar-style class. Inclusion of lists of key concepts, case studies, evaluation sections, and strategically significant endnotes are designed to allow people with a variety of learning styles and reading approaches to master the content fairly easily. Faculty can readily accentuate, elaborate, or co-relate examples that are similar, parallel, or contrary, with a sound framework for student background and on-going reference. With this format, I have sought to engage the interest of, and to motivate, a wide range of readers of varied preparatory background and academic experience, in the vitally interesting subject of terrorism.

ACKNOWLEDGMENTS

University of North Carolina–Charlotte has a strong commitment toward the integration of research and teaching, encouraging faculty to generate materials that are of use in the classroom. I have been particularly fortunate in that the Political Science Department offered me a reduction in course load, a chance to teach a course on this topic each year, and continuous friendly support as I struggled to complete the research, writing, and editing of this text. Particular thanks must go to Cheryl Almond, the secretary without which little of this would have been possible, and to Ted Arrington, who continued to help me stay focused on this task. My thanks also to Richter Moore, of Appalachian State University, for encouraging me to begin this task several years ago.

My husband, Lee, stood before me and behind me, pulling and pushing me forward, editing and encouraging me not to give up in spite of the many frustrations. His help on the computer, particularly, made it possible for me to meet my deadlines in spite of a very crowded schedule. Our daughters, Sara, Elizabeth, and Katherine, with their assessments of the inherent "dullness" of social science from a student's perspective, helped me to remember to try to keep the text interesting and exciting to students, who will be its primary consumers.

INTRODUCTION

To get anywhere,
you have to walk over the corpses.

This ruthless declaration by Ilyich Ramirez Sanchez in 1975, made while holding 11 OPEC ministers hostage, evokes the image of terrorists as they have menaced so many lives during the latter part of the twentieth century. When Sanchez, known to the public as "Carlos the Jackal," was taken from his home in the Sudan by French police in the summer of 1994, it seemed to many that his capture might mark the beginning of the end of terrorism. Just as the end of the Cold War has made many governments less willing or able to engage in state-sponsored or state-protected terrorism, many hoped that the capture of "Carlos" was symbolic of a willingness between states to cooperate to end decades of bloody terrorist acts.

Less than one month later, nations reeled from the alarm of learning that weapons-grade plutonium from former Soviet arsenals was "on sale." During the spring and summer of 1994, German police uncovered four attempts to sell smuggled nuclear material that could have actually been used to make an atomic bomb. On August 10 of that year, Lufthansa Flight 3369 from Moscow to Munich was found to contain 350 grams of atomic fuel aboard in a lead-lined suitcase carrying MOX. A Colombian and two Spaniards were arrested.

A 35–year-old German man was arrested two days later trying to sell an extremely pure sample of plutonium to a police informant.

None of the recovered materials were sufficient to produce even a small, crude atomic bomb. But the fact that weapons-grade plutonium was "on the market" has acted as a red-alert for many experts on terrorism in Western governments. Frightening questions have been raised about the possibilities of nuclear terrorism, a potential threat largely written off during the past few decades as too expensive and too politically costly to be an attractive option for most groups engaged in terrorist activities, especially since most nuclear facilities are heavily safeguarded. Now many of those who study terrorism wonder if, with bomb-grade plutonium finally "on sale," there will be a rogue state or group which will try to buy enough material to build a bomb. While it is reassuring to know that the small amounts of material recovered in Germany are not enough to build a bomb, it is disturbing to think that there may be larger deals for nuclear material taking place undetected in other parts of the world.

Terrorism in the twenty-first century may well be quite different from that experienced in the twentieth. The wave of terror that "Carlos the Jackal" embodied is, apparently, fading. Just as the extreme left-wing ideology which Sanchez and others of the 1960s and 1970s embraced is fading in much of the world, so the terrorism of the extreme left, which plagued much of Europe is also becoming less common. The 1980s witnessed the beginning of the shift in contemporary terrorism from ideologies of the extreme left toward fundamentalism from the extreme right. Both types of terror continue to play an important role in international politics, but the pattern for the twenty-first century is less clear.

In order to understand what terrorism may be like in the twenty-first century, it is important to first examine what is known about terrorism in the twentieth century. Political science is founded upon a need to *explain* and to *predict* actions in the political realm. For that purpose, this text will examine the known facets of contemporary terrorism, attempting to answer the primary questions of **what, who, why,** and **how**. Prediction about forthcoming patterns of terrorism can then be based on an understanding of previous and present patterns of behavior.

Terrorism, in spite of the capture of Carlos, has not gone away. It continues to exist, but it is changing. Evaluating present conditions and attempting to predict future trends can offer useful insights for policymakers and for citizens in the new century.

CHAPTER ONE

AN IDEA WHOSE TIME HAS COME?

KEY CONCEPTS

terrorism

mass terror

dynastic assassination

random terror

focused random terror

tactical terror

CHRONOLOGY OF TERROR

08/31/81   Twenty people are injured when a powerful bomb explodes at the U.S. Air Force base in Ramstein, West Germany. The Red Army Faction claimed responsibility.

01/18/82   Lt. Col. Charles Robert Ray is shot and killed while walking to his car in Paris. The Lebanese Armed Revolutionary Faction claimed responsibility.

08/09/82   Gunmen throw a grenade into a Jewish restaurant in Paris and then fired with automatic weapons, killing six people and wounding 27 others. The leftist group, Direct Action, first claimed, and then denied, responsibility for this attack.

09/23/83   One hundred eleven people are killed when a bomb explodes on board an Omani Gulf jet en route from Karachi to Abu Dhabi.

01/18/84   Malcolm Kerr, President of American University in Beirut, is shot and killed as he steps off the elevator to his office on the West Beirut campus. The Islamic Jihad claimed responsibility.

06/14/85   Shi'ite gunmen hijack TWA Flight 847 from Athens. The hijackers shoot and kill one passenger, then disperse the remaining hostages throughout Beirut.

10/07/85   Four Palestinian gunmen hijack the Italian cruise ship *Achille Lauro* off the coast of Egypt. One passenger, a wheelchair-bound American, is shot and killed before the hijack ends.

12/27/85   Palestinian gunmen attack airports in Rome and Vienna with grenades and automatic weapons, killing men, women, and children. Abu Nidal's Revolutionary Army Fatah group claims responsibility.

04/02/86   Four people are killed, including one infant, and nine are injured in a bomb explosion aboard TWA Flight 840 en route from Rome to Athens. The Hawari Group, a radical Palestinian organization, claims responsibility.

04/05/86   A Turkish woman and two U.S. Army sergeants are killed, and nearly 200 people are injured in a bomb explosion in a West Berlin discothèque. Intelligence data links Libya to the bombing.

04/17/86   Peter Kilburn, a librarian at the American University of Beirut, Lebanon, and two British school teachers are killed by their captors in apparent retaliation for the U.S. air raids on Libya on April 15. The pro-Libyan Arab Fedayeen cells claim responsibility for Kilburn's death.

09/05/86   PanAm Flight 73 is hijacked in Pakistan. At 5:55 P.M. (Washington time), four members of Abu Nidal's organization seized a 747 at Karachi International Airport. The hijackers held 374 passengers and 15 crew members hostage for 16 hours. When the ground power units ran out of gas and the lights dimmed on the plane the second night, the gunmen panicked and began firing indiscriminately at the huddled passengers. Twenty-one hostages were killed and more than 60 were seriously injured.

12/27/87   Ronald Strong, an American sailor, died from wounds received on December 26 in a grenade attack on a temporary USO club in Barcelona, Spain. The Catalan Red Liberation Army claimed responsibility.

04/05/88   Hizbollah fighters hijack Kuwait Airways Flight 422 en route from Bangkok, Thailand, to Kuwait. Two Kuwaiti passengers were killed in an effort to dramatize the hijackers' demands.

04/14/88   A car bomb explodes outside the USO club in Naples, Italy, killing five people. The Organization of Jihad Brigades (a Japanese Red Army associated group) claims responsibility.

05/15/88   ANO members fire machine guns and throw grenades in the British Sudan Club and the Acropole Hotel in Khartoum. Eight people are killed.

12/21/88   A PanAm 747 passenger aircraft was destroyed in flight over Lockerbee, Scotland, by a bomb, killing 259 people on board and another 11 on the ground. Two Libyans have been indicted for this operation.

Were the 1980s truly a decade of violence? Perhaps. But it was clearly less violent than those decades during which the world experienced the trauma of global war. There was certainly less loss of life than during the years in which the Indochina conflict raged. Fewer lives were claimed by political violence during the 1980s than are lost annually due to traffic accidents on U.S. highways.

So why is so much attention directed toward developing policies to cope with the terrorist violence of recent years? It has, as experts such as Walter Laqueur point out, attracted what could be considered an inordinate amount of attention, compared with other major problems of our times, such as global debt and world hunger. Terrorism has been the subject of countless speeches by political leaders throughout the world, and the impetus for numerous initiatives and conferences by foreign policy experts. The drama of terrorist-directed events such as those outlined above attracts enormous attention in the press and on television worldwide. Terrorist violence, some have argued, became an accepted method of warfare during the latter part of the twentieth century.

Certainly terrorism has been waged by a wide variety of individuals and groups. It has become a favored tactic by national and religious groups, by groups on both the left and the right of the political spectrum, by nationalist and internationalist movements. It has been used as an instrument of state policy. It has been directed against autocratic as well as democratic regimes, although political democracies have been the most frequent targets. At times it has been an instrument of last resort for movements of national liberation whose political attempts to change the system have failed; and at other times it has been deliberately chosen by such movements *before* other such political options have been attempted.

States have sponsored terrorism outside their own frontiers, and have used terrorism as a weapon against their own citizens. Terrorism has become, paradoxically, both an instrument designed to force radical social and political changes, and an instrument of oppression in seeking to prevent such changes.

Even with the increased use of terrorist violence, or perhaps *because* of its proliferation, there remains a great deal of confusion as to what the term "terrorism" really encompasses. Many definitions of terrorism are, in fact, encoded political statements. Too often the term is used in a pejorative sense, attached as a label to those groups whose political objectives one finds objectionable. In order to study this phenomenon, we must first establish a workable and useful definition—workable in that it has sufficient precision to allow us to identify the phenomenon when it occurs, and useful in that it is acceptable to a fairly broad range of political persuasions. For terrorism is a politicized term, just as terrorism is a political crime. Its definition must therefore be politically acceptable.

MODERN DEFINITIONS OF AN OLD CONCEPT

Terrorism is a phenomenon that is becoming a pervasive, often a dominant influence in our lives. It affects the manner in which governments conduct their foreign policy and the way corporations transact their business. It causes alterations in the role and even in the structure of our security forces. It forces us to spend huge amounts of time and money to protect our public figures, vital installations, citizens, and even our system of government. It influences the way we travel and the choices we make when we travel. It even affects the manner in which we live our daily lives. Our newspapers, radios, and televisions inundate our every waking moment with vivid details of spectacular terrorist news from all corners of the globe.

But what *is* "terrorism"—this "it" to which we attribute so much influence today? Before we can assess just how great a threat "it" poses and exactly whom "it" threatens, we need to determine what "terrorism" is. And it is precisely this problem of definition that has caused political, legal, and military leaders to throw up their hands, metaphorically, in discouragement and dismay.

Because terrorism is a political as well as a legal and a military issue, its definition in modern terms has been slow to evolve. Not that there are not numerous definitions available—there are hundreds. But few of them are of sufficient legal scholarship to be useful in international law, and most of those which are legally useful lack the necessary ambiguity for political acceptance.

Thus, the problem of defining terrorism is not insuperable, but it must be handled with caution in order that the subsequent use of the term will have meaning. To say that the number of terrorist incidents is rising annually would have little clear meaning unless it is clear precisely what such a terrorist incident *is* and *is not*.

Moreover, it helps to put the term into a historical perspective. Terrorism is not a modern phenomenon. The admixture of religion and politics fomenting terrorism in many areas today has a counterpart in the Hashashin of the Middle Ages. Incidents such as the *Achille Lauro* hijacking have precedents dating back many centuries. The statement that "one man's terrorist is another man's patriot" illustrates the historical continuum of conflict under which terrorism is operationally defined.

Ideology has always had an ambiguous relationship with terrorism—at one point justifying and at another condemning the same act. Theorists (and practitioners) of both the left and right have advocated the use of what has been termed "terrorist" violence. Understanding the context of the ideological debate helps to deal with the "justifications" offered in contemporary times for terrorist acts.

It also helps to assess the ideological commitment of the perpetrators of terrorism. Profiling modern terrorists is one way of assessing what terrorists are committed *to* today. An understanding of the impact of group dynamics is also useful in critiquing the rationale behind such acts. Patterns in the type of recruiting done among groups committing terrorist acts lends substance to these "profiles" of modern terrorists.

But terrorism is not strictly a phenomenon committed by individuals or groups. In fact, terrorism as a political term derived from *state* terror. So analysis of ways in which states use "terrorism" as an instrument of foreign and domestic policy offers interesting insights.

Some states are even involved in the network emerging among individuals and groups today involved in the commission of terrorist acts. Opinions differ as to the extent, cohesiveness, and ideological commitment of this network, but evidence of its existence is beyond reasonable dispute. Nations such as Libya, Syria, and Iran have repeatedly been accused of involvement in state-sponsored terrorism. The linkage between these states and terrorism will be explored in depth later, focusing on questions such as: How is the terrorism financed? What are its targets? These and other fascinating questions offer opportunities to plumb the murky depths of the terror network.

Understanding of *why* and *who* leads to questions of *how*. Profiles of terrorist events offer thumbnail sketches and interesting insights into the *how* of terrorism. The depth of media involvement in the making of a "terrorist spectacular," for instance, can provide useful clues to understanding why this is so sensitive an area of democratic policymaking. Analysis of potential targets and weapons raises crucial and frightening questions for democratic systems.

The responses of the systems—legal, military, and political—to the threat and reality of terrorism is, of course, crucial to any understanding of the problem of terrorism today. The willingness as well as the capacity of a nation to respond to this form of "warfare" is critical to any assessment of the role of terrorism in shaping our world. The differences between the responses to domestic as opposed to international terrorism may also be critical as democratic nations seek ways to respond to terrorism without sacrificing fundamental principles of democracy.

Ultimately, the question may not be how nations can eliminate terrorism—since it is indeed a centuries-old practice and well entrenched as a useful tool in warfare—but rather how much terrorism a state can tolerate today. New laws and new technology are changing the face of terrorism, but if it is not vanishing, then new thresholds for "acceptable" violence may well be emerging.

This book in no sense covers *all* that could be said about terrorism. It is a contemporary review of current acts of terrorism. Definitions of "terrorism," like the act itself, continue to undergo changes. The definition suggested in the following unit highlights certain important facets of the issue, answering some questions while raising a multitude of others. Such a study can only provide a frame of reference from which it should be possible to analyze this phenomenon—the instrument and the nemesis of rulers, governments, and citizens.

CRUCIAL COMPONENTS OF TERRORISM

Whereas it certainly is not possible, yet, to create a universally acceptable definition of "terrorism," it is both possible and necessary to specify certain features common to the phenomenon. This in turn makes it feasible to create an operational definition of this term. Acts possessing *all* of these attributes could then be identified as "terrorists" acts with some consistency. Without falling into the political quagmire of attempting to label individuals or groups as "terrorist," certain types of *actions* could be identified as "terrorism," regardless of who commits them, for however noble a cause.

Let us consider a loose definition of contemporary terrorism. It must of necessity be "loose," since its elements tend to form a wide variety of compounds which today fall within the rubric of "terrorism." For the purposes of this investigation, **terrorism** will be defined as *a synthesis of war and theater, a dramatization of the most proscribed kind of violence—that which is perpetrated on innocent victims—played before an audience in the hope of creating a mood of fear, for political purposes.*

There are, in this description of terrorism, a number of crucial components. Terrorism, by this definition, involves *an act of violence, and audience, the creation of a mood of fear, innocent victims, and political motives or goals.* Each of these elements deserves some clarification in order to formulate a clear set of parameters for this frequently misunderstood and misused term.

Violence, Audience, and a Mood of Fear

First, it is important to note that terrorism is fundamentally a violent act. Sit-ins, picket lines, walk-outs, and other similar forms of protest, no matter how disruptive, are *not* terrorist acts. Violence—the threat of violence and the capacity and the willingness to commit violence—is endemic to terrorism. The violence need not be fully perpetrated—that is, the bomb need not be detonated or all of the passengers aboard an airliner killed—in order for it to be considered a "terrorist" act. But the capacity and the willingness to commit a violent act *must* be present.

This means, then, that it is the *perception* of the audience of that violent potential that is crucial to classifying an act as terrorism. Terrorism is, essentially, theater, an act played before an audience, designed to call the attention of millions, even hundreds of millions, to an often unrelated situation through shock—by doing the unthinkable without apology or remorse—thereby producing situations of outrage and horror. Unlike similar acts of murder or warfare, acts of terrorism are neither ends in themselves, nor are they often more than tangentially related to the ends sought. They are simply crafted to create a mood of fear or terror in that audience.

This mood is not the result, moreover, of the *numbers* of casualties caused by the act of violence. Automobile accidents cause greater numbers of injuries and deaths each year in the United States without necessarily invoking a mood of terror among other drivers or pedestrians. Nor is it the deliberate nature of the death inflicted which causes the audience response. Individuals are murdered in nonpolitical, nonterrorist acts throughout the world each year without provoking widespread fear.

Victims: The Right Place—
But It Must Have Been the Wrong Time

Instead, the creation of this mood of intense anxiety seems to be specifically linked to the nature of the victim of terrorist acts. As one scholar notes,

> To qualify as an appropriate victim of a terrorist today, we need not be tyrants or their sympathizers; we need not be connected in anyway with the evils the terrorist perceives; we need not belong to a particular group. We need only be in the wrong place at the wrong time.[1]

Terrorism is thus distinguished from guerrilla warfare by deliberate attacks upon innocent persons and the separation of its victims from the ultimate goal—the "playing to an audience" aspect of a terrorist act. Terrorism can be distinguished from legal acts of warfare and ordinary crimes of murder. As David Fromkin points out,

> Unlike the soldier, the guerrilla fighter, or the revolutionist, the terrorist
> . . . is always in the paradoxical position of undertaking actions the im-
> mediate physical consequences of which are not particularly desired by
> him. An ordinary murderer will kill someone because he wants the per-
> son to be dead, but a terrorist will shoot somebody even though it is a
> matter of complete indifference to him whether that person lives or
> dies.[2]

Put more simply, the difference between a terrorist act and a similar crime or war activity is that terrorist acts are perpetrated *deliberately* upon innocent third parties in an effort to coerce the opposing
party or persons into some desired political course of action. Victims
are thus chosen, not primarily because of their personal guilt (in terms
of membership in an opposing military or governmental group), but
because their deaths or injuries will so shock the opposition that con-
cession can be forced to prevent a recurrence of the incident, or in
order to focus attention on a particular political cause. Terrorist acts,
in other words, are constructed to deliberately "make war" on innocent persons.

This distinction needs some explanation. The laws of war permit waging war between national armies, within certain humanitarian limits. Even against an enemy in a violent protracted conflict,
some types of behavior (such as genocide and torture) are expressly
forbidden, and certain basic amenities are required to be preserved
(regarding such issues as the treatment of prisoners-of-war).[3] "War"
as waged by terrorist acts violates these rules in that those deliberately destroyed are not principally armed military opponents, but
hapless civilians. Rules of international behavior, particularly those
which pertain to political responsibility and military obligations, offer
maximum protection to the innocent person. Terrorism makes a practice of persistent, deliberate harm to precisely that type of person.

The distinction between a terrorist act and a legitimate act of
guerrilla warfare is not always clear. General George Grivas, founder
and head of the Cypriot EOKA asserted in his memoirs: "We did not
strike, like a bomber, at random. We shot only British servicemen who
would have killed us if they could have fired first, and civilians who
were traitors or intelligence agents."[4] The French Resistance, the Polish Underground, and the Greek Guerrillas were called "terrorists" by
the Nazis of the occupation; yet they, like the EOKA, attacked primarily military personnel, government officials, and local collaborators.

During World War II, the Polish-Jewish Underground planted explosives at the Cafe Cyganeria in Cracow, a meeting place for Nazi
officers, which no doubt resulted in injury to Polish waiters as well as
to the desired military targets.[5] The point here is that the terrorist deliberately chooses to invoke injury on the innocent in an effort to

shock the "guilty" political or military audience. Injury to the innocent thus is not an undesirable accident or byproduct, but the carefully sought consequence of a terrorist act.

A "terrorist" act is committed not against a military target necessarily—as the individual or group perpetrating the act does not seek to overthrow by military force—nor against the person in direct opposition to the perpetrators, as the ultimate goal is not usually the death of one leader. Unlike the "terrorism" practiced by nineteenth-century anarchists, twentieth-century terrorist acts have been deliberately aimed against noncombatants, unarmed third parties whose loss of well-being can be expected to evoke a desired response from the opposition or from the "audience" watching the event throughout the world.

Until recently it appeared that, although most of the victims of terrorism were innocent of any crime, they were also relatively few in number. In those terrorist incidents recorded in the 1950s and 1960s, the actual number of casualties was relatively small. It has been speculated that perhaps the terrorists felt a need to avoid alienating certain groups of people or portions of society. Perhaps it was also true that terrorists ". . . want a lot of people watching, not a lot of people dead."[6]

But the recent bombings of crowded passenger airplanes and the slaughter of family groups at airports would appear to herald a loosening of the threads which have constrained terrorists in their search for victims. As the craving for a worldwide audience increases among groups utilizing terrorism, the increasing tolerance of that audience for violence may actually be pushing terrorists to widen their target range, to create a more "spectacular" event for their audience.

Thus, as the violence becomes more randomized, it is being directed against a wider range of innocent persons. Children are becoming targets, as the massacres at the Rome and Vienna airports demonstrated. Ironically, this increase in innocent targets may well be a direct result of a viewing audience which is no longer as interested in attacks on military attachès or political figures.

"Political" Quicksand

Terrorism, then, is an act of violence, perpetrated on an innocent person in order to evoke fear in an audience. There is, though, one further component necessary to this definition. As it stands, such a definition could reasonably be applied to actions taken by professional sportsmen on the playing field!

But the addition of a "political purpose" to the concept of terrorism continues to create enormous legal problems. While it is obviously crucial to establish parameters for this concept of "political purpose," particularly in light of the fact that "political" crimes and criminals have enjoyed special status under international law for centuries, the concept remains largely undefined.

Much of the confusion today results from a misperception that the presence of political *motivation* is sufficient to establish the political character of an action. A recent extradition case clearly stated that "an offense is not of a political character simply because it was politically motivated."[7] The prevailing Anglo-American rule of law has been derived from *in re Castroni*, in which two basic criteria were given for determining the political quality of an action. These requirements, simply stated, were that (a) the act at issue must have occurred during a political revolt or disturbance, and that (b) the act at issue must have been incidental to and have formed part of that same revolution or disturbance.[8]

A political motive thus may be termed *necessary* but it is not *sufficient* to earn for an action a "political offense" status under international law. Nicholas Kittrie has suggested that a "pure political offense" would consist of acts "which challenge the State but affect no private rights of innocent parties."[9] By this definition, a political revolution or disturbance is an essential ingredient, in which the "political offense" plays only a part. Moreover, the offense must bring harm *only* to the State, while protecting innocent parties from harm through reasonable precautions. This has the effect of narrowing the classes of acceptable victims and of eliminating the random acts of lone assassins.

Political assassination by committed revolutionaries careful to cause as little harm as possible to innocent persons remains thus protected to some extent within the "political offense" provisions of international law. Hence, the assassination of the Grand Duke Sergius might qualify for "political offense" status, while the mob violence of the Paris Commune would certainly not.

Obviously, the "political" element of an act of terrorism adds considerable confusion, both in the legal and the political realm. While it is a necessary component to a definition of terrorism, it is so ambiguous a concept that it is often a two-edged sword, offering insights into the causes of an act while providing gaping loopholes in the law through which perpetrators of heinous acts continue to slither.

One legal expert has described the problem in this manner:

> In order to maintain a proper balance between human rights and world order, it is imperative that the world community in rejecting the proposition that all forms of violence are justified if supported by political goals, avoid the trap of supporting the other extreme, that violent opposition to an established regime is never permissible by international standards. Consequently, the principles of self-defense and the require-

ment of proportionality need to be reexamined, refined, and injected more vigorously into this area.[10]

What distinguishes terrorism, then, from purely political actions may be the illegality of the violence employed, primarily in terms of the victims of the offenses. As noted earlier, many activities, including some sports and many movies, have as a goal the instilling of fear in an audience or opponent. What distinguishes the terrorist of today from the football player, the political assassin, and the revolutionary engaged in regular or irregular warfare may be the *lack* of legitimacy which his actions enjoy under international norms. By its very nature, terrorism involves the deliberate disruption of norms, the violation of generally accepted standards of decency, including the laws of war as they apply to the innocent and helpless.[11]

Since the definition of terrorism is very confusing and contradictory, it is useful to review the issue once more. What is it, then, which distinguishes the terrorist act from other acts of war, as well as from other political or common crimes? Wars, whether between or within states, cannot occur without violence, without the inflicting of injury and death. As individuals we may deplore this violence, but as nations we have recognized its inevitability, and accorded it a limited legitimacy. International rules have been created and accepted that govern the acceptable types of violence, even in war. The international community does not forbid the use of *all* violence; it does, however, suggest basic rules for the use of violence. Many of these rules are directed toward the protection of innocent persons. Even in the life-and-death struggles between nations, these laws focus on minimizing the injury or death of noncombatants, civilians without neither military nor political rank or involvement in the conflict.[12]

Political motivation, then, is *not* a lever by which acts of terrorism can be justified under international law. On the contrary, international law makes it clear that, regardless of the motive, there are some acts of political violence which are never acceptable.

TYPOLOGIES OF TERRORISM: USEFUL TOOLS

It is appropriate at this point to look at some typologies of "terror" which may serve to help us distinguish between types of terrorism as they pertain to revolutionary and guerrilla movements. Feliks Gross, a leading authority on revolutionary terror, has suggested that at least five types of terror-violence exist:

1. **Mass terror** is terror by a state, where the regime coerces the opposition in the population, whether organized or unorganized, sometimes in an institutionalized manner.

2. **Dynastic assassination** is an attack upon a head of state or a ruling elite, precisely the kind of terrorism which the international community tried to criminalize in the mid-nineteenth century.

3. **Random terror** involves the placing of explosives where people gather (such as post offices, railroads, and cafes) to destroy whoever happens to be there. "Algerian revolutionaries left bombs in public places," one scholar notes, "in Paris, apparently convinced that one Frenchman blown to bits was pretty much like any other."[13]

4. **Focused random terror** restricts the placing of explosives, for example, to where significant agents of oppression are likely to gather (as in the aforementioned case of the Polish-Jewish Underground's attacks on Nazi officers).

5. Finally, **tactical terror** is directed solely against the ruling government as a part of a "broad revolutionary strategic plan."[14]

It is obvious that such a typology leaves some guerrilla activity enmeshed in the "terrorist" label. Although similar difficulties afflict other such typologies, some important points can be derived concerning the phenomenon of terrorism by examining some of them. J. Boyer Bell's excellent study of terrorist types yields many insights into the kinds of terrorism prevalent today, and thus contributes to an understanding of what is encompassed by the modern meaning of the term.[15]

In addition to **psychotic** and **criminal terror**, which Bell links to air piracy and kidnaping, four other categories are suggested: endemic, authorized, vigilante, and revolutionary. **Endemic terror** in terms of societal anarchy offers an interesting insight into the internal chaos that has characterized Uganda under Idi Amin, for example. **Authorized terror** is used by the state to intimidate internal enemies or hostile governments, whereas **revolutionary terror** is, like Gross's **tactical terror,** "purely political."

Unlike Gross, however, Bell suggests that this final category could be subdivided into at least six types of terror: **organizational, allegiance, functional, provocative, manipulative,** and *symbolic.* These subdivisions, however, overlap with the types of terrorism discussed in general by Gross, particularly the focused random type. Bell's typology adds, in effect, diversification as to the specific targets and audiences of focused random terror and broadens the spectrum of types of state terror.

Although numerous other typologies of terrorism have been offered by various scholars, review of them in detail would not significantly contribute to the development of a workable definition of contemporary terrorism. A few important points of interest, however, can be made about these typologies. One item of interest is the fact that *virtually every major typology developed today includes some form of state terrorism as well as individual and group terrorism.* What Gross terms "mass terrorism" and Bell calls "authorized" or even "endemic" terror is described by U.S. State Department analyst Thomas Thornton as "enforcement" terror,[16] and by political scientist Paul Wilkinson as "repressive" terror.[17] Whatever the label applied to this particular type of terror, it is obvious that some consensus exists on the propriety of including some repressive state tactics in the classification of terrorist acts.

The typologies also suggest that a wide variety of acts have been encompassed under the rubric of "terrorism," including many engaged in by revolutionary groups, and encompassing both internal activities and activities which cross state lines; but all of which are politically motivated, and all of which are directed toward some end other than the immediate act of violence. These observations serve both to fortify the conclusions already drawn concerning the distinctive nature of terrorist acts, and to highlight certain points of dissension which may contribute to cloud our understanding of this term.

Table 1.1 summarizes some of the typologies of terrorism in use today. Whereas not all of the possible categories of terrorism are included, it is useful to compare the tactics, targets, and perpetrators of such types of terrorism.

Table 1.1

Type	Committed by	Target	Tactics
Mass terror —*endemic* —*authorized* —*enforcement* —*repressive*	political leaders (Example: Idi Amin's rule in Uganda)	General population	Coercion, organized or unorganized
Dynastic assassination	Individuals or groups (Example: Russian anarchists)	Head of state or ruling elite	Very selective violence
Random terror	Individuals or groups (Example: bombing of PanAm Flight 103)	Anyone in "the wrong place at the wrong time"	Bombs in public places, such as cafes, markets, and airports
Focused random terror	Individuals or groups (Example: PIRA and UDF bombings in Northern Ireland)	Members of the "opposition"	Bombs in *specific* public places frequented by the "opposition"
Tactical terror —*revolutionary*	Revolutionary movements (Example: M-19's attacks on Colombian justices)	The government	Attacks on politically attractive targets

TACTICS AND LABELS

Before summarizing the conclusions concerning a working definition of terrorism, one further point needs to be emphasized. Both the typologies of terrorism and the working definition of terrorism being offered treat terrorism as a *tactic*, not as a *goal*. This is important to remember, if the term "terrorism" is not to be used or misused by governments unsympathetic to a group's cause. To describe a particular *action* as a "terrorist" action does not, and should not, in any sense define either the group or the cause for which it uses that tactic as "terrorist."

If an individual, group, or government chooses to use this particular tactic repeatedly, there is every chance that those observing the actions will associate the tactic with those individuals. Continued or prolonged use of such a tactic by any group or government contributes to the perception of that group or government as "terrorist" by the audience who witnesses the crime committed. This is not necessarily accurate, nor is it inaccurate: It is simply a natural phenomenon. A congressman or congresswoman who repeatedly supports war efforts and defense buildups may well expect to be labeled a "hawk" both by those who agree with his or her position, and by those who disagree with it. It is simply a recognition of his patterns of action.

The same is to some extent true of groups which repeatedly engage in terrorist *acts*. The frequency with which they engage in such actions, and to some degree the openness with which they do so, will certainly have an effect on whether their audience views them as being terrorists. This does not mean that the ends toward which they strive are "bad," somehow tainted with the opprobrium of "terrorism." It simply means that the audience for whom the terrorist acts are generally staged have associated in their minds the actors with the actions taken in pursuit of that cause.

This is, of course, a very narrow line of reasoning, one not clearly understood by the general public, which is often the audience for terrorist events. That same public frequently attaches a "terrorist" label to individuals and even to groups who engage on a fairly regular basis in terrorist acts. But in practical terms, acceptable in the legal and political community, it is only the *act* which can accurately be labeled as "terrorist," not the individual, or the group, and certainly not the cause for which the tactic is employed.

But it is true that members of a group cannot engage in questionable or even blatantly illegal actions on a regular basis and not be tainted with the negative labels associated with such actions. Members of Mafia families, while they may themselves be several steps removed from the actual commission of organized crimes, are nevertheless viewed by both the general public and by law enforcement agencies as being linked to, and a part of, those deplorable actions.

So it is with terrorism. Those who commit it, and those whose groups or governments have chosen to use it as a tactic, cannot escape the label of "terrorist" given them, not by governments, but by the very audience toward which such acts are directed. The justice of a cause rarely is sufficient, in that audience's view, to excuse the use of such a tactic. While politicians and ideologues may accept the rationale, covertly or openly, that the ends for which the terrorists struggle justify the means which they choose to employ, most of the civilized world remains unwilling to accept this rationale. Certain acts can be described by definition as *terrorist acts,* whether they are carried out by democratic governments in pursuit of reasonable policy goals, or by armed revolutionaries fighting for freedom against tyranny.

CONCLUSIONS

Terrorism, then, is an *act* comprised of at least four crucial elements: (1) It is an act of violence; (2) it has a political motive or goal; (3) it is perpetrated against innocent persons; and (4) it is staged to be played before an audience whose reaction of fear and terror is the desired result. This definition eliminates from the label of "terrorist" football players, lunatics on a killing spree, and the assassin who tries to kill a "bad" ruler. All acts of violence are not terrorist acts, however heinous the acts may be.

The lines between acceptable types of violence and unacceptable types is, unfortunately, not always clear. Violence by revolutionaries and by the state is sometimes difficult to categorize clearly as "terrorist," even given the working definition evolved here. Further study of the history, ideology, and individuals involved in terrorist acts may increase our understanding of this important but confusing term.

EVALUATION

Using the definition in a practical application is one method of increasing one's understanding of the usefulness and limitation of the definition. Listed below are two brief sketches of what were termed by some observers to be "terrorist" acts. Use the four criteria in the definition of terrorism suggested in this chapter to decide whether these incidents were, in fact, "terrorist" acts. Try also to decide which type of terrorism, if any, was involved, using any one of the typologies mentioned.

1. At 2:30 P.M. on March 30, 1981, President Ronald Reagan was shot in the chest by a gunman. The would-be assassin, John W. Hinckley, Jr., shot the President as he walked to his limousine after addressing the AFL-CIO meeting at the Washington (DC) Hilton Hotel. Shooting from a distance of about ten feet, Hinckley shot President Reagan, Press Secretary James Brady, Secret Service Agent Timothy J. McCarthy, and Washington policeman Thomas K. Delahanty. Evidence at the subsequent trial indicated that Hinckley was motivated by a desire to impress movie actress Jodie Foster.

2. Just before dawn, on October 23, 1983, a suicide vehicle laden with about 2,500 tons of TNT blew up the U.S. Marine headquarters near the Beirut, Lebanon, airport. Around 230 persons were reported killed, most of them as they slept. The Free Islamic Revolutionary Movement claimed responsibility for the action.

SUGGESTED READINGS

Leeman, Richard W. "Terrorism," in *Morality and Conviction in American Politics: A Reader,* Martin Slann and Susan Duffy, eds. Englewood Cliffs, NJ: Prentice Hall, 1990.

Wilkinson, Paul. *Terrorism and the Liberal State.* New York: New York University Press, 1979.

Schmid, Alex. *Political Terrorism.* New Brunswick: Transaction Books, 1983.

Jenkins, Brian, and Janera Johnson. *International Terrorism: A Chronology, 1968–1974.* A report prepared for the Department of State and the Defense Advances Research Projects Agency, R-1587-DOSIARPA (March 1975). Santa Monica, CA: Rand, 1975.

Friedlander, Robert. *Terrorism: Documents of National and International Control,* vol. 1. Dobbs Ferry, NY: Oceana, 1979.

ENDNOTES

1. Irving Howe, "The Ultimate Price of Random Terror," *Skeptic: The Forum for Contemporary History,* no. 11 (January–February 1976) p. 14.
2. David Fromkin, "The Strategy of Terror," *Foreign Affairs,* 53 (July 1975) p. 689.
3. See T.I.A.S., no. 3365.
4. Robert A. Friedlander, *Terrorism: Documents of National and International Control* (Dobbs Ferry, NY: Oceana, 1979) vol. 1, p. 40.
5. Howe, "The Ultimate Price of Random Terror," pp. 14-15.
6. Brian M. Jenkins, *International Terrorism: A New Kind of Warfare,* P-5261, (Santa Monica, CA: Rand, June 1974) p. 4.
7. *Escabedo* v. *United States* 633 F2d. 1098,1104 (5th Cir. 1980).
8. *In re Castroni* 1 Q.B. 149, 156, 166 (1891).

9. Nicholas N. Kittrie, "Patriots and Terrorists: Reconciling Human Rights with World Order," *Case Western Reserve Journal of International Law*, vol. 13, no. 2 (Spring 1981) p. 300.

10. Kittrie, "Patriots and Terrorists," p. 304.

11. Friedlander, *Terrorism*, p. 286.

12. *Principles of the Nuremberg Charter and Judgment,* formulated by the International Law Commission, 1950 (U.N. General Assembly Records, 5th Session, Supp. 12 A/1315).

13. Howe, "The Ultimate Price of Random Terror," p. 15.

14. Feliks Gross, *Political Violence and Terror in 19th and 20th Century Russia and Eastern Europe* (New York: Cambridge University Press, 1990) p. 8

15. J. Bowyer Bell, *Transnational Terror* (Washington, DC: American Institute for Public Policy Research; and Stanford, CA: Hoover Institution on War, Revolution and Peace, 1975) pp. 10–25.

16. Thomas Thornton, "Terror as a Weapon of Political Agitation," in *Internal War*, H. Eckstein, ed. (London: International Institute for Strategic Studies, 1964) pp. 77–78.

17. Paul Wilkinson, *Political Terrorism* (New York: Harvard University Press, 1974) pp. 38–44.

CHAPTER TWO

NOT A MODERN PHENOMENON

KEY CONCEPTS

assassination
hashashin
fedayeen
tyrannicide
Juan de Mariana
divine right of kings
political asylum
state terrorism
privateers
guerrila warfare

IMRO
Saint Elliah's Rebellion
Comitatus
Black Hand
IRA
cycle of violence
Russian anarchists
Zemiya I Volva
Union of Russian Men
Okrana

Even though the word "terrorism" originated during the French Revolution and the Jacobin Reign of Terror (1792-1794), individual acts of terror-violence can be traced back at least to the ancient Greek democracies and Roman republics. By definition, the assassination of Julius Caesar in 44 B.C. was an act of terrorism in so far as a modern political assassination is defined as terrorism. Modern political science, at any rate, tends to treat **assassination,** *the murder of a head of state or other state official,* as a terrorist act.[1]

Group terrorism became more common as early as the Middle Ages. In fact, the word "assassin" comes from an Arabic term **hashashin**, which literally means "hashish-eater," or "one addicted to hashish."[2] It was used to describe *a sectarian group of Muslims who were employed by their spiritual and political leader (the local caliph) to spread terror in the form of murder and destruction among religious enemies, including women and children.*

Accounts of Marco Polo's travels include lurid tales of murder committed by these assassins, acting, it was supposed, under the influence of hashish or other such drugs. It was reported that these early terrorists were motivated not only by religious promises of eternal reward, but also by promises of unlimited access to hashish (and other drugs). Even the Crusaders made mention of this group of fanatics and the terror they inspired.[3]

The potent combination of religious and political fanaticism with intoxicating drugs made the legacy of the Brotherhood of Assassins formidable. It is still evident to some extent in the unrest that plagues the Middle East today. **Narco-terrorism**, as the *linkage between drugs and terrorism* is often termed today, will be described in more depth in a later chapter. Suffice it to note here that the region from which the original Assassins emerged is in the modern nation of Iran. The former Ayatollah Khomeini, leader of the Shi'ites in this nation during its revolution in the late 1970s, was from the same area that hundreds of years before was the home of the infamous caliph who brought about the Brotherhood of Assassins.

Another Brotherhood of Assassins emerged from a combination of religion and politics in the 1890s. The Hur Brotherhood, whose roots were in the Sind region of British India, resembled the earlier Islamic Brotherhood of Assassins. While this latter Brotherhood was suppressed, after considerable bloodshed, another Hur rebellion occurred in Pakistan in the mid-twentieth century. Indeed, much of modern Pakistan's terrorism from its Sikh minority derives from that group's religious and political dissatisfaction with Muslim Pakistan's leaders. Religion and politics continue to take innocent lives in this turbulent region of the world.

Islam is not, in any sense, a violent religion. Nor are Christianity, Judaism, or any of the other religions in whose name violence has been carried out. However, the mixture of religion and politics has quite often resulted in violence, frequently against innocent victims, which makes it, according to the definition suggested in the preceding chapter, terrorism. The Middle East, as the home of three major world religions, has been plagued by a variety of violent sects. Today, nations such as Iran have witnessed, and perhaps fostered, the creation of several violent sects, whose blending of religion and politics looks a lot like that of the Brotherhood of Assassins. Table 2.1 offers a brief insight into two of the larger of these radical groups, their location, and their violent activities.

The **fedayeen**, *the Islamic "self-sacrificers,"* in the "holy war" being waged by more militant sects today are similar in many respects to the Assassins of the Middle Ages. Like the Assassins, modern fedayeen find strength in the promise of a reward in "paradise" after death. Unlike the earlier sect, however, these modern zealots believe that they will receive their reward in a spiritual paradise, not in the courtyard of the caliph. Religion is the "narcotic" which serves to both motivate their terrorist actions, and to deaden their consciences to the horror of the slaughter which they inflict on innocent persons.

Thus, the mixture of religion and politics in the commitment of terrorism today is not new, but continues to be quite deadly. History enables us to place current mixtures such as these in context, making understanding easier. It has not yet made it possible for governments or organizations to prevent the explosion of these potentially lethal elements.

TYRANNICIDE: "TO GO TOO FAST"

Assassination, in fact, has become both an ideological statement and a powerful political weapon, using the vehicle of the doctrine of **tyrannicide**, *the assassination of a (tyrant) political leader.* Throughout Italy

Table 2.1

Group	Description	Activities
Hizbollah (Party of God), a.k.a. Islamic Jihad, Revolutionary Justice Organization	Radical Shi'ite group; formed in Lebanon; close ties to Iran	—bombing of U.S. Marine barracks in Beirut (1983) —held most, if not all, Western hostages in Lebanon
Sikh Groups Includes, among others: *Dashmesh* (active in India, Germany, and Canada)	Several domestic and international groups	—regular and bloody attacks against Hindu
Dal Khalsa (active in India, Pakistan, and Germany)	Seek to establish an independent Sikh state called Khalistan	—blamed for bombing of Air India aircraft (329 people killed)
Babbar Khalsa (active in India, Germany, and Canada)		—desecration of Hindu holy places, bombings, and assassinations
The All India Sikh Students Federation		—hijacked an Indian aircraft to Pakistan (1981)

during the Renaissance, tyrannicide was fairly widely practiced, whereas in Spain and France during the Age of Absolutism it was at least widely advocated. The leading advocate of the doctrine of tyrannicide as an acceptable solution to political repression was a Spanish Jesuit scholar, **Juan de Mariana**, whose principal work, *De Regis Intsitutions*, was banned in France.[4]

In the words of Mariana we find much of the same political justification used by leaders of national liberation movements today. Mariana asserted that *people necessarily possessed not only the right of rebellion but also the remedy of assassination,* stating that "if in no other way it is possible to save the fatherland, the prince should be killed by the sword as a public enemy."[5]

Only ten years after Mariana's words were uttered, King Henry III, of France was assassinated by the monk Francois Favaillac. Many leaders since that time have been struck down by persons who have claimed to have acted as instruments of justice against a tyrant. Even President Lincoln's assassin, John Wilkes Booth, saw his act in such a light, as evidenced by his triumphant shout, "*Sic semper tyrannis!*" ("Thus always to tyrants!").[6]

Political assassins, like those committing murder in the name of religion, have frequently claimed to be acting as "divine instruments" of justice. At the very least, such assassins have viewed themselves as the chosen instruments of a popular legitimacy, rightly and even righteously employed in the destruction of illegitimate regimes and tyrannical rulers. The robes of martyrdom have been donned as readily by political as by religious zealots. Like the religious fanatics, political assassins have had no hesitation in acting as judge, jury, and executioner, assuring themselves and others that their appointment to these offices was made, not by themselves, but by a "higher" will or authority.

During the latter part of the eighteenth century and the nineteenth century, the **divine right of kings** theory, stating *that kings rule by divine appointment*, began to lose its political grip on Europe. As the theory of the existence of a social contract between a people and their government began to gain acceptance, those who carried out political offenses such as tyrannicide gradually found a more benign atmosphere in which to act.

As one acting to "right the wrongs" committed by government, the political assassin was no longer regarded with universal disfavor. Vidal, a leading French legal scholar, has noted that

> Whereas formerly the political offender was treated as a public enemy, he is today considered as a friend of the public good, as a man of progress, desirous of bettering the political institutions of his country, having the laudable intentions, hastening the onward march of hu-

manity, his only fault being that he wishes to go too fast, and that he employs in attempting to realize the progress which he desires, means irregular, illegal, and violent.[7]

Not until the middle of the twentieth century was the murder of a head of state, or any member of his family, formally designated as terrorism. Even today, those who commit the "political" crime of murder of a head of state can often enjoy a type of special protection, in the form of **political asylum**, *a type of sanctuary or refuge for a person who has committed such a crime, granted by one government against requests by another government for the extradition of that person to be prosecuted for this "political" crime.*

STATE TERRORISM: FRANCE'S REIGN OF TERROR

The use of "irregular, illegal, and violent means" was not, of course, limited to lone political assassins. The execution of Marie Antoinette on October 16, 1793, was one of the first incidents actually called terrorism. In this instance, the terrorists were not trying to *overthrow* the government: they *were* the government! The Committee of Public Safety, led by Robespierre, chief spokesman of the Jacobin party, governed France during the tumultuous period known as the Reign of Terror (September 1793–July 1794). It is from this period, during which an estimated 20,000 persons were killed, that the word "terrorism" has evolved.

It is interesting, is it not, that modern terrorism derives its name from a gross example of **state terrorism**, *acts of terrorism which a state commits against defenseless victims,* rather than from terror-violence by a lone assassin or small, fanatic, nonstate group? States have been, and continue to be, involved from time to time in a wide variety of violent acts against their own citizens and those of other nations.

Consider the case of piracy. From the sixteenth century onward, pirates have been considered by law-makers to be the "common enemies of humanity." Blackstone's *Commentaries* referred to piracy as "an offense against the universal law of society."[8] Yet both England (for whom Blackstone wrote) and America (whose law frequently cites his precepts) licensed **privateers**, *private ships which were outfitted as war ships and given letters of marque and reprisal, allowing them to make war on vessels flying foreign flags.*

Under the reign of Queen Elizabeth I of England, the **Elizabethan Sea Dogs**, privateer ships sailing under the protection of the English flag, carried out violent acts of piracy against the Spanish fleet. American privateers, too, played a fairly significant role in both the American Revolution and the War of 1812. Both nations, then, have commissioned pirates to carry out acts of terror-violence on the high seas, acts which both nations publicly deplore as "offenses against humanity" in their courts today. Modern terrorism continues to occasionally take the form of piracy, but today the piracy is often of aircraft rather than sea vessels. This interesting change will be discussed later, with particular attention to its impact on legal remedies for terrorism.

GUERRILLA WARFARE: SELECTIVE VIOLENCE

Since the French Revolution, terrorism and guerrilla warfare have become increasingly difficult to separate clearly. **Guerrilla warfare** is, essentially, *an insurrectionary armed protest, implemented by means of selective violence.* To the extent that the violence remains "selective" and the choice of targets military rather than civilian, then it is possible to distinguish between guerrilla warfare and terrorism.

The term "guerrilla," meaning "little war" evolved from Spanish resistance to the invasions of Napoleon in 1808. This war on the Iberian Peninsula, in which Spanish "guerrillas" were aided in making increasingly successful attacks on French encampments by the British military, has become in some measure a prototype for the twentieth-century wars of national liberation. In contemporary guerrilla struggles, indigenous vigilante groups are often supported openly (as were the Spanish) or covertly by the military of other nations.

Ideology and nationalism combined with terror-violence in the **Internal Macedonian Revolutionary Organization (IMRO)**, a group which made its first appearance in 1893. For several years the IMRO waged guerrilla warfare, sometimes employing terrorist tactics, against the Turkish rulers of their region. As in the Iberian conflict, other nations both assisted and interfered in the struggle. Bombings and kidnappings, as well as the murder of civilians and officials, were frequent in this "little war." Violence escalated into the **Saint Elliah's Rebellion** in August of 1903, which was ruthlessly dealt with by Turkish authorities. This struggle left thousands dead on both sides, at least 70,000 homeless, and 200 Macedonian villages in ashes.

Turkey's suppression of similar nationalist struggles on the part of its Armenian population in the early part of the twentieth century helped to create Armenian groups willing to engage in terrorist activities today. These activities, which include bombings and murder reminiscent of the IMRO, have been directed less by nationalism than by a desire for revenge for the ruthless suppression of that earlier nationalism. In this case, savagely suppressed nationalism has spawned vengeful terrorism, whose perpetrators' demands are perhaps even harder to satisfy than were those of the nationalists of earlier decades.

Events in the 1990s in the former Yugoslavia give credence to the concept that repressed nationalism can, in a resurgent form, exact a bloody toll on innocent civilian populations. In the turbulent years before the outbreak of World War I, the Balkan states were engaged in a wide variety of revolutionary violence. Terrorist brigands, calling themselves **Comitatus** ("Committee Men"), covertly sponsored by Greece, Serbia, and Bulgaria (which was also involved in the IMRO struggles), roamed the countryside. In the worst, not the best, tradition of revolutionaries, these brigands terrorized their own countrymen—burning, murdering, and robbing all who stood in their way. The incredible destruction and genocidal murders which took place in the Balkans in the 1990s parallel, and even exceed, this pattern.

World War I was, in fact, triggered by a transnational assassination which had its roots in revolutionary terrorism. A secret Serbian terrorist organization, popularly known as the **Black Hand**, was both an organization employed by the Serbian government as an unofficial instrument of national foreign policy and a lethal weapon of political protest against the Austro-Hungarian Empire. On June 28, 1914, a 19-year-old Serbian trained by the Black Hand murdered the heir to the imperial throne of that empire, Archduke Franz Ferdinand, in Sarajevo. This assassination was the catalyst for a series of events which, within a month's time, grew into a global conflagration. Revolutionary terror-violence triggered international devastation on a scale unprecedented at that time.

Conflict in and around Sarajevo in the 1990s is partially explained, too, by this early pattern of revolutionary terror-violence. At least twice within the twentieth century, revolutionary terror-violence has been unleashed by groups, governments, and militias against a civilian population. This type of violence makes reconciliation extremely difficult, if not impossible, to achieve. Memories of violence against women and children within families are hard to relinquish, and repetition of such violence within less than a century makes the creation of a sense of common identity (nationalism) and reconciliation between populations within that region perhaps an impossible goal.

Revolutions are *not* by definition terrorist events! Indeed, some have been successfully carried out without resort to terrorist tactics. It is increasingly difficult, however, for an untrained and sparsely equipped indigenous army to wage a successful guerrilla war against a national standing army. With mounting frustration in the face of apparently insurmountable odds, it is increasingly easy to resort to terror-violence to achieve by psychological force what it is not possible to achieve by force of arms.

Perhaps nowhere else in this century has the role of liberationist combined more thoroughly, until recently, with that of terrorist than in the actions of the militant group usually known as the **Irish Republican Army (IRA)**. This group's guerrilla campaign of murder and terror, growing out of the Sinn Fein political movement in 1916, provoked the British to respond in kind, with a counterterror campaign. While this revolutionary terrorism may be said to have stimulated the creation of an independent Irish Republic, the violence did not end with this success. In the mid-1950s the Provisional IRA began a second wave of anti-British terror, which still continues.

This struggle offers insights in several historical respects. In addition to being, in part, a blend of nationalism and terrorism, it is also a contemporary example of the potent mixture of religion and politics. Catholic Ireland has long resented Protestant Britain's domination of its politics. Northern Ireland, which remains under British rule, is predominantly Protestant, with a large Catholic minority.

Thus, the lines of battle are drawn along both nationalistic and religious lines. Catholics in Northern Ireland have tended to support a unification of those northern provinces with the Irish Republic, whereas Protestants in Northern Ireland have demanded continued British rule. The legacy of hatred and mistrust bred by generations of violence is so bitter that an end to the violence seemed, until the end of the twentieth century, unlikely. The cyclical nature of violence can indeed create a deadly spiral.

CYCLICAL NATURE OF TERROR

Violence, particularly terrorist violence, has too often created a **cycle of violence**, *with those against whom the terror-violence is first carried out becoming so angered that they resort to terrorism in response, directed against the people or institutions regarded as being responsible for the initial terrorist acts.* Each violent act frequently causes equally violent reactions. When the violence is unselective, when innocent people are victimized, the reactive violence is also likely to "break all the rules" in the selection of targets, and thus be terrorist violence.

Most revolutionary groups assert that it is terrorism by the *state* which provokes, and by its presence justifies, acts of terror-violence by nonstate groups seeking to change the government or its policies. The relationship between terror-violence by the state and that of nonstate groups and individuals is evident in the history of many modern nation-states. But the nature of that relationship is still the subject of much debate.

From the time of the French Revolution, terrorism and guerrilla movements have become inextricably intertwined. Perhaps the most prominent proponents of individual and collective violence as a means of destroying governments and social institutions were the **Russian anarchists,** *revolutionaries within Russia who sought an end to the Tzarist state of the late nineteenth century.* "Force only yields to force," and terror would provide the mechanism of change, according to the Russian radical theorists Alexander Serno-Solovevich.[9] In the writings of two of the most prominent spokesmen for revolutionary anarchism, **Mikhail Bakunin** and **Sergei Nechaev,** one finds philosophies often echoed by modern terrorists. Bakunin, for example, advocated in his *National Catechism* (1866) the use of "selective, discriminate terror." Nechaev, in his work, *Revolutionary Catechism,* went further in advocating both the theory and practice of pervasive terror-violence. He asserted of the revolutionary:

> Day and night he must have one single thought, one single purpose: merciless destruction. With this aim in view, tirelessly and in cold blood, he must always be prepared to kill with his own hands anyone who stands in the way of achieving his goals.[10]

This is surely a very large step in the evolution of a terrorist from the lone political assassin of earlier centuries. Even the religious fanatics of the Assassins genre and the privateers of Elizabethan times were arguably less willing to kill "anyone" to achieve a political objective. But his difference may well have existed more on paper than it did in practice. In spite of this written willingness to kill "anyone" who stood in the way, even the Socialist Revolutionary Party resorted primarily to selective terror-violence, and took special pains to avoid endangering the innocent bystanders. For instance, the poet Ivan Kalialev, who assassinated the Grand Duke Sergius on the night of February 2, 1905, had passed up an opportunity earlier that evening to throw the bomb because the Grand Duchess and some of her nieces and nephews were also in the Grand Duke's carriage.[11]

Although an attempt was made to kill Tzar Alexander II as early as 1866, the first generation of Russian terrorists generally resorted to violence only to punish traitors and police spies, or to retaliate against brutal treatment of political prisoners. (Odd, isn't it, that these same reasons are frequently quoted today as justifications for similar use of "extra-legal violence"?)

With the creation of the **Zemiya I Volva** (The Will of the People) in 1879, political assassination of a wide range of targets began to become a normal form of political protest, becoming part of an intense cycle of terror and counterterror. This revolutionary group believed that terrorism should be used to compromise the best of governmental power, to give constant proof that it is possible to fight the government, and to strengthen thereby the revolutionary spirit of the people and its faith in the success of the cause.[12]

It is quite easy to note the blending of revolutionary and state terror-violence during this time. The assassinations of Tsar Alexander II in 1881 and of First Minister Peter Stolypin in 1911 were incidents which produced periods of counterterrorism (in the form of state repression). This repression probably accelerated the revolutionary movement responsible for those assassinations. Thus, the terrorist acts of assassination, inspired by brutal repression in the Tsarist state, provoked further state terrorism, which in turn the inspired revolutionary movement to further acts of violence.

The formation of the **Union of Russian Men** to combat the growing revolutionary movement "by all means" was not only sanctioned by the Tsar, but granted special protection by him. This reactionary group engaged in a variety of terrorist activities, including but not limited to political murders, torture, and bombing. The **Okrana** (the Tsarist secret police) also wreaked fierce counterterror against the militant revolutionaries in an unabated attack until World War I.

George Kennan, commenting on the rising tide of "terrorism" in Russia during the last half of the nineteenth century, explained the relationship of state and revolutionary terrorism in this way:

> Wrong a man . . . deny him all redress, exile him if he complains, gag him if he cries out, strike him in the face if he struggles, and at the last he will stab and throw bombs.[13]

Still, whereas some of the seeds of a more widespread and random terror-violence were sown in the revolutionary and anarchistic movements of the late nineteenth century, by the beginning of the twentieth century, terror-violence was still principally directed toward political assassination. Between 1881 and 1912, at least ten national leaders had lost their lives to assassins, as Table 2.2 (on page 30) indicates.

The cyclical nature of terror is also evident in the events surrounding the creation of the state of Israel. The terrorism spawned in Nazi Germany helped to create a cycle of violence which still grips the Middle East today. After the military collapse of the Central Powers and the Armistice Agreement of November 1918, within Germany a large number of largely right-wing paramilitary organizations grew. In ideology, terrorist method, and political role, these groups were in many respects the historical heirs of the Brotherhood of Assassins. They were also the nucleus for the German *Reichswehr*.

TABLE 2.2

Individual	Nation	Date of Death
President James Garfield	United States	1881
Tsar Alexander II	Russia	1881
Lord Frederick Cavendish, Chief Secretary	Ireland	1882
President Sadi Carnot	France	1894
Premier Antonio Canavos de? Castillo	Spain	1897
Empress Elizabeth	Austria-Hungary	1898
King Umberto I	Italy	1900
President William McKinley	United States	1901
Premier Peter Stolypin	Russia	1911
Premier Jose Canalejas y Mendez	Spain	1912

Under the leadership of the *Reichwehr*, Germany perpetrated upon innocent persons the greatest atrocities the world has ever recorded. Organized state terrorism reached its zenith in Nazi Germany, and its victims numbered in the millions. Of those victims, the majority were Jewish. Many Jews who sought to flee the terror tried to emigrate to Palestine, which at that time was under British mandate. But the British Mandate Government, by 1940, was engaged in closing the gates to Jewish immigration into this land, which was, in fact, already occupied by Arabs. As the population balance began to swing away from the indigenous Arab population toward the immigrant Jews, the British government sought to stem the tide of refugees.

The *Haganah*, a Zionist underground army, and the *Irgun Zvai Leumi*, a Zionist militant force willing to use terrorist tactics, waged terrorist warfare on the British forces in Palestine. Bombing, murder, and assassination became the order of the day, as British counterviolence met with escalating *Haganah* and *Irgun* intransigence. With the *Irgun* bombing of the King David Hotel, in which many innocent persons died or were seriously injured, British determination to quell the rebellion diminished.

But during the struggle to gain a homeland free of Nazi terror, the *Irgun* had practiced terror against the indigenous population. When Israel declared itself to be an independent state in 1948, some of the dispossessed people within its borders and those who fled to surrounding states began a war of revolution and terror against Israel.

Israel's revolutionary terror-violence against the Palestinian people has spurred a conflict which continues to rend the fragile fabric of peace in the Middle East. Born in bloodshed, violence, and desperation, Israel continues to struggle against the terrorist violence which its very creation evoked.

CONTEMPORARY EVENTS: HISTORICAL ROOTS

Is contemporary terrorism different? In what ways? One reason for briefly reviewing the historical pattern and roots of terrorism is to be able to discover whether that pattern remains accurate in the contemporary world. If terrorism today is just like the terrorism of previous centuries, then we can use historical patterns to predict behavior and to construct responses based on successful attempts to combat this phenomenon in the past.

If terrorism today is different, however, then historical patterns will be less useful in designing responses, although such patterns may still be of use in understanding the dynamics of the phenomenon. Terrorism has clearly existed before this century. What we need to know as we prepare for yet another century is whether twentieth-century terrorism was significantly different from its historical counterparts.

We have established that prior to the twentieth century, terrorism has existed in many forms: political assassins, lethal groups of religious zealots and drug-crazed murderers, state-sponsored as well as nonstate pirates, and dedicated revolutionaries, whose resort to violence is tied to state repression. All of these forms of terrorism still exist in the modern world. But there are important differences. Examination of these differences may help us to understand our contemporary terrorism.

A. Political assassinations   Terrorist acts are no longer directed solely or even primarily at heads of state. Security precautions to guard such persons against attack have made it very difficult for a lone assassin to successfully murder such a person. The assassination in 1995 of Yitzak Rabin, Prime Minister of Israel, demonstrated that it is not, of course, impossible for such an attack to occur with success. However, in the latter part of the twentieth century, attacks have been made with greater frequency on individuals of less significance but who were easier for the assassin to attack. This broadens the range of acceptable *victims* well beyond the realm justified under the doctrine of tyrannicide.

B. Drugs, religious fanaticism, and political murders While this lethal combination still exists in the contemporary world, the relationship between these elements has changed considerably. During the Middle Ages, the Caliph rewarded his Assassins with drugs for successfully completed murders of his religious opponents. Today, drugs are used to finance the lethal expeditions of religious zealots, whose targets are not only those of another religion within their community, but include whole nations or groups of nations whose citizens are regarded by the zealots as legitimate targets for murder. Again, this is a drastic broadening of the category of acceptable potential victims.

C. Piracy While piracy on the sea has waned somewhat in recent years (although the incident involving the *Achille Lauro* has reminded us that such piracy still occurs), air piracy has more than taken its place. During the 1970s and 1980s, airline hijacking has become a fairly commonplace occurrence. Whereas pirates of old sought primarily material gain (with political gain a pleasant byproduct for certain governments), modern air pirates have tended to seek political gain first. So although the treatment of victims of piracy has remained essentially the same (pirates throughout the ages have tended to treat their victims as completely expendable), the *purpose* or *goal* of the act has changed radically.

D. State-sponsored terrorism Modern governments have expanded the concept of "licensed" pirates. Terrorism has, in fact, become an institutionalized form of foreign policy for many nations. Governments privately and sometimes publicly sponsor groups involved in terrorist activities. Moreover, in the latter half of the twentieth century, governments increasingly became involved in revolutionary movements, providing assistance for either the foreign revolutionaries or the foreign regime against which the revolution was fighting. This has blurred the lines between those involved in the fighting of a war, and those who are merely innocent bystanders.

Related to these differences between historical and modern terrorism are important developments in the contemporary world. *Modern methods of travel,* for example, make it possible to carry out an assassination in the morning in Country Q, and be halfway around the world from that nation within a matter of hours.

Modern communication, too, has made this a "smaller world" in that events in, for instance, Nigeria, are of immediate notice and interest in New York. Such communications, too, have served to expand the theater and enlarge the audience to which the terrorist plays. Thus, to catch the attention of America, the Nigerian terrorist need not travel to New York City with a bomb; he need only plant a bomb in Lagos.

The dramatic *increase in the arsenal of weapons* available to modern terrorists is also worth noting. No longer need the would-be assassin rely on a small handgun to eliminate his victim. A letter bomb will do the job without endangering the perpetrator, as the Uniabomber in the United States has demonstrated. Revolutionaries are no longer confined to simple rifles; SAM's (surface-to-air missiles) are all-too-accessible.

The potential for destruction through chemical and biological weapons has not yet been fully tapped, although the *sarin* gas attacks in subways in Japan in 1995 gave ample evidence of the potential for such weapons when used in the very vulnerable mass transit systems of a modern nation. Perhaps, until recently, the consequences of using such weapons were too dramatic for most groups to contemplate. But modern technology has certainly put at the terrorist's disposal a vast array of lethal and largely indiscriminate weapons, of which the sarin toxin apparently used in Japan represents only a very simple example. With this arsenal, the selection of victims has become devastatingly indiscriminate. One can be a victim simply by riding a subway train to work—a necessary act for millions of innocent people.

As historical precedents for terrorism grow, it becomes very hard to distinguish between legitimate and illegitimate violence. As the nations born of illegitimate violence, such as Ireland and Israel, become themselves illegitimate, it is increasingly difficult to condemn the terrorist methods employed in the struggles for independence and survival. The longer the history of terrorism grows, the harder it is to make a label of "terrorism" stick to the actions of any group or nation.

EVALUATION

October 1985—the news flashed across the world—a group of American and European tourists had been taken hostage aboard a pleasure ship, the *Achille Lauro*, by a handful of Palestinian terrorists. The ship wandered north along the coast of Lebanon as the hijackers sought safe haven. Bit by bit, news of the horror aboard leaked out: 69-year–old wheelchair-bound Leon Klinghoffer of New York City was murdered.

The Egyptian government called in a negotiator, Abbu Abbas, leader of the Palestinian splinter group to which the hijackers claimed to belong. He ordered them to release the ship and come into Cairo, where they were promised safe passage out of Egypt.

At the same time, U.S. intelligence sources, who were monitoring the exchanges between President Mubarak of Egypt and Yassir Arafat, leader of the Palestinian Liberation Organization, gained enough information to enable the United States to spring a bold trap. The EgyptAir plane aboard which the hijackers were being smuggled out of Egypt was ambushed by U.S. war planes and forced to land in Italy, where the hijackers were taken into custody by the Italian government.

This modern incident of terrorism and counterforce raises some important questions for discussion:

1. Were the hijackers pirates, "common enemies of mankind," or revolutionaries using the means at their disposal to wage war on oppressive governments?
2. In order to secure the release of the rest of the hostages, was it wrong of Egypt to allow the hijackers into port and then to assist them in leaving the country?
3. Was the United States justified in its actions against the hijackers, or was it guilty of state terrorism as well?
4. Do, in fact, "rights" (to commit acts of terror-violence) derive from "wrongs"?

SUGGESTED READINGS

Schultz, George. "Low-Intensity Warfare: the Challenge of Ambiguity." Address to Low-Intensity Warfare Conference, Washington, DC, January 15, 1986.

Rose, Paul. "Terror in the Skies." *Contemporary Review*, no. 248 (June 1986).

Slann, Martin. "The State as Terrorist," in *Multidimensional Terrorism*, Martin Slann and Bernard Schechterman, eds. New York: Lynne Rienner, 1987.

Maranto, Robert. "The Rationality of Terrorism," in *Multidimensional Terrorism.*, Martin Slann and Bernard Schechterman, eds. New York: Lynne Rienner, 1987.

ENDNOTES

1. Robert Friedlander, *Terrorism: Documents of International and Local Control* (Dobbs Ferry, NY: Oceana, 1979) p. 7.
2. Funk and Wagnall's *Standard Dictionary: Comprehensive International Edition*, vol. 1, p. 86, col. 3.
3. See M. Hodgson, *The Order of the Assassins* (1960); B. Lewis, *The Assassins: A Radical Sect in Islam* (1968).
4. Cf. O. Zasra and J. Lewis, *Against the Tyrant: The Tradition and Theory of Tyrannicide* (1957).
5. Quoted by B. Hurwood, *Society and the Assassin: A Background Book on Political Murder* (London: International Institute for Strategic Studies, 1970) p. 29.
6. Carl Sandburg, *Abraham Lincoln: The War Years* (Cambridge: MIT Press, 1939) vol. 4, p. 482
7. Vidal, *Cours de Droit Criminal et de Science Pententiare*, 5th ed. (Paris: Institute de Paris Press, 1916) pp. 110–112.

8. William Blackstone, *Commentaries on the Laws of England* (1749) vol. 4, p. 71.

9. Quoted by F. Venturi, *Roots of Revolution: A History of the Populist and Socialist Movements in Nineteenth Century Russia*, F. Haskell, trans. (London: International Institute for Strategic Studies, 1966) p. 281.

10. Venturi, *Roots of Revolution*, p. 366.

11. Irving Howe, "The Ultimate Price of Random Terror," in *Skeptic: The Forum for Contemporary History*, no. 11 (January–February 1976) pp. 10-19.

12. Sandra Stencel, "Terrorism: An Idea Whose Time Has Come" in *Skeptic: The Forum for Contemporary History*, no. 11 (January–February 1976) pp. 4–5.

13. Quoted by Friedlander, *Terrorism: Documents*, p. 26.

CHAPTER THREE

IDEOLOGY
AND
TERRORISM

Rights from Wrongs?

KEY CONCEPTS

anarchism
jus ex injuria non oritur
right of self-determination
image of the enemy
images of themselves
nature of the conflict
image of victims
theme of millenarianism
religious fanaticism

neo-nazism
neo-fascism
separatism
nationalism
issue orientation
ideological mercenaries
pathological terrorists
counterterror terrorists

Can rights ever derive from wrongs? Can one injustice truly justify the commission of another injustice? There are, of course, no easy answers to such loaded questions. In the same manner, there may be no clear or absolute answer to the question of whether there could be a justifiable terrorist act.

Most individuals or groups which claim that an act is justified, mean that it has a purpose which is just, one which can be given a reasonable explanation. So to determine whether or not terrorism is justified, we must study the reasons or justifications given for the terrorist acts. Since we have already reviewed the transformation of terrorism over the centuries, from the lone assassin "executing" an unjust ruler to the revolutionaries of modern Russia, we will confine our study to the reasons for the terrorism that has existed in *this* century.

This will not limit the usefulness of our observations, since the basic reasons for terrorism have not, in fact, changed as rapidly as have the tactics of terror. The forces of oppression which have caused men to rebel have not changed over the centuries; what has changed is the willingness of the oppressed to use previously unthinkable means to achieve their objectives.

The reasons for this willingness to use extraordinary means are important; they are, in many ways, the justification for modern terrorism. It has always been possible to murder innocent persons. Why is it no longer an unthinkable option for so many revolutionary groups? This is the crucial question. It is unarguable that states throughout history have used terrorism on their citizens, on the citizens of other nations, and as an instrument of war. Biblical and historical accounts abound of conquering armies who slaughtered innocent men, women, and children; who took slaves and captives and perpetrated all manner of atrocities on their innocent heads. But those rebelling against such tyrannous brutality have heretofore eschewed a comparable brutality. Indeed, the lodestar of revolutionary theory has been its vehement condemnation of the brutality of the existing regime. Why, then, during this century have revolutionary groups become more and more willing to perpetrate equally brutal acts against similarly innocent persons? Oppression is not new, nor is the presence of a few desperate persons willing to risk all to oppose a system they abhor. What is new is the willingness of these desperate people to use tactics which, until very recently, were the sole provence of the despised state?

This, it seems, is the phenomenon of modern terrorism: that revolutionaries, those rebelling against state oppression, are now willing to use weapons of terror against an innocent citizenry. In the past, revolutionaries and the theorists who espoused their causes have defended their actions in terms of ridding the world of oppressive states whose leaders committed "unthinkable, barbarous acts upon the citizenry." By committing similar "unthinkable, barbarous acts upon the citizenry," revolutionaries have fundamentally altered their philosophy. It is important to understand the substance of this changed philosophy, and the reasons for the change, in order to understand modern terrorism.

THE RATIONALIZATION OF VIOLENCE

The terrorist revolution is the only just form of revolution.
—Nikolai Morozov (1880)

Revolutionaries such as Morozov came to view terrorism as the only chance for successful revolution in tzarist Russia. **Anarchism**, which advocated "propaganda of the deed," became increasingly committed to nonselective violence, as the possibility of forcing change within the structure of the existing state became less feasible.

Unlike the revolutionaries of nineteenth-century Russia, anarchists were less strict in their adherence to the idea of injury inflicted upon only "guilty" persons. Louis August Blanqui asserted that the transformation of society could only come about from a small, well-organized group of terrorists acting as the vanguard of the revolutionary process.[1] With the imperial abdication in France in 1870 and the establishment of the Paris Commune in March 1871 (composed as it was of a Blanquist majority) "a red terror once again came into being, accentuated by class division and violence."[2]

The anarcho-syndicalist credo expressed by American revolutionary propagandist Emma Goldman offers another insight into the transition of revolutionary theory. Goldman advocated "direct action against the authority of the law, direct action against the invasive meddlesome authority of our moral code."[3] This rejection of our moral code as "invasive" and "meddlesome" and belonging to those in authority is certainly a shift in philosophy. Revolutionaries of previous centuries had claimed that such a code justified their actions against a clearly immoral state. This change in perception of the existing moral code will be explored shortly, in the context of discussion of the self-justification of modern terrorists.

Franz Fanon, the theoretical architect of the Algerian independence movement, also offered some changes to traditional revolutionary theory. He argued for the use of "the technique of terrorism," which, he asserted, consisted of individual and collective attempts by means of bombs or by the derailing of trains to disrupt the existing system.

Both of these theorists express a philosophy radically different from that espoused by the early Russian revolutionaries or earlier advocates of tyrannicide. The legitimate victim of violence need no longer be exclusively either the soldier or the government official. Rather, with increasing frequency, the victim is an innocent civilian, a third party, whose injury or death is intended to hurt or frighten the entire body politic.

In the United States, anarchist philosophy also began to engender radical demands for indiscriminate violence. Anarchist publications in the 1880s were candid in their enthusiasm for the widespread use of explosives. One letter, which appeared in the extremist paper *Alarm,* enthused:

> Dynamite! Of all the good stuff, this is the stuff . . . Place this in the immediate vicinity of a lot of rich loafers who live by the sweat of other people's brows, and light the fuse. A most cheerful and gratifying result will follow.[4]

Anarchist violence did indeed claim innocent lives, often through the use of dynamite, during the following decades. While strains of both nonviolent socialism and violent anarchism mixed in the labor movement, unfairly tainting much of labor's legitimate attempts to organize, acts of random violence were unabashedly carried out by anarchist extremists within the movement.

On October 1, 1910, the *Los Angeles Times* building was destroyed by dynamite. Two young ironworkers eventually confessed to this crime, in which 20 innocent persons died and another 17 were injured. On September 16, 1920, an explosion on New York's Wall Street destroyed an even larger number of innocent lives. Forty people were killed in this blast, and another 300 were injured. A hitherto unknown group, calling itself the American Anarchist Fighters, claimed credit for this devastation, whose victims were ordinary working people. In spite of the fact that anarchists were, in theory, committed to conflict with the "rich ruling elites," victims of its violence were in many cases *not* wealthy or powerful persons, but innocent bystanders.

Violence among groups seeking to correct societal injustices has not been limited to anarchistic rationalization. In Uruguay, terrorism was justified by the Tupamaros on nationalistic and socialistic grounds. Uruguay, until the late 1950s a model of democracy and prosperity in a largely authoritarian sea of South American nations, began to falter economically in 1958.

Young middle-class professionals and intellectuals, hit especially hard by the economic difficulties, and moved by the wretched living and working conditions of many groups in the country, began to seek radical solutions to the nation's woes. Over the next few years, their activities ranged from the hijacking of trucks carrying food (which they subsequently distributed to needy people) to bank robbery and kidnaping for ransom.

These activities alone would not constitute terrorism, perhaps. However, the targets for the kidnappings were frequently foreign diplomats or employees of foreign companies, whose only "crime" was their presence in Uruguay. Assassinations of police officers were so common that some police officers refused, in fear, to wear their uniforms to work.

Attacks on the military are standard and, usually acceptable during a time of revolution and social upheaval. Attacks on unarmed civilian personnel is neither acceptable nor can it be readily justified. Socialism and nationalism in Uruguay combined to create a climate similar to that which prompted the "Macedonia for Macedonians" cry of the IMRO. The desire to drive out foreign influence and to forcibly redistribute wealth served, in this case, as the justification for terror-violence.

REBELLION AND THE RIGHT
OF SELF-DETERMINATION

The evolution of revolutionary violence into terrorism is significant. It has long been a stumbling block in the creation of effective international law concerning terrorism. Revolutions have occurred throughout history without recourse to terror-violence; there needs to be an effort made to understand why such revolutions do not continue to occur without the use of terrorist tactics. Do they not occur, or can they not occur *successfully* without the use of terrorism?

Although rebellion cannot be separated from violence, certain types of violence have, as noted earlier, not been acceptable. Violence that is directed deliberately against innocent parties is destructive not only of law and of legal systems, but also of civilized society, according to one expert on international law.[5] As the United Nations Secretariat, in its study of the nature and causes of terrorism, conlcuded: The legitimacy of a cause does not in itself legitimize the use of certain forms of violence, especially against the innocent." Paragraph 10 of the Secretariat's study notes that this limit on the legitimate use of violence "has long been recognized, even in the customary laws of war."[6]

There are two points here worth noting. One is that *the community of nations regards the limits on the legitimate use of violence as being of long standing, not the product of twentieth century governments seeking to prevent rebellions.* Although many nations have come into being during this century through both rebellion and peaceful decolonization, the customary laws restraining the use of force were not created to harness this explosion of nationalism.

The second point is that *the community of nations, not just in the Secretariat's report but many documents and discussions, has agreed that there are in fact limits to the legitimate use of violence, regardless of the justice of the cause.* Moreover, these limits are acknowledged to exist even in times of war. Indeed, it is *from* the laws of war that we obtain our clearest understanding of precisely what these limits on the use of violence are.

Therefore, a condemnation of terrorism is not a denunciation of revolutionaries or guerrillas. It is only a reiteration of the limits of violence which a civilized society has decided to set. It does not in any sense preclude the right to revolution, which is a recognized and protected right under international law.

As one scholar pointed out, those who attack "political and military leaders . . . will not be called terrorists at all" in international law.[7] Another knowledgeable expert remarked that "today's revolutionaries want to be guerrillas, not terrorists," as there is no stigma attached to the status of rebels.[8]

There is no pejorative status attached to rebels and revolutionaries, but even armies engaged in warfare must by law recognize certain limits on the use of violence. The right to revolution and self-determination cannot be predicated upon the wrongful deaths of innocent persons, nor is this right prevented in any meaningful way from other nonprohibited activity by the condemnation of terrorist tactics.

To cite a venerable legal maxim, ***jus ex injuria non oritur***, meaning "rights do not arise from wrongs." Revolutions have occurred throughout history without depending for success on the use of terrorism. There seems to be no legitimate reason why they cannot continue to occur successfully in spite of a ban on terrorist tactics. The position of governments committed to this concept was stated in part by former U.S. Secretary of State William Rogers when he spoke at the 1972 opening of the U.N. General Assembly:

> Terrorist acts are totally unacceptable attacks against the very fabric of international order. They must be universally condemned, whether we consider the cause a terrorist invoked noble or ignoble, legitimate or illegitimate.[9]

Not all nations, governments, or individuals agree with this assessment. Even the nations who subscribe to this assessment are not unfailingly willing to adhere to it. For instance, during World War II, Nazism was regarded as "an ultimate threat to everything decent . . . an ideology and a practice of domination so murderous, so degrading even to those who might survive it, that the consequences of its final victory were literally beyond calculation, immeasurably awful."[10]

But nonstrategic, random terror bombing by those same nations who have authored and defended the current laws against terrorism resulted in the deaths of thousands of German civilians during World War II. These persons were apparently sacrificed for "psychological" purposes (i.e., to create fear and chaos in an audience). Such sacrifices of civilians and the indiscriminate destruction of civilians today would be roundly condemned by those same nations if they were performed by a revolutionary or guerrilla force or by a rogue state carrying out terror-violence against its own citizens. So the distinction between acceptable and unacceptable use of force is not always clear, and is of course influenced by the nations responsible for making the rules. But as noted earlier, the mores prohibiting certain forms of violence are not of recent vintage: They have been evolving over many centuries.

One of the ingredients in the formulation of the rules that govern civilized society today that *is* new is the **right of self-determination**. The U.N. Charter, written in 1945, states that "people" have a "right" to determine for themselves the form of state under which they choose to live.[11] Since that time, nations and legal scholars have been trying to work out just which "people" have this "right," and how extensive a justification this "right" confers on individuals engaged in wars of "self-determination."

The answers to these and related questions are not readily attainable. As one scholar noted:

> According to United Nations practice, a "people" is any group that august organization wishes to liberate from "colonial and racist regimes." Thus, the Puerto Ricans are a people but the Kurds are not; the Namibians are a people and possess their own state but the population of East Timor (or what remains of it) is without identity and without hope.[12]

Obviously, this "right" is not clearly defined by the concepts essential to it. Nor is it clear just how fundamental or extensive this "right to self-determination" is. Is it more fundamental than the right to life? If not, then the pursuit of self-determination cannot intentionally jeopardize any person's right to life. Does the right to self-determination supercede the right of a state to try to protect itself and to provide for its citizens a safe and stable system of government?

No "people" seeking to exercise their "right to self-determination" do so today in a vacuum. Their actions in the course of their struggle necessarily have an effect, often a negative one, on other persons within their community. As in any other armed struggle, there must remain limits within which their "right" to pursue "self-determination" must operate, in order to limit the adverse effects of such a course of action on the rights of others.

The problem that this newly articulated "right to self-determination" has created in terms of the limitation of armed warfare is important. This right is readily conferred upon, or claimed by, many groups who do not enjoy, and probably can never gain, majority support among the indigenous population of their state. This means that many groups of disaffected persons may claim this right who have no hope of ever waging even a successful guerrilla war against an established state. The argument has of course been made that these groups therefore cannot reasonably be held to conventional rules of warfare, for to hold them to those rules is to condemn them to inevitable failure.

Faced with the overwhelming odds in favor of the well-established and well-armed state, many of the peoples seeking to exercise their right to self-determination have been increasingly willing to use less conventional methods and means of waging war. Lacking significant popular support from the indigenous population, facing a state whose trained army and weaponry make conventional resistance a mockery, such groups are increasingly willing to use "unthinkable" weapons, such as terrorism, to achieve their right to self-determination.

The difficulties facing such groups seeking self-determination are very real, but the problems which they create are also formidable. What happens, for example, if two peoples claim that their right to self-determination gives them the right to occupy and control the same piece of land? Who decides which group's right should prevail? Should it be decided based upon which group can establish control, or which has the better legal claim to the land? Again, who or what is to make such a determination?

This is not a hypothetical situation. There exist such delimmas in the world at this very moment. The rival claims of the Palestinians and the Israelis to the same land have provoked decades of bloodshed and bitter fighting. Each people in this struggle claim an historic right to the land.

For more than four decades, Israel managed to secure its right to determine its own form of government and to exercise control over its own people. But it has had to do so through force, and it has maintained, until the late 1990s, its existence through the occupation of additional land. Peace is seldom achieved, in the long term, through occupation, and Israel has begun the difficult process of pulling out of those occupied lands. But now there are Jewish settlers, who have lived in those lands for decades, whose identity and security as a "people" is threatened by the withdrawal, and whose own right to self-determination may well be lost in the peace process. As long as there exists within, or near, the borders of this troubled land a "people" whose right to self-determination remains unsatisfied, terrorist acts may well continue to be a threat to peace in the region.

The assassination in late 1995 of Yitzak Rabin, prime minister of Israel, by a Jewish student seeking to derail this withdrawal of Israel from the occupied territories, makes this threat very clear. Certainly, the satisfaction of the Palestinians' right to self-determination will be difficult to achieve in any way which is acceptable to all of the people of Israel. One Israeli military officer noted that even children, born and raised in land-locked Palestinian refugee camps, will state that they are from Jaffa and other coastal cities of what used to be Palestine. Since this land is now an integral part of Israel, there seems to be little likelihood that the aspirations of those Palestinian adults who have fostered this sense of "belonging" to old homelands can ever be satisfied.

Violent actions taken during the peace process begun in 1993 have made it clear that some Palestinians do not want "independence" in the West Bank or the Gaza Strip. They want to return to, and to claim, their "homeland" of Palestine, including the land which is today Israel. It would appear to be impossible to satisfy their right to self-determination *without infringing upon Israel's right to exist.* Just as the Jewish people rejected other offers of "homelands" around the turn of the century, insisting on their right to return to the homeland of their theological ancestors, Palestinians have found it difficult to accept alternatives which fall short of a return of *their* homeland.

On whose side does right rest in this conflict? The right of self-determination which the Palestinians seek to exercise is the same one for which the Hagganah fought against the British occupying forces in the 1930s and 1940s. Just as the Jewish Irgun, and its radical offshoot the Stern Gang, used terror tactics to force out an occupying power, the Palestinians have resorted to terrorist acts to rid themselves of what *they* perceive to be occupying powers

This right to self-determination is, by its very lack of clarity, a dangerous justification for unlawful violence. Since neither the peoples nor the extent of the right itself appear to have any specific legal limitations, the exercise of such rights can lead to vicious spirals of violence, as rival peoples seek to claim their rights within an international system whose constant state of flux lends credence to first one and then the other's rights.

TERRORIST BELIEFS AND IMAGES

Terrorism, then, has been justified by relatively sophisticated theories, such as anarchism, and by less well-defined concepts, such as that of the right of self-determination. But how does the modern terrorist justify himself, on a personal level, for his actions? Does he indeed think in terms of broad theoretical justifications, or is his belief system less complex?

The content of terrorist belief systems has not, in fact, been the subject for much systematic study. The reasons for this neglect are in some respects understandable. For one thing, the study of terrorism a relatively new field, with very little emphasis placed thus far on the worldview of terrorists.[13]

Another, more serious, problem in analyzing terrorist belief systems lies in the difficulties in acquiring and interpreting data. Few if any extensive memoirs, minutes of meetings, or interviews with terrorist decision makers are available to facilitate a reconstruction of events. Much of the data which does exist is classified by governments in ways which make it virtually inaccessible to researchers.

This does not mean that no studies exist of terrorist belief systems. Gerald A. Hopple and Miriam Steiner, in 1984, employed content analysis to evaluate 12 factors as potential sources of action, applying the techniques to 46 documents from the German Red Army Faction, the Italian Red Brigades, and the Basque ETA. Their findings indicated that emphasis within belief systems changes over time, and that different groups stress different motivations.[14]

From the studies which have been made, some significant components of terrorist belief systems have emerged. A brief review of these, while not sufficient to explain why *all* terrorists do what they do, or what they all believe, will offer insights into the framework of logic by which a terrorist justifies his or her actions.

One of the significant components of a belief system is the **image of the enemy**. Dehumanization of the enemy is a dominant theme. The enemy is viewed in depersonalized and monolithic terms, as capitalist, communist, the bourgeoisie, or imperialist. It is not human beings whom the terrorist fights; rather, it is this dehumanized monolith.

As one group of researchers noted, for many terrorists, "the enemy is nonhuman; not good enough. He is the enemy because he is not the hero and is not friendly to the hero."[15] This rationalization is particularly prominent among right-wing terrorists, whether neofascist or vigilante. Like other right-wing theorists, such groups tend toward prejudicial stereotyping, based on class or ethnic attributes. The "enemy" thus might be all journalists, lawyers, students, intellectuals, or professors, who are regarded by such terrorists as "leftist" or "communist."

It is all too easy to make war, even illegal, "unthinkable" war, on an "inhuman" enemy. As long as that enemy does not have a face, a wife or child, a home, grieving parents or friends, then the destruction of that "enemy" is a simple matter, requiring little or no "justification" beyond the "enemy" status.

Viewing the enemy in these terms also makes the depiction of the struggle in which the terrorists see themselves relatively simple. It is a struggle in which good and evil, black and white, are very obvious. The enemy is often seen as much more powerful in its monolithic strength, with many alternatives from which to choose. The terrorists, on the other hand, have no choice except to resort to terrorism in confronting this "monster," which becomes, in their view, a response to oppression, not a free choice on their parts, but a duty.

Also of interest in this belief system is the terrorists' **images of themselves.** Terrorists of both the left and right tend to think of themselves as belonging to an *elite*. Most left-wing revolutionary terrorists view themselves as the *victims*, rather than the aggressors, in the struggle. The struggle in which they are engaged is an obligation, a duty, not a voluntary choice, because they are the enlightened in a mass of unenlightened.[16]

Like terrorists of the right, revolutionary terrorists seem to view themselves as *above* the prevailing morality, as morally superior. Normal standards of behavior do not apply to them. They do not deem themselves in any sense bound by conventional laws or conventional morality, which they often regard as the corrupt and self-serving tool of the enemy. It would clearly be useless to condemn as immoral an action by a terrorist, since it is quite likely that the person embracing terrorist tactics has already reached the belief that the morality which would condemn his action is inferior to his own morality.

This view of the morality is integral to the terrorist view of the **nature of the conflict** in which they are engaged. Not only is this a moral struggle, in which good and evil are simplistically defined, but terrorists tend to define the struggle also in terms of elaborately *idealistic* terms. Terrorists seldom see what they do as the murder or killing of innocent persons. Instead, they are wont to describe such actions as "executions" committed after "trials" of "traitors."

Menachim Begin offered insights into this legalistic rationalization. He noted that, in terrorist struggles, "what matters most necessary is the inner consciousness that makes what is 'legal' illegal and the 'illegal' legal and justified."[17]

Also of importance in understanding the belief system of terrorists is the **image of victims** that have. If the victims are fairly easily identifiable with the "enemy," then as representatives of the hostile forces, they are despised and their destruction easily justified, even if such victims have committed no clear offense against the terrorist or his group. Michael Collins, founder of the Irish Republican Army, noted that the killing of 14 men *suspected* of being British intelligence agents was justified because such persons were "undesirables . . . by whose destruction the very air is made sweeter." This remained true, according to Collins, even though not all of the 14 were guilty of the "sins" of which they were accused.[18]

Innocent victims, persons whose only "crime" was in being in the wrong place at the wrong time, are generally dismissed as *unimportant byproducts of the struggle.* "Fate," rather than the acts of man, is often blamed for the deaths of such persons.

This brings up one last important point about terrorist belief systems: the predominant **theme of millenarianism.** Personal redemption through violent means is a millenarian theme which is found in many terrorist belief systems. Violence is often viewed as being essential to the coming of the millenium, whose coming may be hastened by the actions of believers willing to violate the rules of the old order in an effort to bring in the new order (often conceived of in terms of total liberation).

Such beliefs have led to a deliberate abandonment of restraints. Coupled with the tendency to divide the world into clear camps of good and evil, as noted earlier, this abandonment of restraints usually entails a strong conviction that no mercy can be shown to the evil that the enemy embodies. The terrorist is wrapped in an impenetrable cloak of belief in the absolute righteousness of his cause and the ultimate success which will inevitably come. If all violence brings the millenium closer, then no violence, regardless of its consequences, can be regarded as a failure. The terrorist always "wins" in this struggle.

There are other elements common to some terrorist belief systems. Some, for instance, place a premium on martyrdom, suggesting this as a desirable goal. Others suggest the desirability of Marxist revolution.

Understanding at least these few fundamental elements of terrorist beliefs may facilitate an ability to deal with terrorism in its many forms, and to anticipate its future growth patterns. Certainly the modern terrorist appears to hold belief systems very different from that of either soldiers or criminals.

CAUSES OF THE LEFT AND RIGHT

In addition to having belief systems which help the individual to "justify" terrorist actions, there are a wide variety of causes for which men and women have committed terrorism. Let us briefly consider a few of the motives for modern terrorism.

Religious fanaticism The Islamic Jihad has given the world ample evidence of the destructive power of *a committment to waging "holy" war based on religious principles.* The "holy war" waged by Islamic fundamentalists has torn Lebanon apart, has caused the death or continued captivity of numerous Western hostages, and has continued to feed the flames of conflict between Iran and most of its neighbors.

In their righteous fervor, Shi'ite fanatics have been unrepentantly responsible for the loss of hundreds, perhaps even thousands, of lives. Planes are sabotaged, temples stormed, and unrelenting guerrilla warfare waged, all in the name of "religion." It is a war which pits Shi'ite Muslims against Sunni Muslims, as well as against Christians, Jews, and other religious groups. Martyrdom is a compelling lure, and self-sacrifices valued above many other virtues, including mercy or pity. In the name of Allah, rivers of blood have flowed, and will no doubt continue to flow, for fanatics of any sort are seldom ever satisfied by any gains.

Anarchism   Few groups still operate today which hold strictly to this cause. Over the last three decades of the twentieth century, we witnessed the growth and demise of the Weather Underground and the Symbionese Liberation Army in the United States. The Japanese Red Army is one group which, in its rhetoric, has espoused anarchistic beliefs. Such groups have tended to be small and short-lived, perhaps because their goals are somewhat nebulous, and thus they find it difficult to draw others into their ranks. Anarchism's more extreme form, *nihilism*, in which the destruction of *all* structure and form of society is sought, still exists as an ideology among certain Western European terrorist groups.

Neo-nazism and Neo-fascism   There have been, in recent years, a number of groups which have sprung up throughout Western Europe and the United States, which have embraced a neo-fascist doctrine. In the United States, for example, the Aryan Nations and several of its splinter groups, including the Order, the White Patriots Party, the Covenant, the Sword and the Arm of the Lord, and Bruder Sweigen Strike Force II, have been involved in armed conflict with the authorities, and have been responsible for several bombings in which innocent people were killed. Indeed, one White Patriot Party leader has been indicted for helping to arm and train a paramilitary group within the state of North Carolina. The devastating bomb blast in Oklahoma City in 1995, after which a shocked nation watched the bodies of small children carried lifeless or dying from the rubble, was attributed to a member of a paramilitary group in Michigan. Paramilitary, essentially neo-nazi groups such as the Hoffman Sports Group, have also emerged in Germany; and in Italy, in the latter years of the twentieth century, there has been a resurgence of right-wing paramilitary groups, engaging in acts of terror-violence, including the bombing of a train.

Separatism *Seeking separation from an existing state*, is also a prevalent theme. Perhaps the best known separatist group is the ETA, the Basque separatists who seek independence or at least autonomy from Spain. They have used bombs and machineguns to try to force the Spanish government to accede to their demands for independence. The French-Canadian separatists, the FLQ, were less active in the 1980s, but were responsible for several acts of terrorism during the previous two decades. Within the United States, Omega 7, the violent Puerta Rican independence faction, has committed many acts of violence, including the placing of bombs in New York's crowded airports, and the attempted murder of U.S. officials.

Nationalism It is difficult to separate nationalism from separatism as a motivator of terrorism. The distinction is somewhat unclear in many cases. Groups whose motivation is nationalism *are those who seek for their portion of society, which is usually but not always a minority, control of the system of government and the allocation of resources within that nation-state.* Such groups do not seek independence or separation from the nation. With this in mind, the Irish Republican Army, whose terrorist acts in Northern Ireland are the source of infamous legend, could conceivably have been classed in this category, prior to the peace process in the 1990s. Organizations such as the African National Congress, whose members from time to time have been accused of engaging in acts of terrorism, could also have fallen, at one time, within this category.

Issue orientation Within the past few years, *a number of issues have aroused such violent sentiments that adherents to one side or another have resorted to terrorist violence to enforce their beliefs.* Abortion is one such issue: Its opponents have actually bombed abortion clinics and shot the workers in those clinics. Oddly enough, environmental- and animal-protection activists, during the last of the twentieth century, became increasingly militant in their insistence that such protection is crucial and worth fighting for. Placing spikes in trees and in paths through the woods to thwart loggers, and burning down animal testing centers have become all too common actions by such groups. Doctors have been killed to "save the fetuses" that those doctors may have been willing to abhort. Earth Now, one militant environmental group in the United States, rationalized that if it was necessary to kill people to save the trees, then they would be "justified" in killing people! The issue of nuclear power and nuclear weapons, too, has provoked violence. Several modern novelists and screenwriters have created all-too-realistic scenarios concerning the possibility of antinuclear activitists detonating a nuclear weapon to illustrate their contention that such weapons must be banned. Thus far, such an incident exists only in fiction, but the growing intensity of the debate on this issue makes such an incident uncomfortably close to reality.

Ideological mercenaries   The legendary Illich Ramirez Sanchez, known to the world as "Carlos," and the more recent Abu Nidal have given rise to a fear of the proliferation of *terrorists-for-hire*. While it is beyond debate that such persons do exist, and cause considerable violence, there seems little evidence which suggests the development of a mercenary army of terrorists. Indeed, the arrest of "Carlos," from his abode in the Sudan, and his removal for trial in France, indicates that the next century may have less tolerance politically for such individuals in a world in which nations no longer can count on a "cold war" to protect them from direct intervention by a stronger nation if they harbor such a mercenary.

Pathological terrorists   There are, of course, some persons *who kill and terrorize for the sheer joy of terroriszing, not for any cause or belief.* Charles Manson was perhaps one such; those who commit so-called serial murders are of the same cast. They have no cause; they are sick and twisted individuals, whom Frederick Hacker has called "crazies."[19]

Counterterror terrorists   Perhaps the most frightening development toward the end of the twentieth century is the proliferation of so-called counterterror terrorists, *the death squads which meed out summary justice to those judged by their leaders to be "terrorists."* Several authoritarian states, threatened by political change, have resorted to these semiofficial troops, thereby inspiring that spiral of terror-violence discussed earlier. Several countries in Central and South America have fallen prey to the lure of counterterror tactics to control terrorism.

CONCLUSIONS

Terrorism *is* different today, with many different forms and many different causes. The argument continues to be made that the justice of the cause, the nobility of the motive, in some way makes the terrorist act less heinous. To understand the cause for which the terrorist fights, and the belief system in which he or she operates, it is said, makes it less likely that one will whole-heartedly condemn the actions taken.

But does the woman whose legs are blown off in an explosion in the supermarket understand that the bomb was placed by persons who bore her no personal grudge, but were merely seeking independence or separatism for a disenfranchised minority? Will the family of a child killed in an airline explosion accept the explanation that the group responsible for the explosion had not enough weapons to fight a legitimate battle with an authoritarian government?

No cause, however just or noble, can make such actions acceptable. Understanding cannot diminish the horror of the atrocity committed against the innocent. The right of self-determination, if it must be secured by the wrong of the murder and maiming of innocents, is not worth the price in the eyes of the rest of the world.

EVALUATION

If a group is exercising its right to self-determination, does this give it the right to commit a wrong on other persons? To what extent is one justified in committing a wrong in order to secure a right? Is there ever a time in which, as some have argued, the needs of the many—to secure the right of self-determination or freedom—can be said to outweigh the needs of the few—the victims of the violence?

Consider and discuss the following incidents, keeping in mind several questions: Were these acts of terrorism? For what cause were they committed? Were they in any sense justified?

a. **Assassination of Franz Ferdinand**—Shot to death by a man who felt, with some justice, that the rights of the minority of which he was a part were being cruelly ignored in the carving up of Europe by nation states. Ferdinand's death precipitated the events leading up to World War I. His death was, in some ways, the catalyst to that cataclysm.

b. **Assassination of Anwar Sadat**—Shot by men who felt that Sadat had betrayed the Arabs by his willingness to establish a peaceful relationship with Israel. Sadat's death considerably slowed down the peace process in the Middle East. His successor, Hosni Mubarak, was understandably reluctant to take similar unpopular steps.

c. **Bombing of the U.S. Marine barracks in Lebanon**—Carried out by militants who regarded the U.S. military presence in Lebanon as an invasive influence in their civil war. The attack resulted in over 200 deaths and the diminishing of the U.S. presence in that war-torn country. Syrian and Israeli influence and presence remain strong in that country's territory.

d. **Bombing of Hiroshima**—Carried out by U.S. bombers carrying atomic weapons. This attack was designed to bring a quick halt to the devastating war in the Pacific and an end to World War II. It did indeed achieve this, at the cost of countless thousands of Japanese civilian dead or maimed, and many more who bore disease and deformity for generations.

SUGGESTED READINGS

Brown, Michael. "Right-Wing Extremism as an Extention of American Frontier Tradition of Violence." Missouri State University, Academy of Criminal Justice Scientists, 1987.

Crenshaw, Martha. "Ideological and Psychological Factors in International Terrorism." Paper presented to the Defense Intelligence College Symposium on International Terrorism. Washington, DC, December 2-3, 1985.

Hacker, Frederick J. *Crusaders, Criminals, and Crazies: Terror and Terrorism in Our Time.* New York: Bantam Books, 1978.

Jenkins, Brian. *The Terrorist Mindset and Terrorist Decision-making: Two Areas of Ignorance.* Santa Monica, CA: Rand, 1979.

Kidder, Rushworth M. "The Terrorist Mentality." *Christian Science Monitor,* May 15, 1986.

Schechterman, Bernard. "Religious Fanaticism as a Factor in Political Violence." *International Freedom Foundation,* December 1986.

"Turner Diaries: Blueprint for Right-Wing Revolution." *Law Enforcement News,* June 30, 1987.

Wright, Robin. "Holy Wars: The Ominous Side of Religion in Politics." *Christian Science Monitor,* November 12, 1987.

ENDNOTES

1. R. Blackey and C. Payton, *Revolution and the Revolutionary Ideal* (New York: Pergamon Press, 1976) pp. 91–93. See also B. Croce, *History of Europe in the Nineteenth Century,* H. Furst, trans. (London: Hutchinson Press, 1953).

2. Sandra Stencel, "Terrorism: An Idea Whose Time Has Come." *Skeptic: The Forum for Contemporary History,* no. 11 (January–February 1976) p. 51.

3. Emma Goldman, *Anarchism and Other Essays* (New York: Dover, 1969) p. 66. This is a republication of the original 1917 edition. Of particular note to the student of terrorism are Goldman's essays on the meaning of anarchism and the "psychology of political violence."

4. Quoted by Jonathan Harris in *The New Terrorism: Politics of Violence* (New York: Julian Messner Press, 1983) p. 141.

5. Robert Friedlander, "On the Prevention of Violence," *The Catholic Lawyer,* vol. 25, no. 2, (Spring 1980) pp. 95-105.

6. U.N. Secretariat Study, "Measures to Prevent International Terrorism," U.N. Doc. A/C.6/418 (November 2, 1973). Prepared as requested by the Sixth Legal Committee of the General Assembly.

7. C. Leiser, "Terrorism, Guerrilla Warfare, and International Morality," *Sanford Journal of International Studies,* vol. 12, 1985, pp. 39–43.

8. J. Bowyer Bell, "Trends of Terror: Analysis of Political Violence." *World Politics,* 29 (1977) pp. 476-477.

9. For the full text of his remarks, see State Department Bulletin no. 67 (1972) pp. 425-249.

10. Quoted by Robert Friedlander, "On the Prevention of Violence," p. 67.

11. The United Nations Charter entered into force on October 24, 1945.
12. Robert Friedlander, "The PLO and the Rule of Law: A Reply to Dr. Annis Kassim," *Denver Journal of International Law and Policy,* vol. 10, no. 2 (Winter 1981) p. 231.
13. Brian M. Jenkins, *The Terrorist Mindset and Terrorist Decisionmaking: Two Areas of Ignorance* (Santa Monica, CA: Rand, 1979) p. 6340.
14. Gerald W. Hopple and Miriam Steiner, *The Causal Beliefs of Terrorists: Empirical Results* (McLean, VA: Defense Systems, 1984).
15. Franco Ferracuti and Francesco Bruno. "Italy: A Systems Perspective." *Aggression in Global Perspective* (New York: Pergamon Press, 1983) A. Goldstein and M.H. Segall, eds.
16. Martha Crenshaw, "Ideological and Psychological Factors in International Terrorism." Paper prepared for the Defense Intelligence College symposium on International Terrorism, Washington, DC (December 2–3, 1985).
17. Quoted by Martha Crenshaw, "Ideological and Psychological Factors in International Terrorism," p. 8.
18. Rex Taylor, *Michael Collins,* (London: Hutchinson Press, 1958) p. 17.
19. Frederick J. Hacker, *Crusaders, Criminals, Crazies: Terror and Terrorism in Our Time* (New York: Bantam Books, 1978).

CHAPTER FOUR

CRIMINALS OR CRUSADERS?

Nothing is easier than to denounce the evil doer;
nothing is more difficult than to understand him.

—Fedor Dostoevsky

KEY CONCEPTS

criminals	"soldiers of the revolution"
crusaders	group dynamics
crazies	trends in recruitment
characteristics of a "successful" terrorist	trends in membership
fedayeen	Abu Nidal

What kind of person becomes a terrorist? Perhaps an understanding of the dynamics of becoming a terrorist will increase our understanding of this phenomenon. As noted in the previous chapter, there are a wide variety of causes for which terrorist acts are committed. It is also true that there are a wide variety of individuals and groups who commit terrorist acts. While it is not feasible to study all such persons in detail, a brief analysis of some of the important characteristics of modern "terrorists" might be informative.

The political world has changed a great deal in the last two decades of the twentieth century. These political changes have influenced the type of persons more likely to be recruited into terrorist groups. A study of the type of individuals known to be drawn to terrorism in the twentieth century will, perhaps, help us to predict the most probable type of person who would be a twenty-first century terrorist. This could be an extremely useful tool for governments and institutions confronted with the need to cope with terrorism.

PROFILE OF A TERRORIST

Why do people become terrorists? Are they crazy? Are they thrill seekers? Are they religious fanatics? Are they ideologues? Is there any way to tell who is likely to become a terrorist?

This final question provides a clue as to why political scientists and government officials are particularly interested in the psychological factors relating to terrorism. If one could isolate the traits which seem to be most closely related to a willingness to use terrorist tactics, then one would be in a better position to predict and prevent the emergence of terrorist groups.

Unfortunately, the isolation of such traits is not easy. Just as not all violence is terrorism, and not all revolutionaries are terrorists, not all persons who commit acts of terrorism are alike. Frederick Hacker has suggested three categories of persons who commit terrorism: **criminals, crusaders,** and **crazies.** He notes that one is seldom "purely" one type or the other, but that each type offer some insights into why an individual will resort to terrorism.[1]

Understanding the individual who commits terrorism is vital, not only for humanitarian reasons, but also in order to decide how best to deal with those individuals *while they are engaged in terrorist activities.* From a law enforcement perspective, for example, it is important to appreciate the difference between a criminal and a crusading terrorist involved in a hostage-taking situation. Successful resolution of such a situation often hinges on an understanding of the mind of the individuals perpetrating the terrorist act.

Let us consider the three categories of terrorists suggested by Hacker. For the purposes of this study, we need to establish loose descriptions of these three types. Hacker offers some useful ideas on what is subsumed under each label. **Crazies,** he suggests, are *emotionally disturbed individuals who are driven to commit terrorism "by reasons of their own that often do not make sense to anybody else."*

Criminals, on the other hand, *perform terrorist acts for reasons that are understood by most: that is, for personal gain.* Such individuals transgress the laws of society knowingly and, one assumes, in full possession of their faculties. Both their motives and their goals are usually clear, if still deplorable, to most of mankind.

Not so the **crusaders**. These individuals *commit terrorism for reasons that are often unclear both to themselves and to those witnessing the acts.* Their goals are frequently even less understandable. While such individuals are usually *idealistically inspired*, their idealism tends to be a rather mixed bag of half-understood philosophies. Crusaders, according to Hacker, seek not personal gain, but prestige and power for a collective cause. They commit terrorist acts in the belief "that they are serving a higher cause," in Hacker's assessment.

What difference does it make *what* kind of terrorist there is behind the machine gun or bomb? To the law enforcement individuals charged with resolving the hostage situation, it can be *crucial* to know what type of person is controlling the situation. Criminals, for instance, can be offered sufficient personal gains or security provisions to induce them to release the hostages. Crusaders are far less likely to be talked out of carrying out their threats by inducements of personal gains, since to do so they would have to betray, in some sense, that "higher cause" for which they are committing the action.

For the same reason, it is useful to security agents to know what type of individual is likely to commit a terrorist act within their province. A criminal, for example, would be more likely to try to smuggle a gun aboard an aircraft than a bomb, since the criminal usually anticipates living to enjoy the reward of his or her illegal activities. Crusaders, however, are more willing to blow themselves up with their victims, since their service to that "higher cause" often carries with it a promise of a reward in the life to come.

The distinction between criminals and crusaders with respect to terrorism needs some clarification. Clearly, when anyone breaks the law, as in the commission of a terrorist act, he or she becomes a criminal, regardless of the reason for the transgression. The distinction between criminal and crusader, however, is useful in understanding the differences in the motives and goals which move the person to commit the act.

The majority of the individuals and groups carrying out terrorist acts in the world in the last decade of the twentieth century are crusaders. This does not mean that there are not occasional instances of individuals who, due to some real or perceived injury, decide to aim a machine gun at the target of their anger, and to kidnap or destroy anyone in sight. Nor does it mean that there are not individual criminals, and criminal organizations, who engage in terrorist activities.

Nonetheless, it is true that the majority of individuals who commit modern terrorism are, or feel themselves to be, crusaders. According to Hacker, the typical crusading terrorist *appears* to be normal, no matter how crazy his cause or how criminal his means. He or she is neither a dummy nor a fool, neither a coward nor a weakling. Instead, the crusading terrorist is frequently a professional, who is well trained, well prepared, and well disciplined in the habit of blind obedience.

Table 4.1 indicates a few dramatic differences between the types of terrorist Hacker profiles. One is that crusaders are the *least* likely to negotiate a resolution to a crisis, both because such an action can be viewed as a betrayal of a sublime cause, and because there is little that the negotiator can offer, since neither personal gain nor safe passage out of the situation are particularly desired by true crusaders. Belief in the "cause" makes death not a penalty, but a path to reward and glory; therefore the threat of death and destruction can have little punitive value. What can a police or military negotiator offer to a crusader to induce the release of hostages or the defusing of a bomb?

Similar problems exist with crazies, depending upon how much in touch with reality such an individual is at the time of the incident. Negotiation is difficult, but not impossible, if the negotiator can ascertain the goal or motive of the perpetrator, and offer some hope (even if it is not real) of success in achieving that goal by other, less destructive means. One of the critical elements is that crazies, according to Hacker's evaluation, have a limited grip on the reality that they themselves may die in the course of this action. Thus, the threat of death by superior police or military force carries diminished weight if the perpetrator cannot grasp the fact that he or she may die in this encounter. Just as the reality of "death" for very young children is a dif-

TABLE 4.1

Type of Terrorist	Motive/Goal	Willing to Negotiate	Expectation of Survival
Criminal	personal gain/profit	usually, in return for profit and/or safe passage	strong
Crusader	"higher cause" (usually a blend of religious and political beliefs)	seldom, since to do so could be seen as a betrayal of the cause	not substantial, since death offers reward in "afterlife"
Crazy	clear only to perpetrator	possible, but only if negotiator can understand motive and offer hope/alternatives	strong, but not based on reality

ficult concept to grasp, Hacker suggests that crazies offer serious difficulties for negotiators because they can often not grasp this reality.

Criminals, then, are the preferred perpetrators, because they will
negotiate; their demands are quite logical (although often outrageous), and they are based in terms which can be met. Or perhaps rational alternatives can be offered. Criminals know that they can be
killed, and they have a strong belief and desire to live and to enjoy
the rewards of the actions they are taking. Thus, negotiators have specific demands to be bartered, and their "clients" can be expected to
recognize superior force, and to respond accordingly in altering demands and resolving the incident.

These differences are critically important to those agencies entrusted with resolving situations in which hostages are held by terrorists. The type of terrorists engaged in the incident significantly impacts the successful, peaceful resolution of the situation.

How is this information useful? To political scientists, as well as
to military, police, and other security and intelligence units assigned
the task of coping with terrorism, an understanding of the type of person likely to commit acts of terrorism is invaluable. As our understanding of a phenomenon increases, our ability to predict its behavior with some accuracy also increases. Thus, as we try to understand
who terrorists are and what they are like, we should increase our ability to anticipate their behavior patterns.

CAN WE GENERALIZE ABOUT A "TYPICAL" TERRORIST?

What, then, do we know about the type of individual who becomes a
terrorist? About the successful terrorists we frequently know very little, in terms of personal data, since successful terrorists depend upon
secrecy for protection. Through the capture of those less efficient in
the art of terrorism, we have learned some useful information; and
our security and intelligence organizations have added substantially
to that data pool.

Nevertheless, it remains true that to generalize about the "typical" terrorist can be very difficult with any degree of accuracy. The
search for a "terrorist personality" is a legitimate exercise, but it is
unlikely to produce any common denominator capable of uniting a
wide variety of countries, periods of time, cultures, and political alliances. In other words, the community of nations is unable, at this
point, to agree on such a profile.

Some scholars have, of course, attempted to create a profile of a
"typical" terrorist. Their successes are mixed, at best, but do offer some

ideas which help us not only to understand what a "typical" terrorist may be like (if such a creature can be said to exist), but also to evaluate how terrorists as well as terrorism have changed in recent years.

Edgar O'Ballance offers one such critique of what he calls a "successful" terrorist (by which he appears to mean one who is neither captured nor dead). In his book, *The Language of Violence*, O'Ballance suggests several essential **characteristics of the "successful" terrorist**. These include:

1. **Dedication**—To be successful, a terrorist cannot be a casual or part-time mercenary, willing to operate only when it suits his convenience or his pocket. He must become a **fedayeen**, a "man of sacrifice." Dedication also implies absolute obedience to the leader of the political movement.

2. **Personal bravery**—As the terrorist must face the possibility of death, injury, imprisonment, or even torture if captured, O'Ballance regards this trait as important, to varying degrees, depending upon one's position within the terrorist group's hierarchy.

3. **Without the human emotions of pity or remorse**—Since most of his victims will include innocent men, women, and children, whom he must be prepared to kill in cold blood, the terrorist must have the "killer instinct," able to kill without hesitation on receipt of a code or signal. As this expert notes, many can kill in the heat of anger or in battle, but few, fortunately, can do so in cold blood.

4. **Fairly high standard of intelligence**—As the would-be terrorist has to collect, collate, and assess information, and devise and put into effect complex plans, and evade police, security forces, and other hostile forces, intelligence would appear to be a requisite.

5. **Fairly high degree of sophistication**—This is essential, according to O'Ballance, in order for the terrorist to blend into the first-class section on airliners, stay at first-class hotels, and mix inconspicuously with the international executive set.

6. **Be reasonably well educated and possess a fair share of general knowledge**—By this, O'Ballance means that the terrorist should be able to speak English as well as one other major language. He asserts that a university degree is almost mandatory.

O'Ballance notes that "all terrorists do not measure up to these high standards, but the leaders, planners, couriers, liaison officers, and activists must."[2] This is an assertion which is difficult to challenge effectively, since if the terrorist is "successful," then the implication is that he or she has succeeded in evading law enforcement, security and intelligence officers, and hence the information about any "successful" terrorist is necessarily either scant or unconfirmed.

We could conclude, with some justice, that most of O'Ballance's assertions, like most generalizations, are at least half-true, half-false, and largely untestable. But these generalizations, with their grains of truth, are still useful in analyzing terrorism and terrorist behavior. Let us instead examine each of his suggested "attributes" of a terrorist to discover whether they can be substantiated by insights into contemporary behavior.

Dedication certainly appears, on the surface, to be characteristic of modern terrorists. The Palestinians involved in various groups, for example, have indicated a willingness to wait for as long as it takes them to realize their dream of a return to a nation of Palestine. They have been willing to wait as long as the Zionists waited, or longer, and many are reluctant to settle for the current peace settlements, since that represents at this point less than full national independence for a nation of Palestine. Like the Zionists, they have unbounded faith in the justice of their cause, and seem willing to die to achieve it.

The progress toward a comprehensive peace settlement in the Middle East in the last years of the twentieth century indicates that this tenacity for the realization of a Palestinian nation may be a liability to the emerging government being established by Yassir Arafat in the Gaza Strip and in parts of the West Bank, since the current settlement represents only a portion of the land that was Palestine, and does not constitute full sovereignty from Israel for the Palestinians. Anger by the Palestinian group of Hamas, a radical movement supported throughout the Middle East by Iran, indicates that a significant portion of the Palestinians remain committed to the full restoration of Palestine to the Palestinian people. The suicide bombings in 1994 and 1995, which claimed the lives of many innocent men, women, and children, has given credence to this "absolute" resolve.

Nor is such dedication limited to Palestinians. Observers in Northern Ireland have suggested that religious fanaticism is handed down from generation to generation in this region as well, carrying with it a willingness to fight and die for a cause. School children in Northern Ireland have exhibited an intolerance and a bitterness which is too often translated into violence. Where children, preachers, and priests join in willingness to commit murder in a "holy" cause, dedication has produced countless bloody massacres and seemingly endless terrorism.

However, as is the case in the Middle East, progress is being made toward a political settlement of the problem of Northern Ireland. Like the situation of Palestine, however, the solution will probably not satisfy all of the truly dedicated terrorists. The IRA's willingness to negotiate a peace has angered absolutists in the Catholic community, and the movement of the British to negotiate with the IRA openly has raised equal anger in militant Protestant groups. If a resolution of the dispute of the British with the IRA *is* reached, and a merging of Northern Ireland with the Republic of Ireland planned, there is reason to fear that a similarly dedicated group of terrorists will emerge, determined to force the United Kingdom into retaining sovereignty in Northern Ireland (thus keeping Protestant control over the region).

Such dedication is not always directed at so specific a nationalist cause. The Japanese Red Army, for instance, founded in 1969, described themselves as **"soldiers of the revolution,"** and *have pledged themselves to participate in all revolutions anywhere in the world through exemplary acts.* This group was responsible for the massacre of 26 tourists at Lod Airport in Tel Aviv, Israel. These dedicated revolutionaries have undertaken numerous terrorist attacks, many of which, like the Lod Airport massacre, were essentially suicide missions, since escape was scarcely possible.

Personal bravery is also a characteristic which has often been attributed to modern terrorists. There are, however, two views of the "bravery" with which terrorists may be said to be endowed. One might argue, with a great deal of justice, that it can scarcely be termed "brave" to use weapons mercilessly against unarmed and defenseless civilians. The men, women, and children at Lod Airport were wholly unable to defend themselves against the vicious attack of the Japanese Red Army. Was it "brave" of the JRA to slaughter these innocent and unarmed people?

The opposing view, which does in fact attribute "bravery" to those perpetrating acts of terrorism, is that to be willing to carry out "missions" in which one's own death or at least imprisonment are inevitable argues no small degree of personal courage. A willingness to give one's life for a cause has, throughout history, commanded at the very least a reluctant admiration, even from one's enemies.

Bravery is, at best, a very subjective term. One may feel oneself to be very cowardly, but be perceived by others to be quite fearless. The audience for one's deeds are often able to judge one's "bravery" only by the commission of the deed, and are unaware of the inner doubts or demons which may have driven one to the act. Nor is the individual necessarily the best judge of his or her own personal bravery, since a person's capacity for self-deception makes it so difficult to assess one's true motives and fears.

The question as to whether or not terrorists who murder innocent persons, with the knowledge that their own survival is problematic, are "brave" may never be answered to anyone's satisfaction. Much depends on the way in which one describes the situation.

According to O'Ballance, a "successful" terrorist should be *without the human emotions of pity or remorse.* Given the necessity of being able to kill, in cold blood, unarmed and innocent persons, this would appear to be a reasonable assumption regarding terrorist personality. Unlike the criminal, who may kill to prevent someone from capturing him, or to secure some coveted prize, a terrorist must, by the very nature of the act which he is often called upon to commit, kill persons against whom he has no specific grudge, whose life or death is not really material to his well-being or security.

Hacker states that

> Often, the terrorists do not know whom they will hurt, and they could not care less. Nothing seems important to them except they themselves and their cause. In planning and executing their deeds, the terrorists are totally oblivious to the fate of their victims. Only utter dehumanization permits the ruthless use of human beings as bargaining chips, bargaining instruments, or objects for indiscriminate aggression.[3]

This description creates a vivid portrait of a ruthless and, one would think, thoroughly unlikable killer. Yet those guilty of such acts have not always presented to the world such a vision of themselves.

Consider the following case: On July 22, 1946, an Irgun team, dressed as waiters, rolled seven milk churns full of dynamite and TNT into the empty Regency Grill of the King David Hotel in Jerusalem. At 12:37 P.M., the TNT in the milk cans exploded, creating pressure so great that it burst the hearts, lungs, and livers of the clerks working on the floors above.

Thurston Clarke gives a gruesome description of the fate of the people in the King David Hotel at that time:

> In that split second after 12:37, thirteen of those who had been alive at 12:36 disappeared without a trace. The clothes, bracelets, cufflinks, and wallets which might have identified them exploded into dust and smoke. Others were turned to charcoal, melted into chairs and desks or exploded into countless fragments. The face of a Jewish typist was ripped from her skull, blown out of a window, and smeared onto the pavement below. Miraculously it was recognizable, a two-foot-long distorted death mask topped with tufts of hair.
>
> Blocks of stones, tables and desks crushed heads and snapped necks. Coat racks became deadly arrows that flew across rooms, piercing chests. Filing cabinets pinned people to walls, suffocating them. Chandeliers and ceiling fans crashed to the floor, empaling and decapitating those underneath.[4]

Ninety-one people died in that bomb blast. Of these 28 were British, 41 were Arabs, and 17 were Jews. Another 46were injured.

Listen to the words of the person who commanded this attack:

There is no longer any armistice between the Jewish people and the British administration of Eretz Israel which hands our brothers over to Hitler. Our people are at war with this regime—war to the end. . .[5]

Was this bombing the deed of a fanatic, a person who could murder in cold blood many innocent people in this "war to the end?" Certainly it would seem to be the case.

And yet the perpetrator of this atrocity, the man responsible for the terrible destruction of 91 lives, was none other than Menachim Begin, who in the 1970s served as Prime Minister of Israel. The Irgun terrorist who plotted to destroy the Hotel is the same man who, working with President Carter of the United States and President Anwar Sadat of Egypt, made significant efforts to move Israel on the road to peace with its Arab neighbors, signing the famous Camp David Accords and bringing a measure of peace between Israel and Egypt.

Is a terrorist a cold-blooded killer only at the time of the commission of his or her crime, or is that a trait which is endemic to his or her character? Does the terrorist, in fact, commit such acts because of a fatal flaw in character, which makes him or her unable to feel pity or remorse? Or is the terrorist driven by circumstances and forces to commit acts which are personally abhorrent?

Just as there is no safe generalization with regard to the personal bravery of terrorists, so there seem to be pitfalls in making too broad a characterization of a terrorist as "incapable of pity or remorse." Perhaps of all that O'Ballance had to say about this particular aspect of a terrorist's characteristics, it is accurate only to say that terrorists appear to have a "killer instinct," simply in the sense that they are willing to use lethal force.

Some may indeed kill without pity or remorse, and may in fact be incapable of such emotions. But to say that terrorists as a whole are so constructed is a generalization for which there is insufficient data, and conflicting indicators in known cases.

The characteristics which O"Ballance suggests of sophistication and education are less true of post-1970s terrorists than of terrorists prior to that time. Many nineteenth-century revolutionary terrorists were indeed intelligent, sophisticated, university-educated, and even multilingual. Those responsible for the murder of Tsar Alexander II of Russia in March 1881 were men and women who possessed a much higher level of education and sophistication than most other young people of their nation. They were led by Sophia Perovskaya, daughter of the wealthy governor-general of St. Petersburg, the empire's capital.

Similarly, the Tupamaros of Uruguay were primarily composed of the young, well-educated liberal intellectuals, who sought, but never fully gained, the support of the less educated masses. The

Baader-Meinhoff gang in West Germany, which terrorized that nation throughout the 1970s, was also composed of middle- and upper-class intellectuals. This gang's master strategist was Horst Mahler, a radical young lawyer, and it drew its membership and support system heavily from the student body of German universities.

The founder of one of Italy's first left-wing terrorist bands, the Proletarian Action Group (GAP), was Giangiacomo Feitrinelli, the heir to an immense Milanese fortune and head of one of Europe's most distinguished publishing houses. Like the Red Brigades, which would succeed this group as Italy's leading left-wing terrorist group, Feitrinelli drew much of his initial membership from young, often wealthy, intellectuals.

Terrorists, in fact, until the 1980s tended to be recruited from college campuses. Many came from well-to-do families, so that sophistication and an ability to mix with the international set were well within their grasp. Intelligence, sophistication, education, and university-training—not only the leaders but also many of the practitioners of both nineteenth-century anarchism and contemporary terrorism possessed these attributes.

But standards and modes of behavior among terrorists as we move toward the twenty-first century are changing. The French anarchists would not have abducted children and threatened to kill them unless ransom was paid. The Narodnaya Volya would not have sent parts of their victims' bodies with little notes to their relatives as the right-wing Guatemalan MANP and NOA did. Neither French nor Russian anarchists would have tormented, mutilated, raped and castrated their victims, as too many terrorist groups have done in the latter part of the twentieth century.

As Walter Lacquer pointed out:

> Not all terrorist movements have made a fetish of brutality; some have behaved more humanely than others. But what was once a rare exception has become a frequent occurrence in our time.[6]

According to Lacquer, the character of terrorism has undergone a profound change. Intellectuals, he contends, have made "the cult of violence respectable." In spite of the violence which characterized their movement, he asserts that no such cult existed among the Russian terrorists, a difficult claim to either prove or disprove. Nevertheless, Lacquer is correct in his assertion that the terror of recent decades is different. That much has already been established in preceding chapters. It is also true that *modern* terrorists are significantly different, and that the differences found in the type of person becoming a terrorist today have a great deal to do with the differences in modern terrorism generally.

TERRORISM IS DIFFERENT TODAY!

Motivation

The motives which drive individuals to embrace terrorism today are different from the motives of the past. Again Laqueur sums up the situation very well:

> Whatever their motives may be, the "ardent love of other" which Emma Goldman observed is not among them. The driving force is hate not love, ethical considerations are a matter of indifference to them and their dreams of freedom, of national and social liberation are suspect. Nineteenth-century nationalist terrorists were fighting for freedom from foreign domination. More recently, appetites have grown, the Basques have designs on Galicia, the Palestinians not only want the West Bank but also intend to destroy the Jewish state, and the IRA would like to bomb the Protestants into a united Ireland. The aims of terrorism, in brief, have changed, and so have the terrorists.[7]

There appears to be less-than-clear *political* purpose involved in much of the terrorism perpetrated today. Moreover, the motives of individuals involved in a struggle against a cruel oppressor are surely significantly different from those of persons rebelling against a democratically elected government. While idealism, a social conscience, or hatred of foreign oppression can serve to drive one to commit acts of terrorism, so can boredom, mental confusion, and what psychologists term "free-floating aggression."

Certainly religious fanaticism is today as strong a motivator for the commission of terrorism as it has been in previous centuries. The "holy war" waged today by Muslims on Christians and fellow Muslims is no less violent than that waged during the Middle Ages. The mixture of political and religious fanaticism has ever been a volatile and often violent combination.

What difference does it make whether terrorism is committed by social idealists or persons suffering from "free-floating aggression"? We could speculate that a social conscience would be more likely to inhibit the perpetrator and keep the terrorist from using indiscriminate violence against the unprotected masses. Perhaps "mental confusion" contributes to an inability to recognize limits on the use of terror-violence.

Group Dynamics

The previously stated reasons are, at best, only suppositions as to why modern terrorists, if they are indeed idealistic, are more brutal than their predecessors. Before considering demographic information which might help to substantiate and explain this difference, let us first consider the impact of the terrorist *group* upon the terrorist. If **group dynamics** help to shape terrorist thought and action, then its impact must certainly be understood in order to understand the contemporary terrorist.

Modern terrorists are, for the most part, fanatics, whose sense of reality is distorted. They operate under the assumption that they, and they alone, know the truth, and are therefore the sole arbiters of what is right and what is wrong. They believe themselves to be moralists, to whom ordinary law does not apply, since the law in existence is created by immoral persons for immoral purposes.

They are not, of course, consistent in their logic. For example, they demand that governments who capture terrorists treat them as prisoners-of-war, as they are involved in a war against either a specific government or society in general. *But* they vehemently deny the state's right to treat them as war criminals for their indiscriminate killing of civilians. In other words, they invoke the laws of war only in so far as it serves their purposes, but reject any aspect of such laws which limit their ability to kill at will.

Two other points should be made with respect to understanding the contemporary terrorist. The first point is relatively simple and involves what seems like a truism: *The less clear the political purpose which motivates terrorism, the greater its appeal is likely to be to unbalanced persons.* A rational individual will be more likely to require a clear purpose for the commission of an extraordinary act. Thus an act whose motivation is unclear is more likely to appeal to an irrational mind.

As already noted, contemporary terrorism has significantly less clear political purpose than that of earlier centuries. Thus, it seems fair to say that a larger proportion of contemporary terrorists may well be unbalanced persons, the crazies that Hacker described.

The second point relates to what psychologists term group dynamics: *If it is true that a terrorist's sense of reality is distorted, as asserted earlier, then the greater the association the terrorist enjoys with his group of fellow terrorists, the greater that distortion will be.* The more, in other words, an individual perceives his identity in terms of the group of fellow terrorists, the less will be his ability to see the world as it really is. For the terrorist who is a member of a close-knit organization, reality is defined by the group. Remember, too, that this group rejects the reality of laws as they currently exist, and morality, as it is defined by anyone except themselves.

Thus, conventional moral and legal constraints have little meaning to an individual who is deeply involved in a terrorist group. The group determines for itself what is moral and what is legal. An individual who has just joined the group may be able to perceive the difference between what the group declares to be morally or legally justified and what is acceptable for the rest of the world. But the longer he or she remains with the group, or the stronger the individual identifies with the norms of the group, the less the individual is able to see the difference between "reality,"as it is defined by the group and the reality of the world.

The strength of the individual's acceptance of the group's definition of "reality" is particularly evident in situations in which terrorism has been a significant part of the culture for several generations. In Northern Ireland, for instance, young people have been "brought up to think of democracy as part of everyday humdrum existence, but of recourse to violence as something existing on a superior plane, not merely glorious but even sacred."[8]

RELIGION AS A FACTOR IN GROUP DYNAMICS

Consider the case of the individual who commits terrorism as a member of a fanatic religious group. Religions, as a rule, offer to some extent their own versions of reality, as well as a promise of reward for conformity to the norms of that reality. The reward is usually promised for a future time, when the present reality has passed away.

Thus the religious zealot committing an act of terrorism is assured by his religion and its leaders that his acts are acceptable to a "higher morality" than may currently exist. He or she is reinforced in the belief that what they are doing is right by the approval of their fellow zealots. Further, the religious fanatic is assured of immortality and a suitable reward in an afterlife if he or she should die in the commission of the act of terrorism.

It would be difficult if not impossible to persuade such a person our of his or her beliefs by reasonable arguments. There is little that could be offered to such a person as an inducement for discontinuing the act of terrorism. What reward can compete with the promise of immortality, approval by one's peers, and religious sanctification?

Obviously, the dynamics of some groups are much more powerful than those of others whose reward system and expensive spiritual support system may be less organized or persuasive. Certain types of terrorists, thus, are much more difficult to deal with on a rational basis, due to this ability of a group to distort reality.

TRENDS IN TERRORIST RECRUITMENT
AND MEMBERSHIP

Some groups have an impact on modern terrorist behavior; and some groups have more impact than others. Motivation has some effect on the type of individual involved in contemporary terrorism. Yet we have not established what a modern terrorist is really like, beyond a few generalizations. Is it, in fact, possible to be more specific about a "typical" terrorist personality?

It is unlikely that this search for a terrorist personality could be successful in creating a set of common denominators which could span several continents, time periods, cultures, and political configurations. All that most experts seem to agree on regarding terrorists today is that they are primarily *young people.* There are, it seems very few *old* terrorists!

There are, however, some demographic trends in modern terrorist affiliations that offer some clues as to who is currently becoming a terrorist. While this falls short of providing a "profile" of a modern terrorist, it does yield insights into not only who modern terrorists are, but also into the impact of such a demographic configuration on contemporary terrorism.

Age   Terrorism is not only a pursuit of the young, it became in the late 1970s and 1980s a pursuit of the *very* young. While terrorists during the time of the Russian anarchists tended to be at least in their mid-twenties, during the last two decades of the twentieth century, the average age steadily decreased. During the turbulent 1960s, many terrorists were recruited from college campuses throughout the western world. This brought the average age down to around 20, give or take a year, since the leaders were several years older, often in their early thirties.

Research in 1977 indicated that the usual urban terrorist was between 22 and 25 years of age. Among the Tupamaros, the average age of arrested terrorists was around 24.1, while in Brazil and Argentina, the average was 23 and 24, respectively. These figures remained true for the ETA, the IRA, and groups in Iran and Turkey during that time.

As early as the spring of 1976, however, evidence of a change in the age level of terrorists began to emerge. Arrests of Spanish ETA-V members revealed a number of youths in their teens. In Northern Ireland, some of the terrorists apprehended were as young as 12 to 14.[9]

Today, however, while the majority of active terrorists are in their twenties, there has been a tendency, particularly among the Arab and Iranian groups, to recruit children of 14 or 15 years of age. These children are used for dangerous, frequently suicidal, missions, partly because their youth makes them less likely to question their orders and partly because their extreme youth makes them less likely to attract the attention of the authorities.

One explanation of this phenomenon is that the anarchistic-revolutionary philosophy which had begun to infiltrate the province of the university students has now begun to infiltrate the secondary school level. While this may explain part of this demographic trend, another explanation may lie in the number of children growing up in cultures in which violence is indeed a way of life.

In the Middle East and in Northern Ireland, for instance, children growing up in violent community struggles could easily become a part of terrorist activities which span successive generations within the same family. Children were thus recruited, not by a philosophy learned at university or secondary school, but by the dogma and lifestyles of their parents, facilitating a potentially more comprehensive assimilation into the terrorist group.

However, by the 1990s, this trend began to reverse, as peace within those two regions came closer to reality. Religious fanaticism is less likely to be the motivating factor compelling a 12-year-old into terrorism; instead, as Hamas membership indicates, most members are closer in age to that found in the early 1970s terrorist profile. The individuals responsible for the bombing of the PanAm flight over Lockerbie, and those involved in the bombing of the World Trade Center in New York City, were certainly not 12 or 13 years of age!

Sex   During the earlier part of the twentieth century, the leaders of terrorist cadres included some women among their numbers, but the rank-and-file were usually male. In many such groups, women were assigned the less life-threatening roles of intelligence collection, courier, nurse, or medical-aid personnel, and women would often maintain "safe houses" for terrorists on the run.

Terrorism of the late twentieth century, however, has been an "equal opportunity employer." For years the commander of the Japanese Red Army, Shigenobu Fusako, was a woman, and of the 14 most wanted West German terrorists in 1981, ten were women. Moreover, studies have shown that female members of terrorist groups have proved to be tougher, more fanatical, and more loyal. They also possess a greater capacity for suffering. Women have also, in some terrorist groups, tended to remain members longer than men, on the average.

One example serves to demonstrate the difference in the roles played by women in terrorism today. It was a *pregnant* woman who was given the task of carrying a suitcase loaded with explosives aboard an aircraft in the 1980s. Only a few decades ago, she would have been, at best, allowed to provide a safe haven for the man entrusted with that task. This is *not* to suggest that this is in any way "progress," but it does indicate a marked difference in the role women now play in terrorism.

Education Until the mid-1970s, most of the individuals involved in terrorism were quite well educated. Almost two-thirds of the people identified as terrorists were persons with some university training, university graduates, or postgraduate students. Among the Tupamaros, for example, about 75 percent of their members were very well educated, and of the Baader-Meinhof organization in West Germany, the figure reached almost 80 percent.

In the Palestinian groups, most members were university students or graduates, frequently those who had, by virtue of their middle-class wealth, been able to study at foreign universities. By 1969, several thousand Palestinians were studying abroad at universities, particularly in Europe, where they were exposed to anarchistic-Marxist ideas. This group became an important recruiting pool for the Popular Front for the Liberation of Palestine (PFLP). Indeed, the chief for decades of the PFLP, George Habbash, was a medical doctor, who obtained his degree abroad.

But the level of education of the average terrorist is declining today. This is due in part to the trend already noted, in recruitment age of the last two decades of the twentieth century. If young people are being recruited out of secondary school rather than out of college, then the number of individuals in terrorist groups with college education will necessarily decline as well.

This trend brings with it another important decline: a diminishing of the understanding by the rank-and-file among terrorists of the political philosophies which have supposedly motivated the groups to adopt terrorist activities. Elementary school children are clearly unable, as a rule, to grasp the impetus of Marxist philosophy toward social revolution. Unlike the college students of the 1960s who studied and at least half-understood the radical political philosophies, today's new terrorist recruits are fed watered down versions of Marx and Lenin by leaders whose own understanding of these philosophers is certainly suspect.

This downward trend in education and understanding of political philosophy is also exhibited by the terrorist leadership figures themselves, as well as by the cadres' rank-and-file memberships. The notorious terrorist, Abu Nidal, leader of the group bearing his name, only attended college in Cairo for two years. Contrary to his claim in subsequent years, he never obtained an engineering degree, or indeed any other degree. He dropped out and went home to teach in the local school in Nablus.

The rising age level of terrorist recruits does not, apparently, signify a return to highly educated cadres. The individuals responsible for most of the recent bombings and overt attacks have been, for the most part, no better educated than Nidal, having at best acquired part of a college degree. Thus, while age level appears to be rising, education level does not.

Economic status   During the 1960s, many young people joined terrorist organizations as a way of rejecting the comfortable, middle-class values of their parents. They were often children of parents who could afford to send them to private colleges, and they were rejecting the comparative wealth of their surroundings to fight for "justice" for those less fortunate.

Today's terrorists tend to be drawn more from the less fortunate than from the comfortable middle-class homes. While some come from families who have had wealth, but lost it through revolution or confiscation, most come from absolute destitution, for whom terrorism represents the only way to lash out at society's injustices. In the terrorist group, these individuals find a collective wealth and ability to improve one's financial situation that is enormously appealing to the impoverished.

Again, Abu Nidal provides insight into the change in the economic circumstances of the type of person who becomes a terrorist today, in many parts of the world. Nidal, born Sabri al-Banna, was the son of wealthy Palestinian parents who lost everything. From the lap of luxury, his family moved into the extreme poverty of refugee camps. The bitterness and frustration of this life of endless poverty and statelessness may well have produced the catalyst for the terrorist Nidal was to become.

Socialization toward violence   As noted earlier, intellectuals have, during the past few decades, helped to make the cult of violence "respectable." But today's terrorists have been socialized toward violence in ways never experienced before in civilized society. Intellectual terrorists of the 1960s were, for the most part, first-generation terrorists. Today we see an increasing number of third- and even fourth-generation terrorists. Young people recruited in such circumstances have been socialized to accept violence as a normal pattern of life. Peace, as much of the rest of the world knows it, has no meaning for them, and the related values of a civilized society have equally little relevance for their lives.

In Northern Ireland, and in parts of the Middle East, until the peace efforts of the 1990s, this pattern of successive generations of terrorism has produced terrorists who have no understanding of the kind of limits on the use of violence which much of the rest of the world regards as customary. Violence is not only a normal pattern of life, it is a means of survival and its successful use offers a means of security and enhancement of one's own life and one's family's life.

This role of violence is made vividly clear by remarks made by the Reverend Benjamin Weir, an American and a former U.S. hostage held by terrorists in Lebanon. He suggested that, for many Lebanese youths, the only employment open to them, which offered both an income and some form of security for their families, was with one of the warring militia factions. College was for decades either unavailable or unaffordable, and alternative employment in a nation whose economy was in shambles was unlikely. Life as a terrorist was, in some respects, the *only* alternative for many young people in that war-torn country.

TO SUM UP: TODAY'S TERRORIST

These trends present an alarming portrait of modern terrorists. Many are younger, much younger. As any parent (or older sibling) knows, younger children are harder to reach by logical argument. Their values are less clearly formed or understood. They are, as a whole, less rational, more emotional than their elders. They are also less likely to question the orders of their leaders, and more likely to follow blindly those who they trust.

Younger or older, they are less educated, so they are less likely to be following the dictates of their social conscience or their political philosophy, and they are more likely to be simply following orders. It is very difficult to reason with someone who is "just following orders." Some of the world's greatest atrocities have been committed by those who were "just following orders"—who did not even have the excuse of being children!

Individuals committing terrorist acts today are less likely to have a comfortable home to fall back upon or to cushion their failure. Instead, their families are increasingly likely to be extremely poor. For these new recruits, membership—and success—in a terrorist group is the only way out of abject poverty. For them, there can be no turning back.

The most recent terrorist recruits are used to violence; it is for them a daily occurrence. They neither understand nor recognize the need for limits on that violence. They have seen homes destroyed, families killed, in endless wars of attrition. The idea that civilization wishes to impose limits on the types of violence used and the types of victims at risk is beyond their understanding, because they have seen almost every type of violence used against almost every conceivable victim.

These, then, are the new terrorists, and they are a formidable force. Their youth and their patterns of socialization make them unique, even in the long history of terrorism. Whether it is possible for modern civilization to successfully counter this radicalization of the very young toward the violence of terrorism is questionable. What is beyond question is that, unless we *can* reverse these trends, civilization will have to cope with an increasing spiral of terror-violence.

CASE STUDY: ABU NIDAL

In recent years, Sabri al-Banna, a.k.a. Abu Nidal, has become notorious as one of the greatest terrorists of our time. As the architect of the massacres of tourists at the Rome and Vienna airports in December of 1985, as well as the master-mind of countless other atrocities, he makes a fascinating subject for the study of modern terrorism.

Al-Banna was born in May 1937 in Jaffa. His father, Khalil, was one of the wealthiest men in Palestine, with homes in Marseilles, France; Iskenderum, Turkey; and Syria. He also owned several houses in Palestine itself.

All of the al-Banna land in Palestine was confiscated by the Israeli government in 1948 and was acquired by the Jewish state. Sabri's father was dead by this time, and he and his family were forced to flee, first to their house near Majdal, then to the al-Burj refugee camp in the Gaza Strip. In early 1949, they moved to Nablus, on the West Bank.

From a position of incredible wealth, Sabri saw, at age 12, his family reduced to life in the teeming refugee camps. Formally taught at private schools and by tutors, he now entered government school, graduating from the city high school in 1955. Although he entered Cairo University, he returned to Nablus two years later without having completed his degree.

Through his brother, Zakariya, he obtained a job as an electrician's assistant with a construction company in Saudi Arabia. While there, he became involved in the illegal Ba'ath party (which later stood him in good stead with the Iraqi regime). His involvement was noted by his employers and the Saudi regime. He was fired, and later imprisoned, tortured, and expelled from the country.

Sabri returned to Nablus a few months before Israeli tanks rolled in during the 1967 Six Day War. Although he had been a passive member of Fatah for years, he became an active member after this traumatic experience. Again a refugee, he moved to Amman, where he chose the *nom de guerre* **Abu Nidal** (which can be translated to mean "*father of the struggle*").

Of his career since that time, no single account exists, though many stories of his exploits abound. Suffice it to say that he broke with the Palestinian Liberation Organization leadership of Yassir Arafat, contending that it's policy of accommodation and moderation was "selling out the Palestinians." He has established ties with several former communist nations, as well as with some Arab states, between which he has traveled with impunity.

In addition to the attacks on the Rome and Vienna airports, he has directed assaults on a group of British invalids in an Athens hotel, on the Israeli ambassador to London, and on his own nephew's family. He reportedly recruits only Palestinians to his group, whose motivations are similar to his own. He has had them trained in Iraq and Syria, and deploys them throughout the world, primarily against civilian targets.

EVALUATION

The modern terrorist *is* different. The requisites suggested by O'Ballance are met less frequently, even by terrorist leaders, and the trends in terrorist recruitment suggest an increasing deviation from the norms suggested by O'Ballance.

Taking Abu Nidal as an example of a modern terrorist leader, try to resolve the following questions:

a. To what extent does Nidal meet, or fail to meet, the criteria suggested by O'Ballance?

b. To what extent does Nidal exemplify the trends discussed (toward youthful recruitment, toward less education, etc.)?

c. If Nidal is a "typical" modern terrorist, what does that suggest about terrorist acts today? (Is modern terrorism more cruel, more indiscriminate)?

d. Are there other leaders who are more "typical" of modern terrorists?

e. Judging by the trends, from what areas or groups are terrorist recruits more likely to come?

f. Do the individuals who committed the World Trade Center bombings or the Oklahoma City bombing fit the "typical" pattern suggested here for modern terrorists?

g. What does this suggest for those who seek to diminish the incidence of terrorism in today's world?

SUGGESTED READINGS

Hacker, Frederick J. *Crusaders, Criminals, Crazies: Terror and Terrorism in Our Time.* New York: W.W. Norton, 1976.

O'Ballance, Edgar O. *The Language of Violence: The Blood Politics of Terrorism.* San Rafael, CA: Presidio Press, 1979.

Clarke, Thurston. *By Blood and Fire: The Attack on the King David Hotel.* New York: G. P. Putnam, 1981.

Laqueur, Walter. *The Age of Terrorism.* Boston: Little, Brown, 1987.

Russell, Charles, and Bowman Miller. "Profile of a Terrorist," in *Terrorism: An International Journal*, vol. 1, no. 1. New York: Crane, Russak, 1977.

Weinberg, Leonard, and William Lee Eubank. "Recruitment of Italian Political Terrorists," in *Multidimensional Terrorism,* Martin Slann and Bernard Schechterman, eds. New York: Lynne Rienner, 1987.

"Identity Movement Quietly Grows Underground; Bonds Together Far-Right Extremists." *Crime Control Digest*, July 29, 1987.

ENDNOTES

1. Frederick J. Hacker, *Crusaders, Criminals, Crazies: Terror and Terrorism in Our Time* (New York: W.W. Norton, 1976) pp. 8–9.

2. Edgar O'Ballance, *The Language of Violence: The Blood Politics of Terrorism* (San Rafael, CA: Presidio Press, 1979) pp. 300–301.

3. Hacker, p. 105.

4. Thurston Clarke, *By Blood and Fire: The Attack on the King David Hotel* (New York: G.P. Putnam, 1981) p. 45.

5. Quoted by Milton Meltzer, *The Terrorists* (New York: Harper & Row, 1983) p. 111.

6. Walter Laqueur, *The Age of Terrorism* (Boston: Little, Brown, 1987) p. 92.

7. Laqueur, p. 93.

8. Connon Cruise O'Brien, "Reflecting on Terrorism," *New York Review of Books* (September 16, 1976) pp. 44-48.

9. Charles Russell and Bowman Miller, "Profile of a Terrorist," in *Terrorism: An International Journal*, vol. 1, no. 1 (1977) p. 20.

CHAPTER FIVE

TERRORISM
BY THE STATE

Terror is an outstanding mode of conflict in localized primitive wars; and unilateral violence has been used to subdue satellite countries, occupied countries or dissident groups within a dictatorship.

—Thomas Schelling (1966)

KEY CONCEPTS

internal terrorism
intimidation
coerced conversion
genocide
external terrorism

covert terrorism
clandestine state terrorism
state-sponsored terrorism
surrogate terrorism
"fishing in troubled waters"

Individuals and groups are not the only perpetrators of terrorism. Political leaders have used terrorism as an instrument of both domestic and foreign policy for centuries. From the time when centralized governments were first organized, rulers have resorted to the use of terror tactics to subdue their subjects and to spread confusion and chaos among their enemies.

Terrorism remains a formidable weapon in the hands of a ruthless state. It is still used primarily for those two purposes: *to subdue a nation's own people, or to spread confusion and chaos among its enemies.*

Internal terrorism, *practiced by a state against its own people,* has produced some of the most flagrant violations of human rights that the world has ever known. **External terrorism,** *practiced by one state against the citizens of another state,* is less often cited as a form of state terrorism. Its perpetrators tend, as a rule, to try to conceal their roles as the instigators or supporters of the terrorists.

INTERNAL TERRORISM:
THE BEAST THAT LURKS WITHIN

No matter how chilling the atrocities committed by individuals or groups, these crimes pale into insignificance beside the terror inflicted by some states on their own people. Since governments have a much greater array of power, they are capable of inflicting a much greater degree of terror on their citizenry.

A look at casualty figures gives some perspective on the magnitude of the harm states can inflict on their people, compared with the damage caused by nonstate terrorists. In the decade between 1968 and 1978, about 10,000 people were killed worldwide by terrorist groups. In just *one* of those years, 1976-1977, the new military dictatorship in Argentina was responsible for an almost equal number of deaths.

Throughout history, states have used terrorist acts of violence to subdue groups or individuals. States have from time to time used such violence to create a climate of fear in which citizens will do whatever the government wants.

The history of state terrorism stretches back at least into the legacy of ancient Rome. The Roman emperor Nero ruled by fear. He ordered the deaths of anyone who either opposed him or who he felt constituted a threat to his rule, including members of his own family. He was responsible for the slaughter of many of the nobility and for the burning of Rome in A.D. 64. To him, everyone was an "enemy," and with his power he made them all victims of his terrorism.[1]

What a state does to its own people was, until very recently, strictly its own business. Neither the rulers nor concerned citizens in other countries usually interfered with what a sovereign government chose to do with its citizens. Even today such interference is largely limited to diplomatic or economic pressures, and to the problematic effects of an informed world opinion.

At least three levels of internal state terrorism have been identified as useful gradations in understanding the scope of terrorism practiced by the state. The first is **intimidation,** *in which the government tries to anticipate and discourage opposition and dissent,* frequently through control of the media and profligate use of police force. This form of state terrorism has existed in almost every nation-state at some point in its history, most often during times of war. Chile, Argentina, South Africa, and Uganda have offered, at several points in the twentieth century, excellent examples of this type of internal state terrorism. **Coerced conversion**, *involving government efforts to create a complete change in a national lifestyle,* is not unusual in the aftermath of a revolution, as the Soviet Union experienced in the early twentieth century, and as Iran witnessed in the 1980s.

Nations in the twentieth century have also practiced the third level of internal state terrorism, **genocide**, *the deliberate extermination of an entire class, or the extermination of an entire ethnic or religious group,* for ideological reasons, while the rest of the civilized world watched in horror, disbelief, or studied indifference.[2] Nor was this destruction of innocent persons confined to Nazi Germany or Stalin's Soviet Union. Certain tribes in African nations were all but obliterated by rival tribal leaders who grasped the reins of government. Rwanda, in the mid-1990s, experienced at least one wave of this form of terror. Bosnia in the early 1990s was the scene of the mass slaughter of people of one ethnic group by leaders of another. In Argentina, thousands of persons "disappeared" during an oppressive regime.

Let us look at some of these examples of state terrorism a little more in depth, to better gauge a comparison between their destructiveness and the destructiveness of terrorist groups. State terrorism during the twentieth century was not confined to one nation, nor to one continent. While history is sprinkled with examples of gross state terrorism, such as that practiced by Nero, or by the Jacobins during the French Revolution, many modern nations must share the "honors" as terrorist states today.

One of the nations which comes most readily to mind when one refers to a modern terrorist state is Nazi Germany (1933–1945). Hitler moved swiftly after he rose to power to create an authoritarian regime. He suspended all civil rights, eliminated the non-Nazi press, and banned all demonstrations. The Gestapo, his secret police, was given the power to arrest and even to execute any "suspicious person."

Under this regime, in the beginning thousands of people were imprisoned, beaten, or tortured to death. But this did not end Hitler's terrorism of the remaining population. Instead, borrowing the idea of concentration camps from Russia, he created such camps in Germany and in occupied nations, and he gave the Gestapo the power to send anyone they wanted to these camps, without trial or hope of appeal.

These camps became the instruments for Hitler's "final solution" for ridding himself of all his "enemies." It is estimated that during his twelve-year rule of terror, between *ten and twelve million people died.* Some were gassed, others hung; some faced firing squads, and countless others died by other equally violent and vicious means. In twelve years, one state murdered between 10 and 12 *million* innocent people, and was responsible, through the war which it initiated, for the deaths of countless more. It is a record of terror almost unparalleled in history, even by the most vicious terrorist.

But it is only *almost* unparalleled: the Soviet Union under Stalin was responsible for millions of deaths as well. Only estimates can be given for the number of people who fell victim to Stalin's totalitarian society. By the time of Stalin's death in 1953, scholars have estimated that between *40 and 50 million* people were sent to Soviet jails or slave labor camps. Of these, somewhere between 15 and 25 million died there—by execution, hunger, or disease.

In some ways it is more difficult for the world to grasp the magnitude of terror inflicted by such regimes because the numbers are so large and because the masses of individuals remain relatively "faceless." We are able to identify with Alexander Solzhenitsyn in his description of the terrors of the "psychiatric-ward" prison in his book *The Gulag Archipelago,* but we find it difficult to identify with the 25 million who died, unheralded, in the labor camps.

Dictators, as a whole, have found it easier to commit terrorism without world censure than have individuals, for state terrorism is committed, generally, in secret. The shadowy world of state terrorism is thus less susceptible to the pressures of world opinion than the activities of terrorist groups, who actively *seek* this spotlight of global attention.

Cambodia, under the rule of the Khmer Rouge, illustrates this point. During its rule of less than four years, its systematic terrorism was responsible for over 1 million deaths. When one notes that there were only about 7 million people in that land, the magnitude of the terror becomes evident. This regime committed genocide against its own people.

Africa has had its share of state terrorism, too. Colonial powers used terrorism, often in the form of summary imprisonment and execution, to suppress national liberation movements. But this was not the only form which terrorism has taken in Africa. Uganda, under Idi Amin, was clearly a terrorist state. Between 1971 and 1979, over 100,000 Ugandans lost their lives to his barbaric terrorism

Latin America, too, continues to have regimes which practice terror on their people. Five nations on this continent—Argentina, Bolivia, Chile, Paraguay, and Uruguay—have suffered under cruel and repressive regimes. In Uruguay, the terrorism instigated by the leftist

Tupamaros has been repaid a hundredfold by the repressive military regime which came to power in the wake of the collapse of what was, at the time, South America's only democracy.

Argentina suffered under the yoke of a brutally repressive military regime, which finally ended in 1983. Leftist terrorism in that nation provoked a right-wing military-backed response so savage that it staggered the imagination. For a time the press reported the appearance of bodies in ditches and mutilated corpses on garbage heaps and in burned-out vehicles. People "disappeared" by the thousands, abducted by armed men claiming to be members of "security forces." Although the "disappearances" became less frequent as the nation moved toward democracy, the legacy of brutality continues to burden the present government in its quest for legitimacy and acceptance.

In the wake of discovering just how ruthless some rulers could be in dealing with their subjects, leaders of victorious nations after World War II tried to create international laws which would restrict the ability of governments to use terrorism against their citizens. Attempts to create such laws by consensus were only marginally successful.

On December 10, 1948, the General Assembly of the United Nations adopted the Universal Declaration of Human Rights without dissent, calling on all Member countries to publicize the text of the Declaration, and to "cause it to be disseminated, displayed, read, and expounded principally in schools and other educational institutions, without distinction based on the political status of countries or territories."[3]

This document states that "everyone has the right to life, liberty, and security of person," and that these rights may not be taken away by any institution, State, or individual. According to the Declaration, it is not acceptable for states to administer collective punishment, or to punish any person for a crime which he or she did not personally commit. The Declaration, too, emphasizes the necessity of fair trials and equal justice before the law. Since terrorism by a state often involves the summary punishment of individuals, not for any specific crime, but because their deaths or incarceration will result in a climate of fear among other citizens, the Declaration would appear to be significant in the effort to curb state terrorism. However, it has no binding effect in international law. It is, in some respects, only a statement of concern among some states about the presence of state terrorism.

If the Declaration is only a statement of principles lacking mechanisms for enforcement, the subsequent Covenant on Civil and Political Rights has tried to remedy that flaw.[4] But while this Covenant has more explicit provisions for enforcing compliance, it has a much worse record for ratification. Less than one-third of the nations in existence today are a party to this treaty, which is designed to protect individuals from state terrorism. The United States, for instance, refused to ratify the Covenant, just as it also refused for over 40 years to become a party to the anti-genocide convention in the Declaration.

The problem, both in terms of ratification and enforcement, is largely a political one. States do not openly interfere in the domestic affairs of other states, since such interference would leave them open to similar intrusions. Conventions such as those protecting human rights are often viewed as dangerous, even by states with relatively clean records in terms of state terrorism, in that these conventions open avenues for hostile governments to interfere with the internal affairs of the nation.

Kren and Rappoport argue that

> . . . within certain limits set by political and military power considerations, the modern state may do anything it wishes to those under its control. There is no moral ethical limit which the state cannot transcend if it wished to do so, because there is no moral-ethical power higher than the state. Moreover, it seems apparent that no modern state will ever seriously interfere with the internal activities of another solely for moral-ethical reasons.[5]

Most interference in the internal affairs of a sovereign state are based on national security, rather than ethical-moral, grounds. Although the Nuremberg trials offered some evidence that the principle of nonintervention was being challenged by nations motivated by moral-ethical concerns, since that time few nations have indicated that "crimes against humanity" undertaken within a nation's own borders are a basis for international intervention. Even evidence of "ethnic cleansing" in Bosnia during the early 1990s, although generating the formation of an international criminal tribunal, did not produce on the part of nations a willingness to send indicted criminals to the justice process at The Hague. Justice remains largely within the purview defined by the rulers of the individual nation-states.

If it is true, as Leon Trotsky declared at Brest-Litvosk, that "every state is based on violence," does this imply that a state retains the right to perpetrate violence indefinitely? Surely that is extending the right of the state to unnecessary lengths.

The linkage between revolution and violence has already been discussed. A similar relationship exists with respect to the right of a state to protect itself from revolutionary violence. Most modern states have experienced a period of revolutionary violence. During and after such periods, however, the right of a state to protect itself remains restricted by even more rules that those which apply to its revolutionary enemies. In addition to abiding by the laws of warfare, states are entrusted with the responsibility for preserving and protecting human rights and freedoms.

Thus, a state has an abiding obligation to restrain its use of violence against its citizens. Whether at war or at peace, a state is supposed to recognize a legal commitment toward the preservation of the rights of the individual. If it is true that insurgent terrorists frequently try to provoke government repression in the hopes of generating greater sympathy and support for the terrorists' cause, then it is obviously extremely important that governments *not* respond in kind.

This does not mean that governments are or should be held impotent in the face of flagrant attacks on law and order. Certainly a state is responsible for protecting its citizens from violence. But the means used to ensure law and order must be carefully balanced against the responsibility of the government to ensure the maximum protection of civil rights and liberties. Too great a willingness to sacrifice the latter in order to preserve stability within a state would not only be giving the terrorist the impetus for his cause, but would also be placing the state in the invidious position of breaking international law in order to stop someone else from breaking it.

A state which violates international law by committing acts of genocide, by violently suppressing fundamental freedoms, or by breaking the laws of war or the Geneva Convention on the treatment of prisoners-of-war and civilians, can be considered guilty of "state terrorism."[6] If "terrorism" is defined to include acts of political violence perpetrated without regard to the safety of innocent persons in an effort to evoke a mood of fear and confusion in a target audience, then surely states have been as guilty of such terrorist acts as have individuals and groups.

Indeed, it is useful to remember that the word "terror" derives from the actions of a government—the Jacobin government of revolutionary France. In fact, "terrorist" regimes have been far more deadly than group or individual actors in this century, even after the end of World War II.[7] The word "totalitarian" has become part of the political lexicon of this century as a result of state terrorism in Nazi Germany and Stalinist Russia. Both systems relied upon organized, systematized discriminate terror to create a bondage of the mind as well as of the body.[8]

If, as Hannah Arendt suggests, "lawlessness is the essence of tyranny, then terror is the essence of totalitarian domination."[9] In her essay "On Violence," this same expert notes that "terror is not the same as violence; it is, rather, the form of government that comes into being when violence, having destroyed all power, does not abdicate but, on the contrary, remains in full control." State terrorism, thus described, is the quintessential form of terrorism.

State terrorism is frequently a nasty combination of personality and ideology. "Nazism and Stalinism were personifications of the evil genius of their leaders, but they could not have succeeded without a disoriented, terrorized citizenry," according to one expert.[10]

Totalitarianism and state terrorism aim not only at a transmutation of society, but at a fundamental change in human nature itself. The basic goal of terrorist states is mass disorientation and inescapable anxiety. Modern governments whose actions have earned for themselves the sobriquet "terrorist," such as Indonesia in the 1960s or Chile in the 1970s, have employed terror-violence as an integral part of the governing process.[11]

Governments, then, have been, and continue to be, as likely to commit "terrorist acts as individuals and groups. Moreover, it is probably true that "as violence breeds violence, so terrorism begets counterterrorism, which in turn leads to more terrorism in an ever-increasing spiral.[12] So state domestic terrorism not only transgresses international law, but it often creates the political, economic, and social milieu that precipitates acts of individual and group terrorism. It is thus a causal factor in the perpetration of further terrorism.

HOW REAL IS STATE TERRORISM?

In 1972, a young woman named Ayse Semra Eker was abducted off the street by Turkish military police. For the next ten days she was tortured. She was tied spread-eagle to pegs on the floor and beaten repeatedly, on her naked thighs, on her palms, and on the soles of her feet. She was beaten so hard and so often her feet turned black, and she was unable to walk. Electric wires were attached to her fingertips and toes, and she was shocked again and again. Then the wires were moved to her ear lobes, and the current was turned up until her teeth broke and her mouth spewed blood. Electric probes were inserted in her anus and vagina, and she passed out from the pain. She awakened to find her fingernails had been burned with hot cigarettes.[13]

Dozens of nations today use terrorism as (unofficial) government policy to secure and ensure control over their citizens. Amnesty International reports that foreign "experts" in torture have been sent from country to country. Schools of torture teach and demonstrate methods to government officials, particularly electroshock techniques, since that is the easiest and most commonly used form of scientific torture.

Modern torture equipment is exported regularly. Some of the shock machines used by governments to torture their citizens are made in the United States.[14]

Torture is, of course, only one form of state terrorism. In the use of the power of the state, its laws and courts, to stifle dissent and compel the people through fear into compliance, many different tools are utilized. Moreover, the use of murder, slavery, and terror to subjugate people taints the history of almost every modern nation.

Even in the United States, there have been instances of such abuses of power by persons in authority. The U.S. history of violence in the labor movement offers several examples of the abuse of government power. The events in Ludlow, Colorado, offer a poignant vignette of state terrorism. On Easter night in 1914, members of the Colorado National Guard, aided by the company police of the Colorado Fuel and Iron Company (owned by John D. Rockefeller, Sr.), poured oil on the tent city of striking miners and set them ablaze. The miners, who had been on strike and been evicted from their homes in the company town, had dug a cave under the largest tent, and placed the children there for safety. Even so, eleven children and one pregnant mother were burned to death, while five men and one boy were shot to death as they tried to run to safety.

Similar blots on U.S. history in the treatment of blacks also exist. Slavery was enforced by government law and police power for decades. Even with its official end, through the Thirteenth Amendment to the Constitution, unofficial persecution of black citizens continued unchecked. The Ku Klux Klan and similar groups murdered, lynched, beat, and raped blacks in a concerted effort to terrorize the freedmen after the Civil War and Reconstruction. While such groups were not in any sense arms of the state, they were allowed until the 1960s to carry out their terror campaigns relatively unhampered by a sympathetic or uncaring government.

But terrorism in the United States fades in comparison to that practiced by totalitarian states. In the Soviet Union under Stalin, millions of dissenters were murdered or sent to camps in Siberia, where they died. Among these millions were intellectuals, artists, writers, army officers, and small farmers who opposed Stalin's collectivization of farms. Few survived to tell of their afflictions.

There are many weapons used by the state in terrorism. These include arrest (usually in the dead of night to maximize the psychological impact), summary deportation of dissidents or "subversives," incarceration without trial for indefinite lengths of time, and, of course, torture. It is torture which is the ultimate weapon of state terrorism.

Amnesty International's *Report on Terrorism,* published by Farrar, Straus & Giroux of New York in 1975, provides horrifying details of state torture and terror. Included in this report is the following description of torture in Chile:

> Many people were tortured to death by means of endless whipping as well as beating with fists, feet, and rifle butts. Prisoners were beaten on all parts of the body, including the head and sexual organs. . . There were many cases of burning (with acid or cigarettes), of electricity, of psychological threats including simulated executions and threats the families of the prisoners would be tortured. At times the brutalities reached animalistic levels. (p. 27)

The report goes on to tell of rape, sexual depravities, abortions forced by rifle butts, force-feeding of excrement, immersion in ice-cold water or in tanks of gasoline, and countless other atrocities too horrible to recount. They sicken the reader—but they are true, and they are happening now. Such bestiality did not stop with the death of Hitler or Stalin. There still exist many governments today with so little regard for human life and dignity that they are willing to perpetrate such acts of terror on their citizens.

TERRORISM AS AN INSTRUMENT OF FOREIGN POLICY

Coercive measures within the state are only one form of state terrorism. There are at least two other forms of state terrorism which have become prevalent in recent years. Terrorism has also been used by national leaders as an instrument of foreign policy, particularly in the waging of irregular warfare against another state. This has usually taken the form of **covert terrorism**, *terrorism committed without the state being openly involved.*

This covert terrorist behavior can be divided into two categories: **clandestine state terrorism** and **state-sponsored terrorism**. In clandestine state terrorism, *there is direct, but not open, participation by state agents in terrorist activities.* In state-sponsored terrorism, *state or private groups are hired to undertake actions on behalf of the state, which acts as the employer but is not necessarily actively involved in the terrorist acts.*

Unlike the internal coercive diplomacy, (which may be obvious to all observers whether or not they are willing to label it as such), clandestine operations are, by their very nature, conducted in secrecy, and consequently they are very difficult to discern. Thus, there is often little verifiable data which can be used to study this phenomenon.

Clandestine terrorism is primarily used to produce fear and chaos within potentially unfriendly or hostile states. It is used to, for example, weaken the resistance or diminish the intransigence of states, as the cost of such antagonism is made plain. Such activities are also designed to demonstrate the weaknesses and vulnerabilities of opponents, often in the hope of making such adversaries more willing to bargain than to threaten.

Such activities have often been described as attempts to "destabilize" unfriendly regimes. CIA efforts in Chile in the early 1970s took this form. Not only was this organization involved in clandestine efforts, including the assassination of Rene Schneider, the commander-in-chief of the Chilean army, who refused to approve plans to remove Salvador Allende from office, but it was also involved in numerous other efforts to remove Allende. Records indicate that at least $7 million was authorized by the United States for CIA use in destabilizing Chilean society, including the financing of opposition groups and right-wing terrorist paramilitary groups.

Similar clandestine efforts in Nicaragua provoked a great deal of, from the U.S. government's point of view, undesirable attention. Efforts to destabilize the Sandinista regime supposedly came to an official halt in 1982, when the U.S. House of Representatives voted to halt covert activities abroad by the CIA for the purpose of overthrowing the government of Nicaragua. But, as the Iran-contra affair indicated, efforts to conduct clandestine terrorist operations did not cease with the passage of that law. Instead, such activites became one step *more* covert.

Another type of terrorism in which a state may be involved is referred to as **state-sponsored terrorism**. Claire Sterling, in her research into the networks of support and sponsorship which terrorist organizations enjoy, noted that such sponsorship is not only difficult to detect, but that it takes place more in the realm of the third type of state terrorism, called **surrogate terrorism**. *Sponsorship implies direct involvement and a significant degree of control.* Of nations, such as the Soviet Union, which this scholar suggested was heavily involved in sponsoring terrorism, Ms. Sterling states:

> Direct control of the terrorist groups was never the Soviet intention. All were indigenous to their countries. All began as offshoots of relatively nonviolent movements that expressed particular political, economic, religious, or ethnic grievances.[15]

States have chosen to sponsor terrorism abroad either directly or, more often, indirectly. Let us consider at least one compelling reason for indirectly sponsoring terrorism. It may be that such sponsorship offers a low-risk avenue for redressing an international grievance. Some Arab states have chosen to sponsor Palestinian groups engaged in terrorist acts as a less risky method of redressing the Palestinian problem—less risky than provoking another war with Israel.

WAGING WAR BY PROXY: SURROGATE TERRORISM

Other states have found a third form of state terrorism to be a more useful tool in the exporting of a revolution. This form of terrorism has been called **surrogate terrorism**. Such terrorism involves *assistance to another state or terrorist organization which makes it possible for that actor to improve its capability for terrorism either at home or abroad.*

Certainly Iran, under Ayatollah Khomeini, engaged in this practice throughout the Middle East. Some nations within the former communist bloc also offered support to terrorist groups in the form of equipment and training camps, purportedly as a way of exporting the communist revolution, or perhaps as a means for weakening an adversary state (a reason often cited to explain Arab support for terrorist activities against Israel).

Libya has used terrorism as an instrument to help the state track down and eradicate exiled dissidents (or to intimidate them into silence). Libya has also offered sanctuary and assistance to the Abu Nidal Organization and a variety of other Palestinian resistance groups. Moreover, Libya has used terrorism to redress a particular international grievance.

Again we can turn to Claire Sterling's assessment of the Soviet Union's reasons for becoming involved in surrogate terrorism. She suggests that

> The heart of Russia's strategy is to provide the network with the goods and services necessary to undermine the industrialized democracies of the West.[16]

There is, even in the light of information unearthed by Sterling and other journalists who have sought to uncover the support network by which terrorist organizations operate, a significant lack of verifiable data to link states which were thought to have logical policy reasons for supporting such groups with actual instances of substantive support. Whereas few would dispute the evidence of relatively low-level support (providing of safe houses, travel documents, and similar assistance), there is a lack of hard evidence as to any "control" exercised by the Soviets or other states, or participation by those states in any hostile events.

While most researchers recognize that the Soviets had an interest in actions which would spread fear and chaos in the Western world, many are unprepared to go further than that assessment. What is often referred to as **"fishing in troubled waters"**—that is, *the giving of assistance to those already engaged in opposition to states which are one's enemies* —is not an unusual policy, nor is it necessarily illicit. Does such "fishing" make the state giving the assistance culpable for the offenses committed by those receiving the assistance?

Ms. Sterling suggests that ". . . the Soviet Union had simply laid a loaded gun on the table, leaving others to get on with it."[17] By inference, the issue of whether the Soviets *directed* or merely *benefited* from terrorist actions carried out with that "loaded gun," is less significant, while the linkage to the Soviet Union and its state policy is clear. Activities carried out by groups provided with a "loaded gun" are nonetheless instruments of state-supported terrorism.

Other scholars also stress the degree to which the Soviet Union was involved in surrogate warfare through terrorism. Cline and Alexander, in 1984, noted that

> In the 1970s, terrorism, whether backed directly or indirectly by the Soviet Union or independently initiated, appeared to have become an indispensable tactical and strategic tool in the Soviet struggle for power and influence within and among nations. In relying on this instrument, Moscow seems to aim in the 1980s at achieving strategic ends in circumstances where the use of conventional armed forces is deemed inappropriate, ineffective, too risky, or too difficult.[18]

These authors also claim that

> . . . it is obvious from the PLO documents that there exists a carefully developed international terrorist infrastructure that serves Moscow's foreign policy objectives of destabilizing noncommunist governments.[19]

But did the Palestinians commit terrorism only or even specifically at the behest of Moscow? There is little evidence to support such a claim. Moreover, there are many other state and nonstate actors from which the many Palestinian groups receive support. Are they instruments of *all* of their supporters' foreign policies?

Perhaps it would be more accurate to say that they act at times in ways which are beneficial to a particular state's interests, and in recognition of that confluence of interest, they receive support. This still does not clarify the degree of control which the supporting state has over this policy "instrument." It does, however, suggest that the use of such "instruments" can be a hazardous and uncertain foreign policy operation.

One scholar sums up the evaluation of the Soviet's support of terrorist organizations as a foreign policy tool in this manner:

Let us be clear about what we do not know. We do not know the extent, if any, to which the Soviets direct any terrorist organization. Moscow seems to have had great influence over the Popular Front for the Liberation of Palestine (PFLP) but less over other factors within the Palestinian Liberation Organization (PLO). Most of the money for many terrorist groups probably comes, not from the Soviet Union, but from wealthy Arab nations and from criminal activities.[20]

In fact, governments may engage in terrorism for a variety of reasons, which become blurred even in their own minds and are often indistinguishable in the eyes of horrified observers. One cause may be the principal motivator for a particular act, but it may have numerous desirable side effects, which become in time prime motivators, too. A state may, for example, decide to assist an organization carrying out terrorist acts, or field an organization of its own, in order to try to redress a particular international grievance. In the course of events, the state may discover that the terrorism has helped to weaken an adversary state against which it would not ordinarily have had the strength to wage a regular war. After a time, it becomes difficult for the state to decide which is the most important reason for engaging in terrorism by proxy.

In the legions of states who support terrorist groups or nations, there are no villains in black hats. Usually the state is at pains to conceal the linkage, or to rationalize its necessity. Even more often, the links are hidden through many channels and transfers of equipment and assistance.

RELUCTANT BEDFELLOWS: THE ARMS BAZAAR

Let us briefly examine the booming sale of arms to individuals, groups, and nations (such as Iran and Libya) engaging in terrorist acts, who make no secret of their propagation of terrorism. Even among the Western allies, who on paper oppose these regimes and groups, there remains strong support channels. Through these channels, with the knowledge and support of the state, many companies circumvent national law in selling arms to hostile or warring nations or groups.

France sold to Libya dozens of Exocet antiship missiles, which were subsequently used by Qadhafi on the U.S. Sixth Fleet. West Germans traveled to Iran to work out details on a contract for the sale of four diesel submarines, which would presumably be added to the armada with which Iran has threatened shipping lanes in the Persian Gulf. Austria has officially condemned Iraq's use of gas and has offered the use of its hospitals for the treatment of victims of gas attacks. Yet Austria has exported the chemicals used to make the poisonous gas—to Iraq! From West Germany, via Greek suppliers, Iran obtained optics and range-finding equipment. Iran has procured as well the G-3 assault rifle, its standard infantry weapon, from Germany.

Nor is it only Iran and Iraq who have benefited from industrial nations' desires to cash in on the arms market. Libya, which makes no secret of its support for and commitment to groups and individuals engaging in terrorism against the West, has been the recipient of considerable European assistance, only a part of which took the form of arms sales. West Germany, for instance, opposed sanctions against states supporting terrorism each time such sanctions were proposed. It may be fair to assume that part of that opposition stems from the fact that West Germany bought 191,000 barrels of oil from Libya in 1985 alone.

Italy, too, has a strong trade relationship with Libya, averaging approximately $5 billion per year. Libya owned 15 percent of Fiat Corporation. In May 1986, the former chief of the Italian intelligence service admitted that his service had helped Qadhafi get arms and assisted him on intelligence matters. Italy also sold a wide variety of arms to Libya, including Augusta antitank helicopters, Assad-class missile corvettes, self-propelled howitzers, Otomat missiles, and acoustic mines and torpedoes. Many of these weapons have subsequently found their way into the hands of terrorists.

Athens, Greece, the cradle of democracy, has for years been the middleman through which transactions from the West are channeled to various protagonists in the Middle East and North Africa. Members of the Islamic Jihad, Abu Nidal's Organization, and Abbu Abbas have operated freely through Greek borders. Athens itself has been the starting point for airline sabotage and hijacking (as in the June 14, 1985, TWA Flight 847 bombing and the November 1985 EgyptAir bombing, in which 60 persons were killed). It has also been the site of heinous massacres, such as the one perpetrated at the El Al airline service counter, which resulted in the deaths of innocent children and holiday travelers in 1985.

Cooperation between governments in the sales of arms has certainly resulted in some strange bedfellows. None is perhaps stranger that the relationship between Israel and Iran in the 1980s. Israel was one of Iran's biggest suppliers of armaments. In 1984, for example, Israel sold twenty F-4 jet engines to Iran, routing the transaction through Greece to Teheran. In January 1985, Israel offered to sell to Iran (via telexes to brokers, including those in Iran) 150 U.S. Sidewinder air-to-air missiles!

The argument in defense of such sales is that the nations or groups would purchase such arms anyway, so why should Western nations not make the profit that is to be made in these "inevitable" transactions? Such argument is, of course, merely a rationalization of an economic reality which contravenes political policy.

Unfortunately, the economic ties forged by such transactions make it difficult for nations to take firm stands against terrorism or terrorist groups sponsored by the recipient nations. The stronger the economic linkage, the weaker is a government's response to restrict terrorism. The uneasy relationship between these buyers and sellers of arms clouds the issue of each nation's policy on terrorism. The seller nations, the purveyors of arms, find themselves in the dubious position of appearing to sponsor terrorism, indirectly, which is an allegation they cannot completely dismiss.

SILENT PARTNERS:
SYRIA, IRAN, AND LIBYA WAGE SUBTLE WAR

Syrian President Hafez al-Assad has long sought to become the dominant power broker in the Middle East, and until the fall of 1986 he came close to achieving that objective. Until that time Assad contrived to mask his support for terrorists beneath a cloak of state secrecy. By distancing himself from the terrorists, he managed to preserve deniability; and when it seemed strategically expedient, he renewed his credit with the West by intervening on behalf of Western hostages.

Assad's secure power base at home and close ties with Moscow made diplomats hesitant to openly criticize him. In the absence of evidence to the contrary, some observers have even assumed that he was a "helpful partner" in Mideast negotiations concerning Lebanon.

Evidence of his duplicity has, of course, come to light, particularly since the demise of the Soviet Union. As *U.S.News & World Report* noted in an article (November 10, 1986), "even in the diplomatic world of studied indirection and strategic dissembling, the evidence has become impossible to ignore, and it points straight at Syrian strong man Hafez Assad."[21] Secretary of State George Schultz noted that the case of Nezar Hindawi's unsuccessful attempt to blow up an El Al jetliner in London provided "clear evidence" of Syrian involvement in terrorism. Ariel Merari, director of the Tel Aviv University Project on Terrorism, suggested that "there is no doubt that the general policy of sponsoring terrorist activity in Western Europe is done with Assad's approval and probably his initiative." The same report contained one expert's comments that

> For years, Libya's Muammar Qadhafi has been the international out-law, condemned for his wide-ranging support of terrorism. But now it is clear that Qadhafi is an erratic bumbler compared with Assad, a hard-eyed strategist who uses terror as an essential tool of statecraft.[22]

Assad's preferred tool of persuasion has been terror, according to some Middle East experts. During the early 1980s, he began exporting his deadly product, by increasingly indirect means. The CIA has made public evidence that the Syrian intelligence services gave logistical support to the individuals who bombed the U.S. Marine barracks in Lebanon. After the attack, the National Security Agency also intercepted messages showing payments were sent through Damascus to the Iranian-sponsored group responsible for the bombing.

Nor were these the only evidences of Assad's involvement in terrorism. *U.S. News & World Report* (November 10, 1986) published what it termed a "bill of particulars" concerning Syria's links to terrorist events in the early 1980s. Since these events were also noted in the U.S. State Department's annual report on global terrorism, there is little reason to doubt the link to terrorism which this bill implies belongs to Syria. The following are a few of the incidents detailed during that period:

- **September 8–16, 1986, Paris:** Bombings kill ten persons, and injure more that 160 people. An obscure Mideast group, thought to be a cover for the Syria-linked Lebanese Armed Revolutionary Faction, claimed responsibility. The series of bombings were carried out by brothers of jailed terrorist Georges Ibrahim Abdallah, held in French prison.
- **September 6, 1986, Istanbul:** Twenty-two killed, three wounded when Arab terrorists fire on Jewish worshipers at a synagogue. Experts claim the Syrian-backed Abu Nidal group was responsible. (Abu Nidal himself, architect of the Rome and Vienna airport massacres, lived at the time in a heavily guarded apartment building on the outskirts of Damascus.)
- **September 5, 1986, Karachi:** Twenty-one killed, more than 100 wounded in a massacre aboard a hijacked jet. Four gunmen, later linked to Syria, were seized after commandos stormed the plane.
- **November 23, 1985, Malta:** An Egyptian jetliner was hijacked. Sixty people were killed, two by the terrorists and 58 by Egyptian commandos who stormed the plane. The Syrian-backed Abu Nidal group claimed responsibility.
- **April 12, 1985, Madrid:** Eighteen killed and 82 wounded in a restaurant bombing. The Islamic Jihad, backed by Syria, was among the groups claiming responsibility.
- **September 20, 1984, Beirut:** Fourteen are killed and 70 are injured when a car bomb explodes at the U.S. Embassy. The Islamic Jihad claimed responsibility.
- **April 18, 1983, Beirut:** Fifty-seven persons are killed and 120 are injured in the suicide bomb attack on the U.S. Embassy. Responsibility is claimed by the Islamic Jihad.

This is by no means an exhaustive summary of Syria's dealings in terrorism. There were, for instance, five bases near Damascus, and at least 20 other Syrian-controlled camps where instruction in the techniques of terrorism was provided. Yarmouk, in Damascus, was the camp most often used for advanced terrorist training. Skills acquired at these camps were tested in Lebanon's Bekaa Valley, which Syria controlled.

General Mohammed Khouli, at the time head of the Syrian Air Force (which was Assad's personal intelligence service and base of power), directed most of these training operations. One of his deputies, Colonel Haitham Sayeed, was also the intelligence coordinator for Abu Nidal. Khouli and Sayeed, according to Western intelligence agents, directed the Hindawi case.

Yet Assad managed to maintain relatively cordial relations with Western nations. Part of his ability to be acceptable (or at least difficult to avoid condemnation) lay in the care with which he distanced himself from actual terrorist attacks. He also won approval by helping in hostage crises. Indeed, he became a master at the strategy of helping groups to take hostages on one hand and gaining favor with the West by aiding in their release on the other hand. Until the Hindawi case, no one could *prove* that what to the West seemed to be the "helping" hand knew what the "terrorist" hand was doing.

Unlike Libya's Col. Qadhafi, Assad seemed to prefer secrecy to the spotlight of international attention in the drama of terrorist involvement. Assad relied on sporadic, preferably untraceable attacks, which allowed him to avoid retribution. Qadhafi treated terrorism like a banner, to be waved before the troops; for Assad, it was instead as quick and silent as an assassin's bullet.

Assad had no wish to make himself an obvious target for retribution in a terrorist incident, as Qadhafi has done. He did not underestimate the desire for revenge of a nation whose citizens have been attacked, and he clearly did not wish to make himself or his country a tempting target. He preferred to wage a hit-and-run war, in which it was hard to find the guys wearing the black hats. He was, at heart, a pragmatic politician, a survivor.

One expert at the Foreign Policy Research Institute summed up sponsors of terrorism during the 1970s and early 1980s in this manner:

> Of the four major sponsors of terrorism—the PLO, Libya, Iran, and Syria—the first two get all the attention. But it's the other two we should be watching, and particularly Syria. It is quiet and deadly in its effectiveness, and until this slipup with Hindawi, it has always managed to stay in the shadows.[23]

It should be noted that, in the wake of the Gulf War, Syria began to distance itself from its role as a sponsor of terrorism. Seeking to improve its relations with the Western nations, Syria moved away from obvious links with various Middle Eastern groups engaging in terrorism. Whether this move was permanent or only a feint designed to deflect Western criticism remains unclear. The situation in Lebanon has not yet stabilized and the terrorist groups have not yet been forced to leave that country to seek sanctuary and assistance elsewhere. The Middle East peace process tests Syria's willingness to cooperate in the control of violence against Israel. Syria will only pass this test by refusing to provide shelter and assistance to such groups.

By 1993, Iran was clearly the most active state sponsor of terrorism, being implicated in terrorist attacks in Italy, Turkey, Germany, France, Switzerland, Argentina, and Pakistan. Iran's policymakers viewed terrorism as a valid tool to accomplish their political objectives, and acts of terrorism were approved at the highest level of the Iranian government. Iran was also a preeminent sponsor of extremist Islamic and Palestinian groups, providing funds, weapons, and training. The Lebanese Hizbollah, Iran's most important terrorist "client," was responsible for some of the most lethal acts of the 1980s and early 1990s, including the 1983 suicide truck-bombings of the U.S. embassy and U.S. Marine barracks in Beirut, the hijacking of TWA Flight 847 in 1985, the 1992 car-bombing of the Israeli embassy in Argentina, and rocket attacks on civilians in northern Israel.

Iran has openly supported many other radical organizations which have resorted to terrorism, including the Palestinian Islamic Jihad, the Popular Front for the Liberation of Palestine—General Command, and Hamas. The latter group was particularly active during the 1994-1996 portion of the peace process, with numerous car-bombings and suicide bombings carried out in Israel, the West Bank and the Gaza Strip.

Iran's support for terrorism has been open, unlike Syria's more covert assistance. This has made it easier to link the state to the terrorist acts, but more difficult to prevent such support, since the Israeli government appeared unconcerned with international disapproval or condemnation. Moreover, Iran's strong position as an oil-producing nation made many nations unwilling to support direct action against Iran in retaliation for such support.

Libya, while also an oil state, has been less obvious in its support for terrorism since 1985, when linkage to a terrorist act in West Germany evoked a bombing attack on Tripoli by the United States. Indeed, Libya's support for acts of terrorism continued to cause economic and political penalties during the mid-1990s, following the bombing of PanAm Flight 103 in 1988 over Lockerbie, Scotland. The U.N. Security Council passed Resolution 731, which demanded that Libya take steps to end its state-sponsored terrorism, including the extradition of two Libyan intelligence agents indicted by the United States and the United Kingdom for their role in that bombing. The resolution also required that Libya accept responsibility for the bombing, disclose all evidence related to it, pay appropriate compensation, satisfy French demands regarding Libya's alleged role in the bombing of UTA Flight 772 in 1989, and cease all forms of terrorism.

In 1992, the U.N. Security Council adopted Resolution 748, imposing an arms and civil aviation embargo on Libya. This resolution demanded that Libyan Arab Airlines offices be closed, and it required that all states reduce Libya's diplomatic presence abroad. When these measures failed to elicit full compliance from Libya, the Security Council adopted Resolution 883 in 1993, imposing a limited assets freeze and oil technology embargo on Libya and strengthening existing sanctions against that nation.

Since the beginning of this U.N. intervention, the regime in Libya has largely avoided open association with acts of terrorism and terrorist groups. While Qadhafi offered public support for radical Palestinian groups opposed to the PLO's Gaza-Jericho accord with Israel in 1993, and openly threatened to support extremist Islamic groups in neighboring Algeria and Tunisia, the level of practical open support by Libya for terrorism has decreased substantially.

CONCLUSIONS

State terrorism, then, whether it is internal or external, offers a real threat to international peace and security. Internal terrorism breeds resistance movements, which often resort to terrorist tactics. This cycle of terror-violence can result in a whirlwind which will destroy all within its reach, both innocent and guilty.

External terror, as practiced by some states, has resulted in the proliferation of terror worldwide. States whose official policy specifically rejects the use of terror have been guilty of giving aid, often clandestinely, to states or groups which promote terrorism. With the exception of a few states, such as Iran and Libya, most states have sought to keep their dealings with terrorists a secret.

Few states have been as successful as Syria in keeping a foot on both sides of the terrorism issue. Western nations regarded President Assad as perhaps the only one with whom they could deal in attempts to bring peace to Lebanon. These states, to some extent, turned a blind eye to his obvious dealings in the training and equipping of terrorists. They were equally reluctant to take him, as they had Qadhafi, to task over the extent to which he and his military offered intelligence and direction to terrorist attack teams.

EVALUATION

Is terrorism becoming the accepted method of warfare for the future? Given the willingness of states to support terrorism as a form of covert warfare and as an instrument of foreign policy, this is a critical question. In order to assess this possibility, consider the assets of terror as an instrument of war:

Low cost—financially—It offers a relatively inexpensive method of operation for insurgent groups who lack the money, the manpower, and the armament to take on a powerful army. It also offers states a fairly inexpensive way to wage war, openly or clandestinely, on a hostile state whose resources make a full-scale war undesirable.

Low cost—politically—For states, particularly those who engage in clandestine support for terrorist groups, the political cost can be quite low, while the profit in, for example, arms sales, can be temptingly high. As long as the support is not too blatant, as it was in Libya's case, the leaders of other nations have shown a tendency to look the other way.

High yield—financially—States engaged in arms sales to terrorists can profit quite handsomely, while suffering little if any political or economic reprisals. Assad's involvement in the Hindawi affair, for instance, resulted in the recall of a couple of ambassadors, but not the complete rupture of any diplomatic or trade relations.

High yield—politically—For freedom fighters who engage in terrorism, the yields can indeed be significant. Government reaction or overreaction can lead to a weakening or even the fall of a regime. Major concessions or changes can also be "bought" at the price of a successful terrorist incident.

Low risk—politically and financially—Since the financing of these terrorist operations is considerably less than that required for a fully equipped and trained army, the possible loss of the individuals carrying out these operations is minor. If it succeeds, the rewards can be enormous. If it fails, the loss is usually minimal, *unless* the failure is openly linked to a state. Since the end of the Cold War, such linkage has become increasingly costly, both in financial and political terms.

What, then, is to deter individuals and nations from engaging in this high-profit, low-risk form of warfare? If nuclear warfare is unthinkable, and unconventional warfare is, as both Vietnam and Afghanistan have illustrated, expensive and often unwinnable today, will individuals and nations turn more and more often to this equally unthinkable alternative?

SUGGESTED READINGS

Gurr, Ted. *Why Men Rebel.* Princeton, NJ: Princeton University Press, 1970.

Harris, Jonathan. *The New Terrorism: Politics of Violence.* New York: Julian Messner Press,1983.

"Iran's Use of International Terrorism." U.S. Department of State, Bureau of Public Affairs, Special Report No. 170 (October 27, 1987).

Kidder, Rushworth M. "Unmasking State-Sponsored Terrorism." *The Christian Science Monitor,* May 14, 1986.

Kittrie, Nicholas. "Response: Looking at the World Realistically." *Case Western Journal of International Law,* vol. 13, no. 2 (Spring 1981).

Liston, Robert A. *Terrorism.* New York: Elsevler/Nelson Books, 1977.

Meltzer, Milton. *The Terrorists.* New York: Harper & Row, 1983.

"More on State Sponsored International Terrorism." *Contemporary Mideast Backgrounder,* no. 240 (September 29, 1987.)

Norland, Rob, and Ray Wilkinson. "Inside Terror, Inc." *Newsweek* (April 7, 1986).

ENDNOTES

1. Milton Metzger, *The Terrorists* (New York: Harper & Row, 1983) p. 193.
2. Martin Slann, "The State as Terrorist," *Annual Editions: Violence and Terrorism 91/92* (Guildford, CT: Dushkin, 1991) p. 69.
3. This Declaration was adopted with forty-eight states voting in favor, none against, and eight abstentions (including Saudi Arabia, the Union of South Africa, the Union of Soviet Socialist Republics, and Yugoslavia). For a full copy of the text of this Declaration, see Louis Henkin, Richard Pugh, Oscar Schachter, and Hans Smit, *International Law: Cases and Materials* (St. Paul, MN: West, 1980) p. 320.
4. International Covenant on Civil and Political Rights, 21 U.N. GAOR, Supp. (No. 16) 52, U.N. Doc. A/6316 (1966). Entered into force March 23, 1976.
5. George Kren and Leon Rappoport, *The Holocaust and the Crisis of Human Behavior* (New York: Holmes & Meier, 1980) p. 130.
6. See Nicholas Kittrie, "Response: Looking at the World Realistically," *Case Western Journal of International Law,* vol. 13, no. 2 (Spring 1981) pp. 311-313.
7. See, for further documentation of this trend, the Annual Reports by Amnesty International, as well as that organization's Report on Torture (1975).
8. Carl J. Friedrich, "Opposition and Government Violence," *Government and Opposition,* vol. 7 (1972) pp. 3-19.
9. Hannah Arendt, *The Origins of Totalitarianism* (New York: Harcourt, Brace & World, 1973) p. 464.
10. See Erich Fromm, *The Anatomy of Human Destructiveness* (New York: Rinehart & Winston, 1973) pp. 285-288.
11. Ted Gurr, *Why Men Rebel* (Princeton, NJ: Princeton University Press, 1970) p. 213.

12. United Nations Secretariat Study, "Measures to Prevent International Terrorism," U.N. Doc. A/C.6/418 (November 2, 1973). Prepared as requested by the Sixth Legal Committee of the General Assembly.

13. Robert A. Liston, *Terrorism* (New York: Elsevier/Nelson Books, 1977) p. 67.

14. Liston, *Terrorism,* p. 79.

15. Claire Sterling, "Terrorism: Tracing the International Network," *New York Times Magazine,* March 1, 1981, p. 19.

16. Sterling, "Terrorism: Tracing the International Network," p. 54.

17. Claire Sterling, *The Terror Network* (New York: Holt, Rinehart & Winston, 1981) p. 293.

18. Ray Cline and Yonah Alexander, *Terrorism: The Soviet Connection* (New York: Crane, Russak, 1984) p. 6.

19. Cline and Alexander, *Terrorism: The Soviet Connection,* p. 55.

20. James Q. Wilson, "Thinking About Terrorism," *Contemporary Review,* no. 186 (April 1981) p. 36.

21. "The Unmasking of Assad," *U.S. News & World Report,* vol. 101, no. 19 (November 10, 1986) p. 27

22. "The Unmasking of Assad," p. 26.

23. "The Unmasking of Assad," p. 29.

CHAPTER SIX

"TERRORISM, INC."

KEY CONCEPTS

networking
international terrorist congress
strategic planning
revolutionary taxes
bonuses
Libyan connection
fedayeen

fighting fund
Hizbollah
NORAID
internationalize
narco-terrorism
unholy triangle

NETWORKING

The three Japanese who disembarked from Air France Flight 132 (May 1972) at Lod International Airport in Tel Aviv, Israel, appeared no different from the other tourists bound for the Holy Land. Chatting pleasantly to the other passengers, they made their way swiftly to the luggage conveyor belt, where they retrieved their bags.

Opening one suitcase, they extracted a light-weight Czech-made submachine gun and a few hand grenades. They then opened fire on the crowd of disembarking passengers and visitors, using their weapons to strafe the airport lounge from side to side. From time to time they lobbed the grenades into the groups of terrified people.

In this attack, 26-six people died. At least six of them were decapitated. One child of about seven was cut in half twice by the barrage of bullets. More than half of the dead were Puerto Ricans on a tour of the Holy Land. An additional 78 persons were wounded, many of them dismembered. The entire episode was over in seconds.

As an example of the **networking** of international terrorists, that is, as an example of *the creation of an interconnected system linking groups with common goals*, this incident excels. Here, Japanese members of the Japanese Red Army killed Puerto Ricans on behalf of Palestinian Arabs who sought to punish Israelis.

Cooperation between terrorist groups with, if not a common cause, at least a shared hatred, has occurred with alarming frequency. Anti-NATO sentiment, for example, drew several European groups into cooperative action. A communique on January 15, 1986, declared that the Red Army Faction (of West Germany) and Action Direct (of France) would together attack the multinational structures of NATO. Shortly thereafter, assassins killed the general in charge of French arms sales and a West German defense industrialist. On August 8, 1985, two Americans were killed in a bomb blast at a U.S. air base in Frankfurt, West Germany. The Red Army Faction and Action Direct also claimed joint responsibility for this attack. This attack was followed by the bombing of a U.S. antiaircraft missile site.

These French and German terrorists used explosives stolen from a Belgian quarry, suggesting a connection with Belgium's Fighting Communist Cells. This latter group bombed NATO pipelines and defense-related companies. Portuguese and Greek terrorists have also attacked NATO targets in their homelands, although evidence of collaboration in these countries is less clear.

Linkage between terrorist groups *does* exist, however. It appears in the form of shared membership, training camps, weaponry, and tactics. It is obvious in the propaganda being disseminated by the groups.

Study of contemporary terrorist groups suggest that terrorists in the latter part of the twentieth century shared intelligence information, weapons, supplies, training facilities, instructors, sponsors, and even membership. It is true that such frequent ad hoc sharing does not necessarily constitute an organized "network of terror," as some have suggested. But the dimensions of cooperation between groups with unrelated or even opposing ideological bases offer useful insights to police, military, intelligence, and academic personnel who understand the web that does from time to time link terrorists.

That web is tenuous for the most part, constructed in a pragmatic fashion to meet common needs for relatively scarce resources. This tenuity does not, of course, diminish the potential for serious damage posed by such linkages. It simply makes the danger more difficult to assess, as the linkages are not only usually covert, but also appear to be in an almost constant state of flux.

Let us examine, then, some of those linkages as they have been shown to exist (usually after the fact in the case of a terrorist event or confrontation!). It is not necessary to study *all* of the available data on such linkages to establish that such connections exist. A brief survey of some of the evidence of cooperation or collusion will suffice to illustrate both the reality and the hazards of this insidious merging of terrorist interests and assets.

SHARED STRATEGIC PLANNING

In 1975, French police learned that the international terrorist known as "Carlos the Jackal," was running a clearinghouse for terrorist movements. His clients included the Tupamaros, the Quebec Liberation Front, the Irish Republican Army, the Baader-Meinhof gang from West Germany, Yugoslavia's Croatian separatists, the Turkish People's Liberation Army and the Palestinians.[1]

The **international terrorist congress**, *a meeting of terrorists from all over the world to work out agendas and to organize cooperative efforts*, took place in Frankfurt, Germany, in 1986, reportedly attended by no less than 500 people. Meeting under the slogan, "The armed struggle as a strategic and tactical necessity in the fight for revolution," proclaimed the U.S. armed forces in Europe to be the main enemy.[2] At this congress, it was decided that the correct strategy was to kill individual soldiers in order to demoralize their colleagues and lower their collective capacity to kill.

Among those represented at this congress, or present as guests, were German, French, Belgian, Spanish, and Portuguese terrorists, as well as the Palestinian Liberation Organization, the Popular Front for the Liberation of Palestine, the African National Congress, the Irish Republican Army, the Tupamaros (of Uruguay), the Italian Red Brigades, and the ETA (Basque separatists, based in Spain). Most of the manifestos issued by this congress were basically Marxist-Leninist in style. The congress was financed largely by Libya.

Reports which surfaced in May of 1987 tell of Khomeinis making the following offer to Nicaragua: Teheran would raise its $100 million in annual economic and military aid by 50 percent if Nicaragua would help recruit Latin American immigrants in the United States to join Iranian expatriates in forming joint terror squads. The mission of these squads: to strike back if the Americans made any attack on Iran.[3]

While there is some evidence that attempts at coordinating activities have been made by various terrorist groups, concrete proof of shared strategies suggesting a "terrorist conspiracy," perhaps manipulated by a common hand—such as Qadhafi—is insufficient. One prominent expert, James Adams, suggested instead that terrorist groups act more like a "multinational corporation with different divisions dotted around the world, all of which act in an essentially independent manner."[4]

In his book, *The Financing of International Terrorism*, James Adams illustrates his analogy by suggesting that these "independent divisions" offer to the head of another operation, when he comes to "town," the use of the company apartment, an advance against expenses, and perhaps access to local equipment. In a similar manner, terrorist groups carrying out an operation in a foreign country may be granted such assistance by the "host" country's terrorist groups.

This analogy between different divisions in a multinational corporation and terrorist groups is credible, based on the fragmentary and often subjective nature of the evidence brought forth as "proof" of a true "conspiracy" among terrorist groups. The cooperation in terms of **strategic planning** which has been authenticated to date between terrorist groups has been: (1) *ad hoc, focused on the planning of just one particular operation between groups whose other contacts remain fragmentary*; or (2) *bombastic, consisting only in the issuing of declarations by "congresses" or transient alliances between groups briefly united against a perceived common target.*

But contact between various terrorist groups does exist, and has been documented. Thomas L. Friedman, writing for *The New York Times* (April 27, 1987), briefly details this "loose-linked network." Moreover, Western intelligence believes that, between 1970 and 1984, 28 meetings involving different terrorist groups have been held around the world. While these meetings were generally called to discuss cooperation rather than coordination or revolutionary activities, it is difficult to establish precisely what plans and agreements have emerged from these contacts.

TERRORISM IS BIG BUSINESS

If the Palestine Liberation Organization were an American corporation, it would have been on the list of Fortune 500 companies. What was the PLO worth in the mid-1980s? British journalist James Adams calculates the organization's financial empire to be worth $5 billion. Return on investments was the group's largest source of income at that time, bringing in about $1billion per year.

Let's take a look at the financial headquarters of this group, as James Adams describes it:

> Just off Shah Bander Square in downtown Damascus is a five-story building of light brown cement. It looks more like the office of a low-level government department, unpainted since the colonials departed, than the headquarters of one of the wealthiest multinational corporations in the world.[5]

On the top floor of this building were banks of Honeywell computers, which were tended by white-coated young Palestinians. Most of these computer experts have been trained in the United States, some at MIT and some at Harvard. From this world of high-tech and super-efficiency, the Palestinian National Fund managed investments which generated a total annual income which is greater than the total budget of some Third World countries, an income which made the PLO the richest and most powerful terrorist group in the world.

Almost all of the PLO's assets were held indirectly through private individuals and in numbered bank accounts in Switzerland, West Germany, Mexico, and the Cayman Islands. Its primary banking institution was the Palestinian-owned Arab Bank, Ltd., headquartered in Amman, Jordan. The chairman of the Palestine National Fund at that time, Jawaeed al-Ghussein, administered the PLO's finances.

PLO financiers invested money in the European market, as well as in a few blue-chip stocks on Wall Street. The PLO also held large amounts of lucrative money certificates in the United States. These and other investments were said to provide as much as 20 percent of all of the group's revenues.

The PLO, like many multinational corporations, was also involved in a wide variety of business ventures, not all of which generated a monetary profit. Some were primarily political, made to win friends for the PLO. PLO money flowed covertly, through dummy corporations established in such places as Liechtenstein and Luxembourg, into investments in Third World countries. Much of this investment money passed through the Arab Bank for Economic Development in Africa and the Arab African Bank.

The PLO owned dairy and poultry farms and cattle ranches in the Sudan, Somalia, Uganda, and Guinea. It reportedly purchased a duty-free shop, in Tanzania's Dares Salaam International Airport, and then negotiated for similar shops in Mozambique and Zimbabwe.

The point is, that the PLO not only had cash assets of staggering proportions, but also it succeeded in investing them for capital, political, and strategic gains. Its stock and bond investments were exemplary, and brought in considerable revenue; its investment in Third World ventures brought it considerable support and goodwill from many nations; and its ventures into such operations as duty-free air-port concessions provided it with security-proof access through which to transfer materials from country to country. The PLO not only had money—it learned how to use much of it wisely.[6]

Not all terrorist groups are so well endowed. Most have to depend on the largess of patrons, or on their own success in staging robberies and ransom situations. The ETA, which had close ties with the Irish Republican Army and the Palestine Liberation Organization, adopted one of the PLO's less-publicized methods of raising money. Funds for this group, which received training and support from Libya and the PLO, were generate through **revolutionary taxes**. These taxes were levied on Basque businessmen. The PLO had levied such a tax against the wages of Palestinians working abroad throughout the Arab world.

Of the financial patrons of contemporary terrorist groups, two deserve special attention. These two nations alone have been respon-sible for the training and arming of countless terrorist teams during the latter part of the twentieth century. Under their aegis, terrorism took on a truly international flavor.

CASE STUDY 1: LIBYAN PROTECTOR

Under Qadhafi, Libyan agents dispersed huge amounts of aid during the 1970s and 1980s to various terrorist groups. That this dispersal of funds appeared to depend greatly on whim, and consequently caused a great deal of frustration among terrorists dependent upon his sup-port, does not detract from the substantial contributions he made to the financing of terrorism worldwide.

Qadhafi supported Palestinian groups, including the PFLP, the DFLP, and the PFLP-GC with donations of as much as $100 million a year. He also assisted the IRA, the ETA, the Baader-Meinhof gang, the Japanese Red Army, the Red Brigade, the Tupamaros, and the Moros (in the Philippines).

His assistance was not confined to the financing of the terrorist operation itself. Israeli intelligence suggested that Qadhafi paid a $5 million bonus to the Black September terrorists who were responsible for the Munich massacre in 1972. Western intelligence also believed that Qadhafi paid Carlos the Jackal a large bonus, around $2 mil-lion, for his role in the seizure of the OPEC oil ministers in Vienna in December 1975.

Bonuses were given for *success, such as that paid to Carlos, and for "njury or death on the job.* By the 1990s, these bonuses significantly decreased in amount. Qadhafi reportedly paid only between $10,000 and $30,000 to the families of terrorists killed in action in the late

1980s, down considerably from the $100,000 reportedly paid to a terrorist injured in the OPEC incident in 1972.

So Qadhafi has given money to support terrorist groups, and he has furnished monetary incentives for participating in terrorist events. Other leaders throughout history have supported dissident groups, and provided for the survivors of their military or quasi-military activities.

But Qadhafi has since taken his support of terrorists to greater lengths. When the U.S. carried out air raids on Libya on April 15, 1986, Qadhafi was, of course, furious. He offered to *buy* an American hostage in Lebanon, so that he could have him killed. On April 17, Peter Kilburn, a 62-year-old librarian at American University who had been kidnaped on December 3, 1984, was executed after Qadhafi paid $1 million to the group who was holding him. He paid $1 million to be able to kill an elderly librarian, in order to "punish" the United States.

Declining oil revenues, particularly due to U.N. sanctions, have diminished Libya's role today in financing terrorism. In six years, this income fell from $22 billion to about $5.5 billion, seriously reducing Qadhafi's ability to bankroll terrorism. Although he remained after this loss involved in the training of terrorists, his role as "godfather" of terrorism decreased dramatically during the last decade of the twentieth century, making it difficult to predict his role for the twenty-first century.

Libya's role has decreased, but not ended. This became obvious when, after having been expelled from both Iraq and Syria, Abu Nidal, the Palestinian master terrorist who planned the *Achille Lauro* hijacking, was given refuge in Tripoli. Western sources fear that, under Libya's protection, Nidal could repay Qadhafi by striking at more American targets.

Moreover, Libya developed a strong *connection to terrorists in Central and South America through its ties to Nicaragua.* The Sandinista government of Nicaragua was, until the early 1990s, the **"Libyan connection"** in this region, supplying arms, training, and logistical support to revolutionary groups in that region.

In 1986, Daniel Ortega wrote to Libya's leader:

> My brother, given the brutal terrorist action launched by the U.S. government against the people of the Libyan Arab Jamahiriyah, I wish to send sentiments and solidarity from the FLSN National Directorate and the Nicaraguan people and government.

This was not the first time these leaders had pledged friendship and support. Long before they came to power in 1979, Sandinista leaders had been training in PLO camps in Libya and Lebanon. When the Sandinistas finally seized power, Qadhafi promised political and financial aid, promises which he indeed kept over the years.

In the early years, the Sandinistas received a $100 million "loan" from Libya. In 1983, Brazilian authorities inspecting four Libyan planes bound for Nicaragua discovered that crates marked "medical supplies" actually contained some 84 tons of military equipment. This military assistance included missiles, bombs, cannons, and two unassembled fighter planes!

In Managua, leaders from Germany's Baader-Meinhof gang, Spain's Basque ETA, Colombia's M19, Peru's Sendero Luminoso, and El Salvador's FMLN have met with Libyan leaders and the PLO. Through Nicaragua, Libya has been able to funnel arms to many of these groups.

M19's attack on Colombia's supreme court, in which more than a 100 were killed, was carried out with arms supplied, through Nicaragua, by Libya. Many of the guns captured in that raid were linked to Libya, some of which reached M19 through conduits in Vietnam, Cuba and, of course, Nicaragua.

Nicaragua's Libyan connection highlights the continuing spiral of terror funded by Qadhafi. Libya supported a revolutionary terrorist group with money and arms, and when that group had managed to seize control of Nicaragua, Libya used that government as a conduit to funnel arms and support to other terrorist groups engaged in similar struggles throughout Central and South America.

The peaceful end of the Sandinista regime, through democratic elections, brought to an end this "Libyan connection." Since Libya's profile in supporting terrorist groups declined in the latter part of the 1990s, this transition has left several groups without a sponsor or support system. Some have begun to link with the illicit drug cartels in Colombia, providing security for drug lords and the shipment of their goods. This has diminished, to some degree, the revolutionary focus of such groups, but it has helped to fill the gap left by the loss of Libyan patronage.

CASE STUDY 2: IRANIAN FEDAYEEN

As James Adams noted, when one prime supporter of terroritst groups falls away, another tends to rise and take its place. Ayatollah Ruhollah Khomeini was able, to a large degree, to take Qadhafi's place as the leading patron of terrorism in the Middle East, Europe, and America.

In order to understand Iran's commitment to terrorism, one can look back 900 years to the time of al-Hassan ibn-Sabbah. Sabbah, a leader of the dissident Muslim Ismaili group (which in turn is one of the two divisions of the Shi'ite sect), was the founder of the previously mentioned Assassins, the hashish-smoking terrorists who terrorized the Persian Gulf region in the twelfth century. Sabbah called his followers **fedayeen** meaning either *adventurers* or *men of sacrifice*, an acronym adopted by many terrorists today.

Iran is the home of the Shi'ite branch of Islam, which has been in conflict with the majority Sunni branch for many centuries. When Khomeini came to power after the fall of the Shah, he began to rally Shi'ites all over the world to this ancient conflict. In March of 1982, clergy and leaders of Shi'ite revolutionary movements from all over the world came to Teheran. At this meeting, in addition to agreeing to establish a number of training camps for terrorists in Iran (which was afterall the home of the Assassins), it was agreed that $100 million would be immediately allocated as a **fighting fund**, *to support worldwide terrorism.* Moreover, an additional $50 million was projected to be spent each year for an indefinite period of time to bankroll specific acts of terrorism.[7]

From this capital outlay has come a variety of terrorist activities. Several powerful groups operating in Lebanon were financed by Iran during the last two decades of the twentieth century. Bomb attacks on moderate Arab states, such as Kuwait, have caused serious personal and monetary damage. Islamic fundamentalism has risen rapidly in southern Asia, supported by substantial cash infusions. Hit squads have been dispatched throughout Europe to eliminate "enemies" of Shi'ite Islam. And a global network of clergy-dominated religious groups has been formed, whose purpose is to mastermind further terrorism and recruit new "Assassins" to serve in Iran's "holy war."

The French authorities, for example, fear a renewal of the bombing waves that have hit Paris in recent years, first from Palestinian groups and then from Algerian fundamentalisdt Islamic fighters. Terrorists struck twice in September 1987 at two Arab-owned banks—one Saudi, the other Kuwaiti. Both incidents were believed to be the work of pro-Iranian terrorists seeking revenge for the deaths of Iranian pilgrims in Mecca and for Kuwait's pro-Iraq stance in the Iran-Iraq War. In the mid-1990s, France was once again a target of attacks, this time from Algerians angry about France's support for the military regime which prevented the strong Islamic fundamentalist parties from winning the elections in Algeria. Attacks in this case included a hijacking and numerous bomb attacks, including attacks on the subways and monuments in Paris.

Faced with the threat of continuing Iranian-sponsored terrorist bombings and hijackings, some wealthy Kuwaiti citizens began taking extended vacations during the late 1980s in other Arab states and in Western Europe. The Kuwaiti government naturally was concerned that too large an exodus of such persons could set off panic among Egyptians, Palestinians, Pakistanis, and other guest workers, who made up 70 percent of the Kuwaiti work force. Accordingly, Kuwait was forced to moderate its antagonism towards Iran, fearing that Iran's terrorist retaliation might cripple beyond repair the Kuwaiti economy. In light of Iraq's subsequent invasion of Kuwait in the Gulf War, this move to placate Iran by not appearing to favor Iraq too much in the previous conflict appears quite ironic.

Saudi Arabia, which has also been a victim of Iranian-directed terrorism, was also very cautious about taking public stands in the Iran-Iraq War. Although many Saudi officials, including Prince Bandar ibn Sultan, the Saudi ambassador to the United States in the 1980s, urged a tough stance toward Teheran, King Fahd maintained an extremely cautious approach. Remembering the violence of the Iranian-provoked riot in Mecca in July 1987, which left more than 400 dead, the Saudis have been careful not to deliberately antagonize the terrorist state of Iraq in their region. The bombing in late 1995 of the building used as U.S. military training headquarters for years in Riyad indicated that such caution may not have been sufficient.

Months before the bloody street battle on July 31, 1987 between Iranian pilgrims and Saudi security forces, Saudi intelligence knew that a specialist unit of Iran's Revolutionary Guards had been training for a major sabotage action during the pilgrimage season in Mecca. Unable, as custodians of Islam's holiest shrines, to ban Iranian pilgrims, they could only respond to the violence instigated by the Iranian pilgrims in a debacle which left 400 dead.

Even in light of the Saudi political wariness, however, terrorism continues to pour from Iran in an unpredictable flow which encompasses friend and foe alike in the Arab world. Kuwait Airways Flight 422 was hijacked on April 5, 1988, in a plot hatched four months earlier in Teheran by Shi'ite radicals from Bahrain, Lebanon, and Iran. The mastermind of the plot was apparently Immad Mughniye, a Shi'ite religious fanatic responsible for planning the bombings of the U.S. embassy and the U.S. Marine headquarters in Lebanon five years earlier.

The world, with the exception of Iran, watched in horror as the bodies of innocent persons were thrown from the plane by the terrorists, whose demands for the release of other terrorists held in Kuwaiti prisons the Kuwaiti government steadfastly refused to meet. Those imprisoned terrorists were responsible for Iranian-directed bombings of the U.S. and French embassies in Kuwait.

Intelligence sources have indicated that a dozen terrorists drawn from **Hizbollah**—*the Iranian-backed Party of God* —and the Bahrain Front, also led from Teheran, were sent for training in the Bekaa Valley of Lebanon in March of 1988. At the same time, Iranian agents checked Bangkok airport for security weaknesses which could be exploited in a hijacking. A hijacking then took place. So blatant was Iran's involvement in this terrorist episode that, when the hijacked plane reached Mashad Airport in Iran, the Iranians allowed the hijackers to obtain a new crew for the aircraft. It is also thought that the Iranians allowed the hijackers to take aboard sophisticated two-way radios, giving them a link to the persons directing the hijacking during the subsequent negotiations in Cyprus and Algeria.

Iran has indeed been willing to carry its terrorism into all parts of the world. Banks, embassies, airports, even temples are under increasingly violent attacks, organized and supported by this nation.

NORAID—THE U.S. TERROR CONNECTION

According to James Adams,

> From the onset of modern terrorism in Northern Ireland in 1969, the United States has played a key role in its support. The enormous Irish-American population has always felt a strong sentimental attachment to 'the old country,' and this has been translated into a steady stream of cash and guns to the IRA, which has, in part, enabled them to survive.[8]

Irish Northern Aid—generally known as **NORAID**—was established by Michael Flannery, a former IRA member living in New York, in 1969. Its purpose was to facilitate assistance to the IRA. Headquarters were established at 273 East 194th Street, in the Bronx, New York City.

Conflicting reports are offered about the importance of NORAID for the IRA (now known as the Provisional IRA or PIRA, after the 1969 split in the IRA leadership) during the last three decades of the twentieth century. Certainly in the early 1970s, NORAID could be termed crucial to PIRA's survival, since it supplied over 50 percent of the cash needed by the PIRA. By the end of the twentieth century, however, PIRA could expect to receive less than $200,000 of their estimated $7,000,000 budget from NORAID.

NORAID, during the late 1980s no longer supplied only cash to the Provos, as the PIRA terrorist called. Instead, cash raised at traditional annual dinners was frequently used to purchase arms, which were then smuggled to Ireland. Since each dinner was expected to raise between $20,000 and $30,000, and such dinners were held in cities throughout the United States during the 1980s. The supply of arms purchased and smuggled was substantial.

Following the murder of 79-year old Lord Mountbatten and other members of his family, including his 14-year-old grandson, by the IRA in 1979, U.S. intelligence agencies, including the FBI, began to cooperate with the British in attempting to stem the flow of arms from NORAID to the PIRA. Although initial successes in this effort were few, by 1984 the cooperation yielded significant results. In early September of that year, for instance, an 80-trawler, registered in Ipswich, Massachusetts, left Boston bound for Ireland. In its cargo were rockets, grenades made in Korea, 100 German automatic rifles, 51 pistols and revolvers, shotguns, and a 0.50 caliber heavy machine gun. A CIA surveillance satellite tracked the trawler to its rendezvous with an Irish trawler. A report on this cargo and its transfer was made to the Irish government, which subsequently seized the ship and confiscated its $500,000 cargo of illegal arms.

NORAID was crippled in the last two decades of the twentieth century by more than the stepped-up scrutiny and cooperation between intelligence services of the United States and Britain. In the chapter which discusses methods of combating terrorism, more details will be given. Suffice it to say at this point that court challenges to NORAID members in the United States, based on claims for injuries incurred by victims of the weapons purchased by NORAID money, have substantially drained NORAID coffers, making the donation of cash and the purchase of arms difficult, if not completely impossible. Moreover, the peace process, begun in the mid-1990s, has helped to make the transfer of this type of aid to the IRA much less politically acceptable in the United States.

TRAINING—AND EQUIPPING—THE TERRORISTS

"[The Soviets] are involved in conscious policy, in progress, if you will, which fosters, supports, and expands terrorism," according to Secretary of State Alexander M. Haig, Jr., at a press conference on January 28, 1981.

Not all of the networking among terrorists involves outright financing of terrorist operations, as NORAID's activities have shown us. The fact that the former Soviet Union was often not listed as a major sponsor of terrorism can be explained in light of these alternative methods of support, methods not involving simply bankrolling terrorist groups, for terrorism worldwide.

Fidel Castro, president of Cuba, has operated "camps" for the training of terrorists since 1961. Recruits were accepted at first from Latin America and African countries. Later recruits from Palestine, Europe, and North America were allowed to attend these special camps. By 1967, more than a dozen training camps for terrorists and guerrillas from all over the world had been established in Cuba. These camps were, during the 1960s and 1970s, under the direction of Colonel Vadim Kotchergin of the Soviet security services (or KGB). Among those trained at these camps were the Weather Underground members Bernadine Dohrn and Mark Rudd.

The Soviet Union, according to intelligence reports at the time, operated training camps which taught techniques of guerrilla warfare and other skills that are useful for groups engaged in terror-violence. Such skills included the use of explosives, mining techniques, commando field tactics, urban guerrilla tactics, and the use of shoulder-fired rockets. Several camps of this type were located in the Soviet Union itself. Other camps with Soviet instructors, were located in Eastern Europe, Cuba, and several Middle Eastern states, including Syria. Alumni of these camps include the infamous "Carlos the Jackal," leaders of the Italian Red Brigade, and more than 1,000 Palestinians.

The Soviet Union and several Eastern European states also supplied arms directly to groups that engaged in terrorism, including the PLO and Turkish leftists. Evidence also suggests that such aid was given to the Basque ETA and to the PIRA. This supplying of arms to groups engaged in terrorism changed dramatically with the demise of the Soviet Union. While Russia and several other former Soviet states still sell arms prodigiously, neither Russia nor most of the European states who had formerly been part of the training network could, by the mid-1990s afford, financially or politically, to openly operate training camps or supply weapons to terrorist groups.

However, the Soviet Union used other proterrorist states, such as Libya, as conduits in the supplying of arms and training for terrorists. Soviet-manufactured weapons given to Libya, for example, found their way into the hands of the Baader-Meinhof gang and the German Red Army Faction (the successor of the Baader-Meinhof group). These weapons still appear in the hands of many terrorist groups, but they appear now to be *sold,* not given, through conduit states.

As disturbing as the provision of arms and training, however, is the willingness of states to offer *safe harbor* and *freedom of movement* to known international terrorists. According to Claire Sterling, author of *The Terror Network*, known terrorists were able to travel freely through Eastern Europe. In that region, she noted, these persons received medical care for injuries received on "missions," and the acquired false passports and documents which enabled them to again penetrate Western nations. For a time, according to this expert, top Italian terrorists were practically commuting to Prague. While this situation is clearly no longer the case, it is unclear to what extent states within that region have begun to exercise control over the transit and accommodation of terrorists.

Unlike Iran and Libya, the Soviets were more discrete in their support of terrorism itself, instead arguing that they were providing training only for people involved in legitimate struggles for national liberation. Since the United States also, in its School for the Americas, offers training in the use of weapons to leaders and groups engaged in "legitimate" struggles within their nations, it is difficult to establish beyond doubt that such support is, in fact, a form of state support for a terrorist network. Like Syria in recent years, Russia and the United States. have tried to distance themselves from the actual training of terrorists.

There is little evidence to suggest that Russia exercises any form of centralized control over an international terrorist network, in spite of editorial commentary which regularly suggested such a premise. Publicly, neither the Americans nor the Russians sanction all of the actions committed by the groups that are trained or equipped by their militaries. Nor is there any reason to feel that terrorism would vanish without such support. But it is reasonable to assume that terrorism is changing dramatically in its patterns of support since the end of the Cold War.

THE "INTERNATIONALIZATION" OF TERRORISM: RAF CASE STUDY

The Red Army Faction (RAF) is the oldest and the most ruthlessly violent left-wing terrorist movement in Germany in the late twentieth century. Emerging from a small residue of left-wing extremists from the student protests of the late 1960s, it was responsible for half a dozen bombing attacks in 1972. Although it suffered large defeats in 1977, and again in 1982 (due to the arrest of many of the original leaders), it continued to successfully regroup and reemerge as a violent political force until Germany was reunited in the early 1990s.

Early generations of the Red Army Faction were to some degree international in the struggle which they waged against "imperialism." In 1977, the RAF carried out a PFLP plan to hijack a Lufthansa aircraft to Mogadishu. The PFLP plan was designed to capitalize on the Schleyer kidnaping. Two members of the RAF, Hans-Joachim Klein and Gabriele Krocher-Tiedemann, were recruited by "Carlos the Jackal" to assist in the raid on the Vienna OPEC conference in 1975. Another two members of the RAF, Wilfred B'o'se and Brigitte Kuhlmann, participated in the 1976 hijacking to Entebbe.

But in July 1984, West German police found documents indicating that the RAF planned to further **internationalize** their struggle by *uniting with other terrorist groups in attacks on the "representatives of repression,"* specifically NATO allies. This antiimperialism brotherhood of bombers and assassins began to wage war throughout Europe in the 1980s.

German, French, and Belgian radicals assassinated prominent members of Europe's defense establishment and set off explosives at targets such as a U.S. air base, military pipelines, and a variety of other NATO installations. Nor have the targets remained specifically military. A Berlin nightclub filled with off-duty soldiers and German civilians was bombed in 1984, allegedly by this terrorist alliance.

One source close to the German underground noted that

> From the Red Army Faction point of view, the only opportunity to fight NATO suppression around the world is to organize a kind of illegal guerrilla war and get in contact with more and more people.[9]

This transformation apparently took concrete form first in 1981. Italian counterterrorist forces revealed that in that year, exiles from the RAF, the Italian Red Brigade and other groups met in Paris. From this meeting, the order went out to kidnap James L. Dozier, a U.S. Army brigadier general stationed in Rome. From being indigenous terrorist groups, operating primarily on their own soil for essentially nationalistic purposes, these groups began to focus their attention and activities against an international enemy: NATO.

Working together, these European terrorists created an informal network which enable them to strike at a variety of NATO targets throughout that region. With relatively open borders between nations in the EU, these terrorists have managed to operate in a manner that makes it difficult for law enforcement officials to predict and prevent their attacks, or to capture them after the events. Evidence suggests that they share personnel, resources (explosives and weapons), and safe houses, as well as the low-level support system involved in such activities as the production of travel documents.

NARCO-TERRORISM

Terrorists of the future may be even less dependent than those of the present on the sponsorship of patron states. A new source of revenue has come into the hands of terrorist groups in the last decades of the twentieth century, prompting some experts to decry the existence of what they call **narco-terrorism**, *a networking of the trade in illicit drugs and terrorism.* U.S. News & World Report (May 4, 1987), called this "the unholiest of alliances, a malevolent marriage between two of the most feared and destructive forces plaguing modern society—terror and drugs."

The use of drugs to underwrite the costs of terrorism adds a new dimension to law enforcement efforts to combat both drugs and terrorism. The drug trade offers vast profits, too, for nations who, although they want to continue to sponsor terrorist groups, find their coffers seriously depleted in recent years. Syria, for example, and more recently Iran, have engaged in international drug smuggling to help finance their support for terrorist groups.

The nether world of narco-terrorism has three main players: the terrorist groups such as the Tamils, the ETA, or the Sikhs; the government officials and intelligence services of nations such as Iran and Cuba, whose foreign policy includes the exporting of revolution, and the narcotic-dealing gangsters, such as Juan Mata Ballesteros, who also deal in political violence and terror. Through a complex network of contacts, these narco-terrorists deal in weapons, launder money, share intelligence information, trade false passports, share safe havens, and offer other forms of assistance.

It is a loose global alliance of two elements of the criminal world. Those who deal in drugs have long become inured to dealing in death, and find little incongruent in their relationship with terrorists. In spite of the apparent callousness of groups such as the PLO toward the taking of human life, these groups are very sensitive to charges that they deal in drugs.

Indeed, PLO treasurer Jaweed al-Ghussein vehemently repudiated such charges: "We are fighting for our homeland. We are not drug smugglers. That is against our values."[10]

Regardless of such denials, it is true that in war-torn Lebanon, the annual 1500-ton hashish trade (recently supplemented by opium and heroin) has supported terrorists of many ideologies for years. "Lebanese hashish helps to pay for everything from hijacking and bombing spectaculars in Europe and the Middle East to a simmering revolt by Moslem insurgents in the Philippines."[11]

It is certain that Syria would be unable to conduct its assistance to insurgent groups without the infusion of millions in drug profits. Without such profits, the Syrian economy would be even more threadbare than it has become in recent years since the collapse of the Soviet Union. Intelligence agencies suggest that Syrian involvement in the drugs-for-terrorism trade involves persons at high levels of the Syrian government, through the activities of Rifat Assad, the president's brother.

CONCLUSIONS

Terrorism today *is* big businesss. No one country is wholly responsible for terrorism's scope, nor is any single country so essential to the existence of terrorism that the withdrawal of its support would seriously diminish terrorism's spread. The continuation of terrorist attacks, in Europe, in the Middle East, and now in the United States, after the collapse of the Soviet Union, has made it clear that no one state's support is essential to the survival of international terrorism. States like the Soviet Union made it *easier* for terrorists to network, but such support, while no longer available, is clearly not critical to the survival or the networking of many groups.

Moreover, there is evidence that terrorist groups are becoming increasingly self-sufficient. As noted earlier, the PLO blossomed from a group which hijacked planes in the 1960s into a sophisticated multinational corporation that used both terrorism and sound investments to achieve its goals. Unlike its earlier years, when its ability to operate depended upon substantial contributions from sympathetic Arab states, the PLO by the final decade of the twentieth century obtained about five-sixths of its annual expenditures of $600 million from its own operations.

Organizations such as the PLO and the IRA have become increasingly entrenched, both in the communities in which their followers live and in the governments which do business with them. The PLO, for instance, invested in farms, factories, the import-export business, and real estate. These investments provide revenues and jobs; they helped to integrate the PLO into the local economy, and they provided members of the organization with valuable experience as managers of both personnel and money, all of which should benefit the Palestinians as they begin self-government in the West Bank and the Gaza Strip.

Furthermore, governments in Europe now have bureaus which have been created to deal with these groups. The PLO now has a mission to the United Nations in New York, and it has begun to operate as a government over a population and territory. Even before the peace accords in the 1990s, the PLO was able, due to its structure and resources, to act more as a government-in-exile than a terrorist operation. This does not suggest that it automatically abandoned its terrorist operations when it secured funds and investments, just that it, like the government of Syria, began trying to distance itself from the use of terrorist tactics.

There still exist, however, many terrorist organizations which depend heavily on the support of patron states. It is more frequently these groups which commit the small-scale acts of terror, such as hostage-taking in Turkey or Burma, in order to prove to their patrons that they are capable of operating efficiently and are worthy of support. Such groups have also been responsible for bomb attacks—a low-cost but lethal operation.

When terrorists strike, countries like Libya or Iran applaud—and quickly deny that they had anything to do with the attack. All of the major Mideast terrorist groups maintain offices in Tripoli and Teheran. Training camps for terrorists operate openly in the Bekaa Valley of Lebanon—an area controlled primarily by the Syrians.

Terrorism is big business; it does have patron states and sponsors (some of whom are more discrete than others); and there is cooperation on occasion between terrorist groups. It was actually George Habash of the Popular Front for the Liberation of Palestine who masterminded the takeover of the U.S. embassy in Teheran in 1979, for instance.

Two final points need to be made with regard to this concept of a terror network. The first has to do with the transition of terrorist organizations into "corporations." As such groups become institutionalized, in terms of formalized government contacts and offices, entrenched in the local economies of many nations, and independent of a need for sponsor financing, *they become increasingly difficult to destroy.* Its adherents begin to include government bureaucrats whose offices regularly deal with the terrorist groups, businesses who share its joint economic interests, and communities whose livelihood depend upon its employment.

The other point is that, with the increasing contact and sharing of support between terrorists, *there is a potential for greater sophistication in the carrying out of terrorist acts.* Terrorists operating in a foreign country, if they are able to avail themselves of the local expertise of indigenous groups, can carry out more efficient operations.

Thus far, evidence of this increase in expertise is limited. Indeed, there has been evidence that terrorists operating on foreign soil are still receiving inadequate or incorrect intelligence information about their targets and intended victims. On September 3, 1985, for instance, the Palestine Popular Struggle Front, a small PLO faction, carried out what it supposed was an attack on a hotel swimming pool in Athens, Greece, frequented by American military personnel. Instead, the two grenades which this group tossed over the wall killed two and wounded 13 handicapped British trourists! Bungling such as this increases, rather than decreases, the work of security forces charged with combatting terrorism, of course, since the selection of victims is not just arbitrary, it is illogical. Ironically, cooperative assistance may increase the ability of a group to select an appropriate target. But such cooperation also increases the likelihood that the group can in fact penetrate that target, as local expertise is added to fanatical commitment. Sharing information, arms, and training, terrorists of the next century can brandish a stronger, if still not coordinated, array of daggers at the throat of the civilized world.

EVALUATION

Consider these examples of narco-terrorism's lethal harvest:

1. There was evidence of Soviet influence in the operation of Kintex, the state import-export trading organization of Bulgaria. Through this organization, heroin and hashish were funneled into Western Europe, concealed among legitimate cargoes. Profits from the sales of the drugs were used to purchase weapons, which were then shipped to various European and Middle Eastern terrorist groups and to Kurdish and Armenian rebels in Turkey. Bulgaria acquired hard currency; terrorists got weapons; and NATO nations were further destabilized by the influx of drugs.

2. In April 1987, more than 150 people were killed in Sri Lanka when a powerful car bomb, set by Tamil rebels, exploded at a bus terminal in Colombo, destroying at least six buses filled with homebound commuters. The Tamils, an ethnic minority which has been seeking a separate homeland, have been financing their terrorist campaign through heroin sales in Canada, Germany, and France, where authorities arrested almost 200 Tamil drug couriers in the latter part of the 1980s. Also in April 1987, Tamil militants killed 145 civilians in a similar massacre.

3. In 1984, when Indian troops stormed the Golden Temple in Amritsar in an attempt to crush Sikh militants, reports surfaced that the soldiers found "huge quantities" of heroin and hashish. This cache was reputedly going to be sold to finance arms purchases, just as the Tamils in nearby Sri Lanka had planned to do.[12]

4. At a secret meeting in Bogota, Colombia, Cuba's ambassador offered Colombian drug barons safe passage through the territorial waters of Cuba—for the modest price of $800,000 for each smuggler's boat! A modest 25-ton hashish shipment smuggled into Florida or the Bahamas could be worth $12 million. Weapons for insurgents in Guatemala, El Salvador, and (until the mid-1990s) Nicaragua were loaded in Havana for each return trip of the smuggler's boats.

5. Lebanon remains a primary source of hashish for the international market, and both production and trafficking occur either with the permission, or with the collusion of a number of terrorist organizations and Syrian military officers in the occupying forces. Nearly all of the militant groups in the area obtain revenue from the drug industry, either directly or by "protecting" the contraband as it is transported through their area of influ-

ence. This "industry" generates an estimated $1 billion per year, most of which is used to finance the activities of terrorist groups and sponsoring states.[13]

6. Iran, in the late 1980s, began establishing its own smuggling routes from Lebanon's Syrian-controlled Bekaa valley into Europe. The 4,000-strong pro-Iranian Shi'ite militia, at Teheran's direction, began to carve out for Iran a portion of that lucrative trade. Iran used the money to offset the costs of its war with Iraq, and to export terrorism worldwide.

What are the implications of this new source of financial independence for terrorist groups and states? Is this alliance of drugs and terror a result of the temporary coincidence of needs, or does it have longer-term, broader, more strategic aims? It has been said that drugs could destroy the Western world. Is the **unholy triangle** *of drug traffickers, terrorists, and state officials committed to the destruction of the Western world* just a mischance or is it of deliberate design? How will this affect the way nations deal with drug traffic? Will there be any attempts to effect cooperation between agencies charged with combatting drugs and those pledged to combatting terrorism, similar to that attempted between Mexico and the United States in the mid-1990s?

SUGGESTED READINGS

Adams, James. *The Financing of Terrorism.* New York: Simon & Schuster, 1986.

Friedman, Thomas L. "Loose-Linked Network of Terror: Separate Acts, Ideological Bonds." *Terrorism: An International Journal* 8, no. 1 (1985).

Laqueur, Walter. *The Age of Terrorism.* Boston: Little, Brown, 1987.

Raynor, Thomas P. *Terrorism.* New York: Franklin Watts, 1982.

Rosewitz, Barbara, and Gerald F. Seib. "Big Business: Aside From Being a Movement, the PLO is a Financial Giant." *The Wall Street Journal,* July 21, 1986.

Scott, Marvin. "What is the PLO Worth?" *Parade Magazine,* September 21, 1986.

Segaller, Stephen. *Invisible Armies: Terrorism in the 1990s.* New York: Harcourt Brace Jovanovich, 1987.

Wardlaw, Grant. "Linkages Between the Illegal Drugs Traffic and Terrorism." Paper presented at the Conference on International Drugs: Threat and Response, Defense and Intelligence College, Washington, DC, June 2-3, 1987.

ENDNOTES

1. When French police moved in to capture Carlos at his headquarters, he escaped in a spectacular shootout, during which he killed two French police officers. For further information and commentary, see Thomas P. Raynor, *Terrorism* (New York: Franklin Watts, 1982).

2. Walter Laqueur, *The Age of Terrorism* (Boston/Toronto: Little, Brown, 1987) p. 290. Laqueur describes both the participants and the agenda of this "congress" in some detail.

3. "Iran's Offer," *U.S. News & World Report* (May 25, 1987), p. 17.

4. James Adams, *The Financing of Terrorism* (New York: Simon & Schuster, 1986) p. 16.

5. Adams, *The Financing of Terrorism*, p. 107.

6. Marvin Scott, "What is the PLO Worth?" *Parade Magazine* (September 21, 1986) p. 17.

7. Adams, *The Financing of Terrorism*, p. 73.

8. Adams, *The Financing of Terrorism*, p. 134.

9. Charles J. Hanley, "Reborn Terrorist 'Armies' Target NATO," *Winston-Salem Journal,* April 9, 1986, p. 1

10. Scott, "What is the PLO Worth?" p. 18.

11. "Narcotics: Terror's New Ally," *U.S. News & World Report* (May 4, 1987), pp. 36-37.

12. "Narcotics: Terror's New Ally," *U.S. News & World Report,* p. 32.

13. Grant Wardlaw, "Linkages Between the Illegal Drugs Traffic and Terrorism." Paper presented at the Conference on International Drugs: Threat and Response, Defense Intelligence College, Washington, DC (June 2-3, 1987).

CHAPTER SEVEN

HOW DO THEY OPERATE?

So in the Libyan fable it is told
That once an eagle, stricken with a dart,
Said, when he saw the fashioning of the shaft,
"With our own feathers, not by others' hands,
Are we now smitten."

—Aeschylus

KEY CONCEPTS

explosive bombs
incendiary bombs
disguise techniques and
    clandestine travel
recruitment
communication
intelligence-gathering
counterintelligence
OPEC

shaped-charge principle
automatic weapons
"little brother"
precision-guided munition (PGM)
organophosphates
botulinal toxins
threat/hoax
amplification effect

INTRODUCTION

Thus far we have noted who is likely to become a terrorist, who trains a person to become a terrorist, and the purposes for which a person might resort to terrorism. We have, in part, attempted to answer the *who* questions, and some of the *why* questions. Part of the *where* questions—relating to where terrorists operate and where they are trained—have also been discussed.

There remains a need to discuss the important *how* questions. How are they trained—at what sites and on what topics? How are they equipped, in terms of weapons available to them? How do they tend to operate; that is, what tactics do they choose and why do they choose to use or not use certain weapons?

Some of these *how* questions can be answered by briefly listing the important points. Others, such as those relating to the type of weaponry available to contemporary terrorists, require considerable explanation. None of these questions need be answered in depth here, for two reasons. One is that this is, at best, a cursory look at terrorism, a brief sketch of only the minimum points relating to this confusing topic. The second is that, just as terrorism is itself in considerable flux today, so the particulars of training sites and other facets of today's terrorists may well be inadequate for understanding and predicting the actions of tomorrow's terrorists. The particulars of terrorism today are unlikely to become obsolete, but the particulars may well be expanded in the twenty-first century.

TRAINING SITES

There were, until the final decade in the twentieth century, more than a dozen nations which offered training camps for terrorists worldwide. Some of these camps were specifically for terrorists, while others were camps used by the host country for military or intelligence training, as well as by terrorists.

Table 7.1 contains a list which, although not comprehensive, details most of the major training facilities used for terrorist training until the end of the Soviet Union. Sites are listed by country, rather than by size or affiliation with particular terrorists organizations, in order to demonstrate the geographic distribution of these camps.

A number of countries during the 1960s through the 1990s operated training facilities within the structure of their own military services. Names for these terrorist training facilities are still not readily available. But a list of training sites would be inadequate without including at least the names of such countries:

- *Algeria* Offered arms, training, funding (occasionally totaling between $5 and $7 million per year), a safe haven for terrorists, diplomatic assistance, and even assistance in acquiring passports.

Table 7.1

Nation	Location of Training Camp(s)
Bulgaria	Varna
Cuba	Camp Matanzos
Czechoslovakia	Ostrova and Karlovt Varv*$
East Germany	Pankow*$@&
Hungary	Lake Belaton
Lebanon	Boalbok
Libya	Res Hilal*$&
	Misurata
	Sirte
	Tameona
	Focra
North Korea	three major centers (names not available at this time)
South Yemen	Khayat*$
Syria	Bekaa Valley (area under Syrian control in Lebanon)*$&

Note: Four symbols have been used in this list to indicate additional assistance given at and through these camps to terrorists.
* —indicates that terrorists are also provided with arms at these camps.
$ —denotes that money is channeled to terrorists from the host country, usually through these training facilities.
@ —indicates that the host country shares its personnel with the terrorists in the training camp.
& —signifies that the host country provides intelligence information to terrorists at the camp.

- *Iran* In addition to providing training to terrorists, also providing funding (already discussed in a previous chapter), a safe haven for terrorists on the run, and passport and diplomatic assistance.
- *Iraq* In spite of the drain on its resources made by its war with Iran, it still provides some training for terrorists, as well as arms, funding, a safe haven, and diplomatic and passport assistance. This did not end with Iraq's defeat in the Gulf War.
- *The People's Republic of China* Began to offer both training and arms to terrorists during the 1980s.
- *Poland* According to intelligence sources, provided training to certain terrorist organizations.

This is not, of course, a comprehensive list of all locations at which terrorists received training during the latter part of the twentieth century. Some nations were more discrete than others in the training which they provided. Moreover, information concerning such camps necessarily came from some national intelligence services, meaning that the information was certainly biased according to how that particular nation defined "terrorism." It is unlikely, for instance, that such an intelligence assessment of a particular nation would list friendly nations as hosts for terrorist camps. Instead such assessments would cite such camps as training sources for legitimate insurgent or revolutionary groups.

Moreover, the dramatic changes which occurred in the world in the early 1990s have seriously impacted the ability of the listed states to offer training, arms, or specific support to terrorist groups. Of the states on this list, only a few still offered significant levels of training and support in the 1990s. Iran remained a major supporter, providing weapons, funds, and training primarily to Hizbollah, but also to the Palestinian Islamic Jihad, Ahmad Jibril's Popular Front for the Liberation of Palestine—General Command, the Kurdistan Workers' Party, and, of course, Hamas. Iraq, too, continued to defy international concern, as articulated through U.N. resolutions, and it offered training facilities and safe havens to several groups, such as the Palestine Liberation Front (Abu Abbas's organization), the ANO, and the Arab Liberation Front.

Cuba, however, could no longer financially or politically afford to flout Western censure by openly offering training to terrorist groups. While it continued in the 1990s to offer safe haven to members of the ETA (Basque separatists) and to members of the Manuel Rodriguez Patriotic Front (a Chilean insurgent group), as well as to the FARC and the National Liberation Army (from Colombia), Cuba could no longer provide weapons or training on the scale which had been available before the fall of their sponsor, the Soviet Union.

Nations such as Syria and North Korea became similarly unable or unwilling to openly offer terrorist training and support after 1987. While Syria continued to offer safe haven to the PFLP-GC, Hamas, the PIJ, the Japanese Red Army, and other groups, the training assistance and access to weapons was no longer made freely available. The political costs to Syria, lacking the shelter of the Soviet superpower, were simply too high.

Perhaps one of the most dramatic highlights of the diminishing role of states involved in providing sanctuary to terrorists came in August 1994, when the Sudanese government handed over the notorious terrorist Illych Ramirez Sanchez (a.k.a. "Carlos the Jackal"). "Carlos" had been given sanctuary in the Sudan in 1993, but was peacefully handed over to French authorities one year later. Open sanctuary to internationally known terrorists was obviously a less attractive policy option as the twentieth century neared its end.

TRAINING TOPICS:
WHAT DO THEY LEARN AT CAMP?

In June 1967, a Venezuelan, Manuel Carrasquel, told an investigating committee of the Organization of American States about the training his group had received in various subjects. They included tactics, weapons training, bomb making—particularly how to blow up oil pipelines—map reading, cryptology, photography, the falsification of documents, and disguise.[1]

Terrorists do not go to training camps just to acquire arms, intelligence information, or funding. They undergo, at most such camps, a rigorous program of activities, gaining proficiency in a wide variety of skills. A brief review of some of the topics taught at these training camps provides useful insights into the type of tactics which terrorists employ in their ventures.

Such a review of topics also yields a better understanding of the depth and breadth of the training available to terrorists today. It is surprising to note that many terrorists are more highly trained in a wider variety of tactics than the police in the nations combatting terrorism.

Again, it should be noted that the following sketch of training topics is not intended to be exhaustive. It is merely meant to offer a rudimentary understanding of the scope of training available today, with the intent of making one more aware of the potential array of tactics from which contemporary terrorists may choose.

Arson and bombs   Since about 50 percent of all terrorist incidents involve bombings, this ranks as one of the most prevalent and most popular training topics. Terrorists are, as a rule, taught how to make and use two types of bombs: **explosive** and **incendiary.** *Explosive bombs are generally of either fragmentation* or *blast type.* The most commonly utilized fragmentation bomb is the pipe bomb, usually employing gunpowder as the explosive agent. Terrorists are also taught how to use commercial- or military-type dynamite with a blasting cap for detonation in the creation and usage of blast-type bombs.

Terrorists are also taught how to create and use incendiary bombs, as such bombs are quickly and easily constructed. *Incendiary bombs are simply fire bombs.* They are inexpensive, yet capable of inflicting extensive damage. Terrorists are taught how to make a simple fire bomb, consisting of a glass bottle filled with an inflammable mixture, to which a fuse is attached. Fire bombs can vary in sophistication. Some use a time-delay fuse; others a barometric fuse. Fertilizer was mixed with fuel oil in the bomb used in the blast in Oklahoma City in 1995. This was clearly a blast-type explosive bomb, simple in construction but incredibly destructive.

Not every training camp offers instruction on all such bombs, nor is every trainee instructed in the construction and use of all bomb types. But the array of weapons of destruction from just instruction in arson and bomb usage is of great use to every terrorist recruit.

Assassination and ambush techniques   Terrorists are usually taught how to penetrate personal security systems in order to kill at close hand. They are instructed in the proficient use of handguns with silencers. Methods of clandestine approach, disguise, and escape are generally incorporated into this part of every terrorist's training. Increasingly, modern terrorists are being instructed in the commission of flamboyant, execution-style assassinations, instead of the unobtrusive gunman-in-a-crowd techniques favored by the anarchists of previous years.

Extortion, bank and armored-car robberies   Contemporary training courses for terrorists now often include information on how to raise money for indigent terrorist groups. This part of the curriculum also includes instruction on how to extort money from wealthy sources, usually the families or employers of kidnap victims.

In the 1970s, kidnapping was a source of considerable wealth, particularly for groups operating in Central and South Ameria. United States firms in these areas were at first willing to pay large sums for the safe return of their kidnapped executives. However, during the 1980s, businesses began making it a formal part of their policy *not* to submit to ransom demands. As a result, kidnapping for ransom money has become a less profitable enterprise.

In the 1980s, terrorists were also trained in the use of kidnapping for the extortion of *political* rewards or the concessions, as well as money. Although many governments have a stated policy of not conceeding to terrorist extortion demands, most have from time to time found it expedient to yield rather than to allow a kidnap situation to drag on indefinitely or to end disastrously. Events in Lebanon give credence to the profitable use by terrorist groups of this tactic.

Disguise techniques, clandestine travel, recruitment, and communications   Terrorists today are trained in many of the same techniques which the counterintelligence services utilize. They are taught methods of **disguise techniques and clandestine travel**, including *how to travel inconspicuously* (contrary to popular belief, an Arab engaged in a terrorist attack does *not* routinely wear a burnous, nor does he or she travel by camel!). Instruction is also given in *the* *procuring of false passport and indentification papers,* and in *the skill of altering one's appearance to slip through surveillance nets.*

Most terrorists are also trained in the techniques of **recruitment**, as all terrorist groups require *transfusions of new members,* but must constantly beware of the dangers of counterintelligence penetration. The *screening and selection of potential recruits* is thus a vital talent for every successful terrorist group.

Terrorists are also trained in sophisticated methods of **communication**. Recognizing the importance of a *reliable and secure means of communicating during a terrorist incident,* leaders of terrorist organizations are having larger numbers of their recruits trained in the advanced technology of communication. Not for the modern terrorists are the simple two-way radios still favored by many police forces.

Intelligence collection and counterintelligence methods
Not surprisingly, many modern terrorists are more skilled at the collection of intelligence information than are many members of the intelligence organizations of some nations. Terrorists now receive comprehensive training, not only in the techniques of intelligence-gathering, but also in the equally important methods of counterintelligence operations.

Intelligence-gathering means that terrorists are currently being taught *how to infiltrate target areas, gather relevant data, and then return that information to headquarters.* The *use of codes* and the *translation of intelligence data into comprehensible information* is basic to the education of today's terrorist.

Terrorists are also being taught methods of **counterintelligence**, including *how to disseminate misinformation designed to confuse their enemies.* Such instruction generally includes information on *how to protect the organization from infiltration by police, military, and governmental intelligence operatives.*

This does not mean, of course, that all terrorists are trained in all of these methods. Most organizations can usually afford to train only a carefully selected number in these sophisticated techniques. But the ability of most terrorist organizations to have at least a few recruits skilled in these techniques is becoming a matter of survival. Lack of information or misinformation can seriously cripple an organization's ability to carry out a successful operation. So the extent to which a terrorist group can field operatives skilled in intelligence matters is crucial to that group's success today.

Weapons   This last item is by no means the least important in the repertoire of skills acquired by terrorists in training facilities. Over time, the number and variety of weapons available to terrorists through the different training camps has varied considerably, making generalizations difficult. Without detailing all of the weapons available to modern terrorists (which is covered in a subsequent section), it is well to briefly note the types of weapons which terrorists are trained to use.

In addition to training in the use of small firearms, including pistols, rifles, and sawed-off shotguns, terrorists are currently being trained in the use of automatic and semiautomatic weapons. Training is regularly given in the use of machine guns and machine pistols, particularly those manufactured in the Soviet Union and several other countries in Eastern Europe, including Poland and the Czech Republic.

Training is also available in light tank antirocket launchers, principally the Soviet-made RPG-7 and the U.S. LAW. Use of the French Strim F-1 has also been taught at some camps. Such weapons are portable and easy to conceal. The use of surface-to-air missiles, known to be in the hands of terrorists, is also taught in some training programs, including those led by the United States.

There is no available evidence of training being given to terrorists in the use of some of the more exotic weapons, such as chemical or biological agents. Although the use of such weapons remains relatively infrequent today, the use of sarin gas by terrorists in Japan on the Tokyo subway in the middle of the 1990s presented the spectre of appalling destruction. While the twentieth century escaped without many serious successful attempts by groups to utilize chemical or biological weapons, use of such weapons may well be significant in the twenty-first century. Moreover, it should be noted that *states* in the twentieth century have been distressingly willing to use such weapons upon a dissident population, as the Iraqis did on the Kurds in the 1980s.

The training process appears to be quite comprehensive, even formidable, in its potential for turning out proficient terrorists. Let us consider one operation carried out in the 1970s, when training camps were far less organized and their "graduates" perhaps less sophisticated than they are now.

CASE STUDY: OPEC KIDNAPPING IN VIENNA

Carlos the Jackal, who was a graduate of training camps in Cuba and, probably in the Soviet Union, masterminded the OPEC kidnapping in Vienna. Together with a hand-picked assault team, composed of Arabs and members of the German Red Army Faction, Carlos and his five confederates walked into the **OPEC (Oil Producing and Exporting Countries)** conference meeting in Vienna, Austria, in December 1975. They carried sports equipment hold-alls, in which they concealed their weapons and equipment.

As Sheik Yamani, a hostage at the conference described the situation, "There is no doubt that Carlos and his group had made very careful plans. We could tell at once that they knew every detail about the building. They knew exactly where to go, and each member of the gang knew precisely what to do."[2]

These terrorists carried out their plan of attack with ruthless efficiency. Hans-Joachim Klein destroyed the switchboard, preventing a telephone warning from being issued. Gabriele Krocher-Tiedemann calmly shot two men who tried to resist the gang's entrance. A third man, a member of the Libyan delegation, was shot by Carlos as the man attempted to disarm the terrorist leader. Order was restored quickly, and the terrorists were in clear control before the Austrian police teams arrived.

The terrorists had a clear and simple list of demands that they gave the negotiators. Carlos, on his way to Austria, had also arranged for sympathizers to send his demands to radio stations in the event that his mission failed—a back-up plan which has become common among terrorists today. When the Austrian government agreed, with very little argument, to those demands, Carlos moved his group and their hostages into a well-planned escape route.

This whole operation demonstrated to the world that terrorists were indeed capable of carefully planned and brilliantly executed attacks. Reconnaissance, timing, and planning were clearly techniques with which terrorists were becoming increasingly familiar. In a few years, an increasingly sophisticated arsenal of weapons would make such an attack many times more lethal.

POTENTIAL FOR DESTRUCTION: THE TERRORIST'S ARSENAL

Before examining the tactics chosen by trained terrorists, it is appropriate to look briefly at the arsenal of weapons available to the terrorist today. From their use in training camps, certain weapons have become favored by some terrorist groups. Other weapons have gained popularity due to their proven effectiveness or their relative availability.

Explosives   Terrorists worldwide contine to use explosives, frequently in the form of homemade devices. These are most often blast rather than fragmentation bombs. Explosives, as Kupperman and

Trent have pointed out, "offer many advantages to a terrorist: they are available everywhere and crude bombs can be fabricated locally; they are concealable and can be readily disguised so that X-ray and magnometer inspections are ineffective defenses."[3]

The destructive quality of bombs does not depend necessarily on the sophistication of their construction. Trucks packed with forms of TNT have created substantial damage and caused innumerable deaths. One truck laden with fertilizer and gasoline exploded in Oklahoma City in 1995 and destroyed a federal building and left hundreds of casualties, dead or injured.

But the ability of a small amount of explosive to create a large amount of damage has been enhanced by terrorists, using the **shaped-charge principle,** *which focuses the force of the explosion in a desired direction.* Terrorists have shown themselves to be proficient in the use of both conical or "beehive" bombs, which increase the explosive penetration, and linear bombs, which have a "cutting" effect.

Small arms   In recent years, terrorists have continued to use pistols, rifles, and such crude weapons as the sawed-off shotgun. The supply of such weapons is vast, the cost relatively small, and the training for their use fairly simple, making these popular weapons for small or underfinanced terrorist groups.

Handguns continue to be the weapon of the political assassin, but more important in terms of modern terrorism, they are often the preferred weapons of those taking hostages. Moreover, unlike the automatic weapon, laws limiting the sale and possession of handguns are either very lax or nonexistent in many countries.

Automatic weapons   While the automatic weapon is essentially an antipersonnel weapon, it has also been used by terrorists to assault cars and even airplanes. It is a favorite weapon of terrorist groups for several reasons: its availability, concealability, high rate of fire, and, perhaps most important, its psychological impact on unarmed civilians or lightly armed security forces.

There are two basic types of **automatic weapons:** *the assault rifle and the submachine gun.*[4] Both are easily obtained through arms dealers or the militaries of various nations, particularly since the demise of the Soviet Union. The Soviet AK-47 is one of the most popular weapons of terrorists today, due to its accessability and performance record. Assault rifles can be obtained in either their military form, such as the AK-47 assault rifle, or in their semiautomatic commercial version.

In recent years, the *"**little brother**"* of the submachine gun, the machine pistol, has become popular among terrorist groups and police forces. This is particularly true of European terrorists, where such weapons can be easily procured.

Man-portable rockets   In recent years, training of terrorists in the use of *precision-guided munitions (PGMs)—devices which can launch missiles whose trajectories can be corrected in flight*—has increased dramatically. Most, but not all, PGMs are man-portable, meaning that they are fairly lightweight and can be both carried and operated by one or perhaps two persons.

Such weapons are designed to destroy aircraft and tanks. There are documented incidents in which terrorists have attempted to use weapons such as the Soviet-made SA-7 (code-named "Streola") against aircraft. In 1973, for instance, a Palestinian group planned to use two SA-7s to shoot down an El Al aircraft near Rome, but the attempt was foiled. Although a similar plot in Kenya in 1975 also failed, by 1978 an SA-7 was apparently used successfully against a commercial airliner.[5]

Of the surface-to-air rocket systems currently available, the most popular appear to be those manufactured in the United States, Russia, and the United Kingdom. The U.S.-made Stinger (the successor of the Redeye), the Russian-made SA-7, and the British Blowpipe have achieved a considerable degree of popularity among contemporary terrorists.

Most such rockets employ infrared devices, which are heat-seeking sensors that serve to guide the missile to a heat source, presumably the aircraft's engine. They generally weigh between 30 and 40 pounds, with an effective range of at least several kilometers.

Worst of all, from a security stand-point, such weapons are becoming readily available to terrorist organizations. It is interesting to note the observations made by Rand Corporation's terrorist expert, Brian Jenkins, two decades ago, with regard to the proliferation of these weapons:

> First-generation PGMs such as the Streola and the Redeye will be available to 30 or 40 countries in the Third World. It is not realistic to expect that all of these countries will maintain strict security measures; some may find it in their interest to make these weapons available to non-governmental groups. If we postulate a conservative loss rate worldwide, by theft or diversion, of one-tenth of 1percent over the next five years, then man-portable PGMs will be "loose" in the hundreds by the beginning of the 1980s.[6]

Such weapons *were* loose in at least the hundreds if not the thousands in the 1980s. Not only did Third World nations allow and even assist in their dissemination, but Western nations whose laws forbade the sharing of such weaponry were nevertheless guilty of allowing these missile systems to come into the hands of terrorists.

Less sophisticated but nearly lethal are the light antitank rocket launchers, such as the U.S. Viper and the Russian RPG-7, which have been used with increasing frequency by terrorists. Such systems are compact, self-contained, lightweight, and easily transported (once dismantled) in a suitcase. Terrorists could use such weapons with devastating effect against limousines, aircraft, transformer banks, vehicles transporting radioactive wastes, and oil or natural gas pipelines.

"SCIENCE FICTION" WEAPONS

Robert Kupperman, in a report prepared for the Department of Justice in October 1977, made a useful analysis of the devastation which could be wrought by chemical, biological. and radiological weapons and nuclear explosives:

> In terms of fatalities, conventional weapons such as machine guns and small bombs constitute the least threat. They can produce tens or hundreds of casualties in a single incident. Chemical weapons such as nerve agents constitute a substantially greater threat, being capable of producing hundreds to thousands of fatalities. A small nuclear bomb could produce a hundred thousand casualties, but biological agents—both toxins and living organizms—can rival thermonuclear weapons, providing the possibility of producing hundreds of thousands to several millions of casualties in a single incident.[7]

Let us first consider the possibilities (for as yet they remain primarily possibilities, with, fortunately only a few attemped usages) of a terrorist group use of chemical or biological agents of mass destruction. That most groups have not yet done so is less a factor of the difficulties and dangers involved in producing such weapons than of the problems involved in effectively disseminating the toxic material.

There are tens of thousands of highly toxic chemicals, some of which are available to the general public in the form of, for instance, rodenticides. *Organophosphates, the so-called nerve agents*, could be synthesized by a moderately competent chemist, with limited laboratory facilities. Indeed, for terrorist groups lacking a chemist and laboratory, there are some forms of these agents, such as TEPP (tetrathylpyrophosphate), which are available commercially as insecticides.

The use of an organophosphate by a group in Japan in 1995 demonstrated both the effectiveness of the agent and the vulnerability of major urban centers to such attacks. The injury to thousands, generated by a relatively small amount of substance, makes it clear that Kupperman's assessment was distressingly accurate.

But the dissemination of such agents of destruction is not simple. Aerosol dispersal would be difficult and risky in some areas, although subways, trains, planes, and buses make inviting targets. Contamination of a large water supply is normally inhibited by such factors as hydrolysis, chlorination, and the required minimum quantity of toxic material per gallon of water for effectiveness.

Similar problems inhibit the dissemination, if not the production, of even more lethal **botulinal toxins,** *highly toxic nerve agents created by anerobic bacterium,* often found in spoiled or ill-prepared food. Compared with the most toxic nerve agent, botulinal toxin is at least a thousand times more dangerous. Dissemination through the food supply is an obvious route, and one which concerns the food industries considerably. Unfortunately, botulinal toxins are easily produced. There is a vast array of literature on their growth, serological typing for virulence, the techniques for continuous culturing, and separation and purification of the toxin. The toxin that causes botulism is produced by the organism *Clautridium botulinium,* which is found almost everywhere.

Dr. Kupperman produced a useful dataset for the comparison of the lethality of such weapons with more conventional (and better-understood) weapons. It would seem, from his data, that although it would take 320 *million* grams of fuel-air explosives (such as the crude truckload of fertilizer and gasoline which was used in Oklahoma City) to produce heavy casualties within a square-mile area, it would take only 8 grams of anthrax spores to produce the same approximate casualty count. While his dataset postulates "ideal" conditions (including requirements for dissemination), making Dr. Kupperman's projections somewhat suspect, it nevertheless highlights how powerful these small but toxic agents are.[8]

This comparison makes it clear that certain chemical and biological weapons are even more potentially lethal than even a relatively small nuclear weapon. It is startling to note that, according to Kupperman's information, anthrax is *100,000 times more effective* as an agent of destruction than is a highly toxic nerve gas, like the one used in Japan. The pneumonia-like illness caused by *Bacillus anthracis* is apparently almost 100 percent fatal if untreated (which it usually is, since by the time the symptoms appear, antibiotic therapy is no longer useful).

Many chemical and biological agents are readily produced or obtained, often through legitimate sources. They are also incredibly deadly, capable of killing thousands, even hundreds of thousands, of people. Thus far, the difficult step of dissemination may be one of the only remaining reasons why contemporary terrorists have not yet used these agents of mass destruction. The success of the use of such an agent in Japan in 1995 may well encourage other groups to utilize these "science fiction" weapons.

Brian Jenkins, in 1975, suggested that another reason might exist which inhibited the use of such weapons. According to his understanding of terrorism at that time,

> Incidents in which terrorists have deliberately tried to kill large numbers of people or cause widespread damage are relatively rare. Terrorists want a lot of people watching, not a lot of people dead—which may explain why, apart from the technical difficulties involved, they have not already used chemical or bacteriological weapons, or conventional explosives in ways that would produce mass casualties.[9]

However, it is no longer true that all modern terrorists eschew mass violence. Bombs have been placed aboard aircrafts, like the PanAm flight over Lockerbie, Scotland, killing hundreds. Explosives have been used in vast quantities, as in Oklahoma City, resulting in hundreds of casualties (among the injured and dead). Hundreds have been injured on subways with toxic materials.

It seems, then, that Jenkins's premise regarding terrorists' reluctance to use weapons of mass destruction has proven less accurate as the century draws to a close. It may well be that the reason that few groups have yet used such weapons rests upon the difficulty in disseminating the toxic substances in sufficient quantities. That is, surely, a frail defense for those nations who may find themselves the target of such attacks.

For years modern nations have tried both to secure the materials necessary for the production of nuclear weapons, and to remain secure in their belief that, even if some small portions of such materials should fall into terrorist hands, the terrorists would lack the technical skill to manufacture such weapons. These are manifestly false premises, particularly since the break up of the Soviet Union made available to terrorists both the material and the technical skill to produce such weapons.

Experts have estimated that, in order to produce a crude nuclear weapon, terrorists would need perhaps a half dozen technologically trained individuals (with training in subjects like nuclear chemistry, physics, metallurgy, electronics, and perhaps the handling of high explosives), and considerable time, space, and money. Let us consider each of these requisites to determine whether such a weapon does in fact lie within the realm of possibility for some terrorists today.

The *financial resources* of terrorists have already been discussed in some detail. Oil revenues (which had enabled patron states to be generous in their support) and, more recently, money from illicit drugs, have served to swell the coffers of many terrorist groups. An organization such as, the RAF could well afford the necessary funds to procure the materials, trained technicians, and facilities necessary for the building of such a weapon.

For small, poorly financed groups, a lack of time as well as money could well inhibit the production of a nuclear weapon. Such groups are compelled to produce results *at once* if they are to obtain the funding and support which they require to survive from patron states. They cannot afford to wait while technicians are either trained or recruited, and suitable facilities are constructed.

Well-financed groups can, however, afford to wait while personnel are put into place in an adequately constructed facility. With their contacts among friendly governments, they might even be able to secure a safe testing ground for the weapon although such a step would not be essential to its use. Military experts are concerned with such matters as high reliability and predictable yield. All terrorists need be concerned with is that the bomb produces a sufficiently audible "bang" and visible mushroom cloud.

The requirement of *space*, too, is one which well-established and funded groups can manage. Since there are considerable hazards attendant upon working with radioactive materials, it would be necessary to build or obtain the use of a laboratory of fairly substantial size, equipped with specialized equipment. Like the fissionable materials, it has become increasingly probable that the acquisition of such facilities are within the grasp of some groups today. If such groups can gain access to military training facilities, as described earlier, then the possibility exists that terrorists can also gain access to the use of suitable research and development facilities.

Trained personnel are also obtainable for groups and states who can afford market prices for such personnel, especially after the demise of the Soviet Union. According to one study, about one-third of individuals identified as terrorists were persons with some university training, university graduates, or postgraduate students. In some groups, such as the Tupamaros (Uruguay), the Argentine Revolutionary People's Army, and the Monteneros, the figure was nearly 75 percent in the 1970s. Even in Turkey and Iran, university-trained terrorists were the rule rather than the exception, according to this study. In Turkey and Iran, too, the fields of study tended to be the more exact sciences, such as engineering. Yassir Arafat is a graduate-school educated engineer.[10]

Thus, while it might not be feasible to train a recruit with only grade school or even high school education in the technology necessary for the construction of nuclear weapons, terrorists have a large pool of university graduates from which to select, as well as a large number of trained scientists seeking employment following the disintegration of the Soviet system.

But it is important to note that those terrorists which may possess or be able to obtain the necessary resources to construct a crude nuclear weapon are those who are least likely to benefit from the commission of such a barbarous act. Well-established terrorist organizations have tended to try to distance themselves from acts of barbarity, as did the group leadership in Japan following the use of gas on the Tokyo subways. The reasons for such distancing is obvious: These organizations have attachable assets and fixed locations and personnel upon which retribution could be meted.

Yassir Arafat, for instance, would have been extremely reluctant to use the resources of his organization for the construction and subsequent detonation of a nuclear device. To do so, even before the peace process began in the 1990s, would have irreparably damaged his credibility with the United Nations, and would have played into the hands of his enemies, giving them good reason for condemning him as a murderer of unparalleled proportions.

Two forms of nuclear terrorism remain feasible, however. One is the **threat/hoax** *by which leaders are frightened or blackmailed into acceeding to terrorist demands, based on the threat of detonating a hidden nuclear device in a crowded area, such as a city.* While it sounds more like the stuff of which science fiction books and movies are made, such threats have in fact already been made. Leaders in several nations, including the United States, have already had to deal with such threats.

To date that is all they have been: a threat/hoax. But the time may well be at hand when leaders may no longer be so confident that terrorists do not truly possess a nuclear device which they are prepared to detonate. The increasing willingness of some terrorists to commit carnage on a large scale must surely give pause to those who would claim that the devastation wrought by a nuclear device would be on too large a scale for contemporary terrorists. As terrorism continues to become more violent, nuclear terrorism becomes more of a possibility.

The greatest potential for a nuclear disaster, and one which has concerned governments more, is the possibility of either a *takeover or hostage situation at an existing nuclear facility* or the *sabotage of such a facility.* With the growing number of nuclear power plants inside countries (which have for some years produced nuclear power and weapons) and of nuclear facilities in previously nonnuclear states, the possibility of these types of situations has dramatically increased.

In either case, great damage could be done, without the expenditure by terrorists of either a great deal of time, money, or personnel recruitment and training. In other words, such an action is well within the reach of most contemporary terrorists. Security protections at such facilities, while gradually increasing, are at present inadequate to prevent a determined and well-planned assault. Such an assault could be carried out by indigenous or foreign groups, as long as sufficient intelligence-gathering and reconnaissance measures had been taken.

The "science fiction" terrorism of earlier years, then, is rapidly becoming part of the potential pattern of terrorism today and tomorrow. Chemical, biological, and nuclear terrorism is technically within the grasp of some terrorists today. That they have, for the most part, not chosen to pursue such tactics—yet—is a subject for conjecture. It would be unwise to rely, however, on the terrorists' need for popular approval or goodwill as an indefinite defense against an attack with weapons of this kind.

TERRORIST TACTICS

It may be useful at this point to briefly review what we do know about the tactics used by contemporary terrorists. We have already discussed how they are trained and what kind of weapons they use. The tactics chosen, given these variables of training and weapons, should prove illuminating in discerning patterns of contemporary terrorist tactics, and perhaps such knowledge will enable us to more accurately predict patterns of terrorist acts in the twenty-first century.

The following list includes various types of terrorist tactics reported worldwide, together with a few brief remarks about their usage. While not an exhaustive list, it features most of the major tactics employed by terrorists to date.

1. **Bombing**   Bombs are the most common tool of contemporary terrorists. About 50 percent of all terrorist incidents involved bombs. Most recent trends in the use of this tactic include efforts to maximize the casualties, the use of secondary explosives, and the use of highly sophisticated devices. The letter bomb of earlier years has in large measure been replaced (except in the case of the U.S. Unabomber) by vehicle bombs, which can carry a larger charge.

Review of a few examples of the use of bombs by terrorist groups indicates that the use of such weapons is becoming common throughout the world, and that such attacks are extremely lethal. The following examples were selected to give a sense of the scope (geographical), variety (of groups involved and types of bombs used), and lethality of these attacks.

Case Examples

- *April 1983, Beirut* —A car bomb was detonated in front of the U.S. embassy, killing 63 and wounding over 100.
- *April 1985, Madrid* —Bomb explodes at a restaurant frequented by U.S. servicemen. Eighteen Spaniards killed and 82 people wounded.
- *September 1985, Athens*—Two grenades thrown into the lobby of a Greek hotel, wounding 18 British tourists.
- *December 1988, Lockerbie*—PanAm Flight 103 airliner explodes from bomb, killing over 200 people. Responsibility for planning and support for bombing traced to Libya, Iran, and Syria.
- *March 1991, Sri Lanka* —State Minister for Defense Wijeratne killed in a car bombing in Colombo along with 50 other victims. LTTE is responsible.
- *June 1991, Honduras* —The Morazanist Patriotic Front launched an RPG-7 rocket at the U.N. Observer Group headquarters in Tegucigalpa.
- *February 1993, New York*—Explosion of a massive van bomb in a van parked in an underground garage below the World Trade Center. The explosion killed six and wounded over 1,000. Islamic extremists convicted.
- *June 1993, Egypt* —A bomb exploded underneath an overpass as a tour bus was traveling to the Giza pyramids. The explosion killed two Egyptians and injured six British tourists, as well as nine Egyptians and Syrians.
- *October 1994, Peru* —The SL exploded a large bomb under a minibus in the parking lot near the departure terminal at Lima's international airport. The driver of a hotel shuttle bus was killed and about 20 others were injured.
- *August 1995, Oklahoma City* —A truck bomb exploded at a federal building, injuring or killing hundreds, including children in a day-care center. Member of militia group charged with crime.
- *January 1996, Israel* —Suicide bombers continued to cause civilian deaths in Jerusalem and the West Bank. Hamas extremists took responsibility, claiming the bombings were efforts to stop the peace process.

This list does not, of course, detail all of the bombings which have occurred in the past two decades. It is intended only to demonstrate the wide range of bombs used, the variety of targets chosen, and the worldwide nature of the attacks.

2. Arson   Arson accounts for approximately 14 percent of all terrorist incidents. The use of this tactic often involves the employment of an incendiary explosive device.

Again, a brief look at some of the terrorist events in which this method has been employed may offer insights into its usefulness. It is, for example, used more frequently to destroy property and to create a climate of fear than to destroy lives.

- *March 1982, Pusan, South Korea*—A U.S. International Communications Office was burned by a band of youths, killing one visitor.
- *October 1993, Paris*—Terrorists threw a firebomb into the Turkish owned Bosporus Bank. No serious damage was caused.
- *November 1993, Western Europe*—The PKK staged a round of coordinated attacks against Turkish diplomatic and commercial facilities in six countries. The assaults consisted mainly of firebombings and vandalism, but one person was killed and about twenty others injured.

3. **Hostage-taking and kidnapping** This tactic allows terrorists to maximize the publicity surrounding the event. By employing such a tactic, terrorists are able to control both the length of the event and the media coverage, at least in terms of interviews with the hostages. Since the audience is important to terrorist events, this makes this tactic particularly enticing to terrorists. The feelings of power, of being in control, of playing before a worldwide audience are indeed heady sensations for terrorists.

The headlines have been full, in recent years, of spectacular, and not-so-spectacular, hostage-takings. Indeed, as shock has succeeded shock, the taking of yet another individual by "extremists" in Lebanon or Turkey is no longer even newsworthy, in some parts of the world. A brief glimpse at the endless list of hostage-takings give an indication as to why this should be so. Note also that virtually all such reports refer to the incident as "kidnapping."

- *October 1986, Lebanon*—Edward Austin Tracy, an American and long-time resident of Moslem-controlled west Beirut, was kidnapped. A group calling itself the Revolutionary Justice Organization claimed responsibility.
- *June 1991, India*—A Kashmiri separatist group kidnapped one Dutch and seven Israeli tourists in Srinagar. One Israeli was killed in an escape attempt.
- *August 1991, Turkey*—The Kurdish Worker's Party (PKK) kidnapped ten German tourists near Lake Van. The tourists were later released. Later this same month, the PKK kidnapped three American, a Briton, and an Australian near Bingol. They were released a month later.
- *February 1993, Colombia*—Eight ELN terrorists kidnapped U.S. citizen Lewis Manning, an employee of the Colombian gold-mining company Oresom, in the Choco area.
- *March 1993, Costa Rica*—Four terrorists kidnapped 25 persons in the Nicaraguan embassy in San Jose, including the Nicaraguan Ambas-

sador. The hostages were held for several days while negotiations were conducted.

- *October 1993, Algeria*—Terrorists kidnapped from the cafeteria of an Italian construction firm in Tiaret, a Peruvian, a Filipino, and a Colombian, who were technicians employed by the firm. Two days later, the three were found dead with their throats cut. The extremist Armed Islamic Group claimed responsibility for this and other attacks against foreigners.

Unlike hostage-taking, kidnapping is a covert act. Since secrecy is required, kidnapping is usually preceded by considerable planning and rehearsal. Terrorists tended to kill the victims, even if their demands were met. This may be because a dead body is infinitely more dramatic than a quietly released hostage. Terrorism, to be effective, requires an element of drama.

In the news items cited above, the events could in some cases be termed "kidnapping," planned and executed in secrecy. The victims, however, were in a very real sense "hostages" to political or monetary demands made by their kidnappers. Some were killed, others remained in captivity as "hostages" to demands which could not be met.

4. **Assassinations and ambushes**   Targets for such attacks have been selected both for their publicity and for their symbolic value. In Lebanon, victims have included officers involved in peace-keeping efforts, priests, and college personnel. This tactic, since it requires an element of surprise, usually involved careful planning and execution.

Assassins and their victims come in all shapes and sizes. While government officials make attractive targets, a variety of others have come under the assassin's gun. Note in the brief list below the diversity of targets.

- *1994, West Beirut*—Malcolm Kerr, President of the American University of Beirut, was shot and killed as he stepped off the elevator to his office. Islamic Jihad claimed responsibility.
- *1987, Rome*—Leamon R. Hunt, the American director of the Multinational Force and the U.N. Observers Peacekeeping force in the Sinai peninsula, was shot and killed as he drove to his home. A radical offshoot of the Red Brigades claimed responsibility.
- *1985, San Salvador*—Terrorists shot and killed thirteen people as they sat in a sidewalk cafe . Two days later the Urban Guerrilla-Mardoqueo Cruz, associated with the FLMN, took responsibility.
- *1985, Rome and Vienna*—A coalition of Palestinian and Japanese Red Army terrorists attacked airports with grenades and machine guns, killing 18 and wounding 116. Abu Nidal's Revolutionary Fatah group was responsible.

- *1991, Bonn*—The Red Army Faction claimed responsibility for firing approximately 250 rounds of small-arms fire at the U.S. embassy. This was the first RAF attack against a U.S., target since 1985.
- *1991, Paris*—An Iranian dissident leader was stabbed and killed in the lobby of his apartment building.
- *1991, Lima*—Senderao Luminosa killed the Canadian director of the hamanitarian organization World Mission.
- *1992, Southern India*—Former Prime Minister Rajiv Gandhi was assassinated by a suspected LTTE suicide bomber while campaigning in southern India.
- *1993, Algeria*—An Italian businessman was shot and wounded by a terrorist as he left his residence.
- 1993— A police officer was killed and six others wounded when a group of terrorists opened fire on two movie houses that were showing foreign films. Al-Gama's al-Islamiyya claimed responsibility, stating that the attack retaliated for the screening of "immoral" films.
- *1995, Israel*—Yitzak Rabin, Prime Minister of Israel, was assassinated by a Jewish student, claiming that Rabin had given away too much of Israel in the peace process negotiated with the Palestinians.

5. **Aerial hijacking**   Skyjacking, as such events have been called, has been used by terrorists to maximize spectacular situations. This type of event allows the terrorist to maximize shock value and to grab world attention. Moreover, it provides the terrorist with an escape vehicle, until international law closed this loophole.

These "spectaculars" have provided extensive media coverage, at fairly minimal cost to the hijackers. While the psychological costs for the victims may be said to be high, the loss of lives has also tended to be less than in other types of terrorist events—except when things go wrong.

- *1985, Athens, Greece*—Shi'ite gunmen hijacked TWA Flight 847. The hijackers shot and killed U.S. Navy diver Robert Stetham in Beirut, and dispersed the remaining hostages throughout the city.
- *1985, Alexandria, Egypt*—Four Palestinian gunmen hijacked the Italian cruise ship *Achille Lauro* with 80 passengers and 320 crewmen aboard, sailed to Syria and Cyprus (where it was refused port entry) and then back to Egypt. While off the Syrian port of Tartus, the terrorists killed wheelchair-bound American Leon Klinghoffer.
- *1985, Cairo*—Arab gunmen hijacked an EgyptAir flight and landed at Malta after an in-flight gun battle with Egyptian security guards. Five passengers were shot at close range and dumped on the runway.
- *1986, Karachi International Airport*—PanAm Flight 73 was hijacked when at 5:55 P.M. (Washington time), four Arab-speaking gunmen seized a PanAm Boeing 747 as the plane was loading passengers for a flight to Frankfurt, Germany. The hijackers held 374 passengers and 15 crew members hostage for 16 hours while sporadic negotiations were at-

tempted. Suddenly, at 9:45 P.M the following night when the ground power units ran out of gas and the lights dimmed on the plane, the gunmen panicked and began firing indiscriminately at the huddled passengers. Before Pakistani commandos could storm the plane, 21 hostages were dead and more than sixty were seriously wounded.

- *1991, Kuala Lumpur*—Four Pakistanis claiming to be members of the Pakistani People's Party hijacked a Singapore Airlines flight to Singapore and demanded the release of several people reportedly imprisoned in Pakistan.

6. **Sabotage**   Western highly industrialized nations are particularly vulnerable to this type of terrorist tactic. It is possible, for example, to disrupt utility services or shut down industrial complexes. In 1987, Japan suffered a disruption of its commuter rail services by terrorists armed with nothing more than a few sharp blades. Such an incident can clearly have tremendous symbolic value, demonstrating to the watching governments the power which even a relatively obscure group may wield. While such actions serve terrorist goals of disrupting and perhaps destabilizing governments, they are not necessarily "terrorist" acts, since there are no innocent victims injured or killed in the action. (The victims may be disturbed and imposed upon but they are not "casualties.")

7. **Threat/hoax**   This is another low-cost tactic, with varying potential for disruption, without making innocent victims out of anyone. It forces governments to assess the vulnerability of the targets and the history of the group claiming responsibility. The cost of reacting to such a hoax may well be crippling to the authority involved, while the consequences of not responding could be equally dreadful.

8. **Chemical-biological attacks**   Agents for this type of tactic are, as noted earlier, available commercially, or can be developed without undue difficulty by some groups. The possibility of a successful poisoning of the water supply of a city has concerned some governments in recent years. Individuals in the United States have already demonstrated that it is possible to poison medicines on drugstore shelves and food supplies. The toxic agent attack on Tokyo subways in 1995 proved the effectiveness of this tactic, and demonstrated that groups can no longer be assumed to be unwilling or unable to use similar tactics. Use of toxic agents against the Kurds by the government of Iraq during its conflict with Iran had already made it clear that states were increasingly willing to use this type of weapon against their own citizens, including women and children.

9. **Nuclear threat**   As noted earlier, the technology and the materials are available to terrorists today. While the devices may be difficult to manufacture, it is not impossible to do so, and they could be stolen, purchased, or supplied by supporting states. Sabotage or takeover of a nuclear facility is also feasible, and far less expensive for terrorists..

Information regarding these last four forms of terrorism is less readily available. Sabotage, as noted earlier, is not a terrorist act, in the strict definition of the term. Threat-making is not, according to most terror-specific statutes, legally punishable as a crime of terrorism. Thus, the reporting for such crimes is less complete. The use of chemical and biological weapons by terrorists has thus far remained quite limited—no longer a "science fiction" tactic, but not yet widely used. But the increased use of such weapons by nation-states at war make the likelihood of terrorist acquisition and use of such methods much more probable.

In the Iran-Iraq War, as noted earlier, Iraq used poison gas against its enemies. For a time such measures were reserved for "desperate" military situations, when confronted with overwhelming Iranian forces. But there was gruesome evidence of an increase in the use of this lethal weapon against villages and cities. The city of Halabja, near the Iran-Iraq border, was covered with a poison cloud, which one survivor described as "a dense choking pancake that settled over many square blocks."[11] Very few of those left in the center of town survived. Medical evidence suggests that the Iraqi government dropped mustard gas, a relatively common poison; hydrogen cyanide, a chemical combination used for executions in U.S. prisons; and possibly sarin, a nerve gas which is one of the deadliest chemical weapons ever developed by mankind.

When nation-states themselves use such weapons, even on civilian populations, how can the civilized world prevent or even proscribe the use of such weapons by terrorists? Certainly the use of such weapons by nations engaged in conflict lessens the strength of the laws designed to control or prohibit their usage, and it makes more difficult the means by which the production of such weapons are controlled. If production of such chemical weapons cannot be effectively limited, then the dissemination of such weapons becomes even more difficult to control.

Today, intelligence sources say that some 37 countries are full or potential members of the "chemical weapons club."[12] While all but six of these—North and South Korea, Laos, Angola, Albania, and Nicaragua—have signed the 1925 Geneva Convention banning chemical warfare, several signatory nations have been flagrant violators of the pact. Iran's violations are well-documented. Evidence exists that others, including Ethiopia, Mozambique, Libya, Vietnam, and the Soviet Union violated the agreement.

THE MEDIA: ANOTHER WEAPON?

Terrorism has been called "propaganda by the deed." This particularly violent form of propaganda has captured the attention of millions of people today. To what exent has the media today become a weapon of the terrorists about whom it reports? Who is exploiting whom in this vicious scramble for a worldwide audience?

Many of today's terrorists have learned an important lesson about this technological age: that television news organizations can be forced into becoming the link between the terrorist and his audience. What is needed to forge this link is a crime sufficiently newsworthy—which has come to mean outrageous, dramatic, even barbaric.

According to Brian Jenkins, a Rand Corporation expert on terrorism, "terrorists want a lot of people watching and a lot of people listening, not a lot of people dead . . . I see terrorism as violence for effect. Terrorists choreograph dramatic incidents to achieve maximum publicity, and in that sense, terrorism is theater."[13]

Terrorists benefit from what has been called an "**amplification effect**," *when their activities are broadcast through the media to a much larger audience than would be available on the spot where the action occurs.* For instance, insurgents carried on rural guerrilla warfare in several countries, including Angola and Mozambique, for more than a decade, without receiving much attention from the rest of the world. But when a similar number of Palestinians carried their warfare into the urban centers of Europe and the Middle East, their actions and their causes became dinnertable conversation for TV audiences around the world, because in the urban centers of Europe and the Middle East, the terrorists were within reach of TV newsmen and their cameras.

This confluence of interest between the media—who thrive on sensational news—and terrorists—who are only too happy to provide the sensational events—has raised questions about the media's complicity in today's terrorism. Students of terrorism have suggested that the media today *is* in fact a contributing factor, a weapon, in modern terrorism. A quick survey of the opinions of a few of these experts is illuminating:

- Dr. Frederick Hacker, a California psychiatrist who has served as negotiator in terrorist incidents notes that "If the mass media did not exist, terrorists would have to invent them. In turn, the mass media hanker after terrorist acts because they fit into their programming needs: namely, sudden acts of great excitement that are susceptible, presumably, of quick solution. So there's a mutual dependency."

- Walter Laqueur, chairman of the International Research Council of the Center for the Strategic and International Studies, stated that "The media are a terrorist's best friend . . .[T]errorists are the superentertainers of our time."

- Professor Raymond Tanter, political scientist at the Univeristy of Michigan, makes the relationship delimma a bit clearer in his statement that "Since the terror is aimed at the media and not at the victim, success is defined in terms of media coverage. And there is no way in the West that you could *not* have media coverage because you're dealing in a free society."[14]

In Professor Tanter's comments lies a key to the delimma regarding the role of the media in terrorism. Censorship in any form is anathema to most free societies. Instead, it has been assumed that the media should be expected to exercise voluntary self-restraints where necessary in reporting such events.

But the media is not wholly convinced that restraint is either necessary or desirable. There is still considerable conflict over the extent of the public's "right to know" in the coverage of terrorist events. Executives of most of the major news companies have stated that television's "right to report" is absolute; that, in any case, it is better to report than not report. ABC's William Sheehan has said: "I don't think it's our job to decide what people should not know. The new media are not the reason for terrorism even though they may sometimes become part of the story."[15]

Which is the more accurate picture of the role of the media with respect to terrorism today? Is it the responsible means by which the public is kept informed on events and individuals who are interacting in the international arena? Or is it, as one hijacker said, a "whore" whose "favors" are available to anyone with a pistol?[16] If it is indeed true that the media is responsible for amplifying the effects of guerrilla warfare, to what extent is that media responsible for the effects of that amplification? If terrorists have to move on to increasingly more spectacular crimes in order to satisfy the increasingly jaded palette of TV audiences sated with violence, to what extent is the media responsible for whetting that appetite?

Some experts have suggested that the media is acting increasingly like a "loose cannon," a weapon which terrorists are learning to use with rapidly improving sophistication. It is, moreover, a cannon which democratic governments have provided, and continue to provide, essentially without controls. It would indeed be ironic if one of the fundamental freedoms of the free world—free press—were to be instrumental in its destruction, as the Libyan fable suggests.

EVALUATION

Terrorists today have a wide variety of tactics from which to choose, and sufficient training and support systems to make the most of the tactics within their grasp. While most terrorist groups continue to rely on the tactics proven successful in earlier years, such as bombing and hostage-taking, recent developments make it possible that different choices may be made in the near future.

Two potentially conflicting forces seem to be influencing the choice of tactics of terrorists. Consider these factors carefully, and decide what you think will be the trends in future terrorist attacks.

1. Some terrorist groups have become financially stable, with well-established ties to many governments. These governments supply training, arms, personnel, intelligence, and travel assistance. These same governments are, at the same time, somewhat more vulnerable than the group itself to retaliation in the event of a terrorist attack. The U.S. air strike against Libya in 1985 gives credence to this point. Moreover, the demise of the Soviet Union has made the political risks for supporting such groups much higher, and the risks of military retaliation much less calculable.

2. The technology for developing more sophisticated weapons is now more readily accessible to terrorists. At the same time, restraints against the use of widespread violence in terrorist attacks appear to be diminishing. In other words, it is now possible to construct instruments of vast destructive power at a time when inhibitions against the committing of such atrocities seems to be vanishing. If terrorists groups (or states) are willing to be responsible for hundreds of deaths in an aircraft bombing, will they continue to be reluctant to use weapons capable of even greater destruction, such as toxins, if they can obtain them?

3. Terrorists today can inflict more harm with more sophisticated weapons, and with larger quantities of weapons, than ever before in part because of the eagerness of the rest of the world to *sell* arms—to anyone who has the money to buy them. How much responsibility rests with the arms merchants of the so-called civilized world for making weapons so easy to obtain?

4. Dr. David Hubbard, a psychiatrist who has interviewed scores of imprisoned hijackers, contends that TV news broadcasts of ongoing terrorist events is "social pornography" because it "caters to the sick, unmet needs of the public" (*Skyjacker: His Flights of Fancy*). He is convinced that world terrorism would decrease if

televIsion brought its coverage under control. How accurate do you think this assessment is? What kind of controls can a democratic society afford to impose on its media? What are the dangers of such controls? How effective do you think either voluntary or involuntary controls on media coverage of terrorism would be in reducing either the number or the violence of terrorist events?

SUGGESTED READINGS

Dobson, Christopher, and Ronald Payne. *The Carlos Complex: A Study in Terror.* New York: P.G. Putnam, 1977.

Grossman, Lawrence K. "The Face of Terrorism." *The Quill,* June 1986.

Hickey, Neil. "Gaining the Media's Attention," in *The Struggle Against Terrorism.* New York: H.W. Wilson, 1977.

Jenking, Brian. "International Terrorism: The Other World War." A Project AIR FORCE Report prepared for the United States Air Force (November 1985).

———. *Terrorism: Trends and Potentialites.* Santa Monica, CA: Rand, 1977.

———. "Will Terrorists Go Nuclear?" P-5541. Santa Monica, CA: Rand, November 1985.

Kupperman, Robert H., and Darrell M. Trent, eds. *Terrorism: Threat, Reality, and Response.* Stanford, CA: Hoover Institution Press, 1979.

"New Horrors in a Long-Running Horror Show." *U.S. News & World Report,* April 4, 1988.

Russell, Charles A., and Bowman H. Miller. "Profile of a Terrorist," in *Terrorism: An International Journal,* vol. 1, no. 1. New York: Crane, Russak, 1977.

ENDNOTES

1. Christopher Dobson and Ronald Payne, *The Carlos Complex: A Study in Terror* (New York: G.P. Putnam, 1977) p. 34.
2. Quoted by Dobson and Payne, *The Carlos Complex,* p. 104.
3. Robert H. Kupperman and Darrell M. Trent, *Terrorism: Threat, Reality and Response* (Stanford, CA: Hoover Institution Press, 1979) p. 80.
4. Kupperman and Trent, *Terrorism,* p. 54.
5. In that year, evidence indicates that a Rhodesian airliner was shot down with an SA-7.
6. Brian Jenkins, *Terrorism: Trends and Potentialities* (Santa Monica, CA: Rand, 1977) p. 80.
7. Kupperman and Trent, *Terrorism,* p. 83.
8. Kupperman and Trent, *Terrorism,* p. 57. This agent comparison was derived by Conrad V. Chester of the Oak Ridge National Laboratory, transmitted in a June 20, 1975 letter entitled "Perspectives on the CB Terrorist Threat."

9. Brian Jenkins, "Will Terrorists Go Nuclear?" P-5541 (Santa Monica, CA: Rand, November 1975).

10. Charles A. Russell and Bowman H. Miller, "Profile of a Terrorist," *Terrorism: An International Journal*, vol. 1, no. 1 (New York: Crane, Russak, 1977) pp. 27-28.

11. "New Horrors in a Long-Running Horror Show," *U.S. News & World Report* (April 4, 1988) p. 11.

12. "A Plague of 'Hellish Poison'," *U.S. News & World Report* (October 26, 1987) p. 32.

13. "Terrorism Found Rising, Now Almost Accepted," *Washington Post,* December 3, 1985, p. A4.

14. These quotes were gathered by Neil Hickey in "Gaining the Media's Attention," *The Struggle Against Terrorism* (New York: H.W. Wilson, 1977) pp. 113-114.

15. Hickey, "Gaining the Media's Attention," p. 117.

16. Hickey, "Gaining the Media's Attention," p. 112.

CHAPTER EIGHT

LEGAL PERSPECTIVES ON TERRORISM

International and transnational terrorism are nothing more nor less than the wanton and willful taking of human lives, the purposeful commission of bodily harm, and the intentional infliction of severe mental distress by force or threat of force.

—Robert Friedlander

KEY CONCEPTS

innocent persons
innocence
civilians
special provisions in
  the Geneva Convention
protected persons
rule of proportionality
hostis humanis generis
skyjacking
novation

jurisdiction
provisions for jurisdiction
extradite
"gentlemen's agreements"
attentat clause
"political"crime
political offenders
loophole in the law

If Dr. Friedlander's assessment of the nature of terrorism is correct, then one would assume that such acts would already be designated as common crimes in the legal codes of most countries today. One could also be forgiven for assuming that international law, if it truly reflects the laws and mores of the international community, would reflect a similar tendency to declare such acts illegal.

The fact that this is not the case is perhaps due less to a lack of consensus about the desirability or even the criminality of "the wanton and willful taking of human lives" than to the nature of the international legal system itself. In the international community, while there may well be general agreement on the undesirability of such things as war, racial discrimination, genocide, and other violations of basic human rights, there has been a significant reluctance to translate that agreement into workable treaties with enforcement powers.

Why, if nations generally agree with the idea of reducing the incidence of such evils, cannot workable methods of getting rid of these evils be constructed? The answer to this question must be the same as that given by municipal leaders when confronted with the question as to why a society's evils (such as poverty, unemployment, and discrimination) are not being effectively eliminated. Unfortunately, consensus about the undesirability of these things at any level is often difficult to translate into acceptable, enforceable rules and regulations that might remedy the situation. General policy directions are always easier to formulate than specific legislation.

Moreover, the constraints that make progress in creating such legislation difficult at the local and national level are magnified many times at the international level. An examination of at least a few of these constraints may help us to understand the dearth of international law on terrorism.

The first problem involves a lack of legislative authority. However inept one may consider state and national legislators to be, at least three law-making bodies can be said to exist at such levels. But on the international level, there is no body invested with such authority. The United Nations was certainly never designed to "rule" the nations of the world or to created rules for its governance.[1] The United Nations offers a forum for discussion, for cooperation and consensus-building on issues. It does not "make laws" in the sense that governing bodies make laws for subordinate individuals and groups in the national arena.

There is, too, a distinct lack of central authority in the international community. To describe it even as a confederation is to invest it with properties which it does not really possess. In a confederal system there are mechanisms for governing at the top level, while no such "governing" system exists in any real sense at the international level. Not only is there no legislative body empowered to make laws, there is also neither an autocratic nor a democratic chief executive who is able to speak with authority for, and issue commands to, the community of nations.

Moreover, there is no judicial system to which all have recourse and whose decisions are binding at the international level. The International Court of Justice's decision-making authority depends for the most part on the willingness of states to amicably resolve a difficulty, and on their willingness to submit their disputes to the Court for adjudication.[2]

So the most serious infractions of international law often go untouched by the Court, since many states are not willing to submit their disputes for adjudication. A voluntary judicial system which can neither hail an offender to the bar of justice, nor inforce compliance with its judgments, and which has no provisions by which entities other than states (such as individuals, groups, or corporations) can seek recourse for injustice, seems to be sadly lacking in judicial accouterments.

The international system, then, has no central authority figure or figures, provides only a forum for debate rather than law-making, and possesses only a voluntary (and frequently ineffective) judiciary. It is thus even less able than municipal governments to deal with the difficulties inherent in enacting and enforcing laws designed to eliminate societal problems. The political and enforcement problems which hamper the making of effective laws within nations are even more capable of preventing the successful completion of treaties capable of dealing with sensitive issues in the international community.

This incapacity is made worse by the absence of law enforcement officers. With the possible exception of INTERPOL (which is strictly charged to stay out of political problems), there does not appear to be, at the international level, anyone with the authority to act in this capacity. Just as there are few procedures for bringing a miscreant to justice, there is no one who is authorized to physically do so.

Lacking these instruments of governance most commonly found at the national level, the construction of rules at the international level has become an extremely delicate and difficult task. Political considerations of the nations in the international community are usually accommodated as fully as possible, since compliance with any rules is largely voluntary.

The more highly politicized the issue, the greater the perception of the "national interests" involved and the more difficult it becomes to construct an effective treaty—that is, one which is both strong and acceptable. This may, as one scholar suggests, derive from the nature and scope of national interests' inevitable tension with political reality. When diverse national interests appear to oppose perceived common goals, as they often do in discussions on terrorism, then this "tension" becomes heightened to unworkable levels, according to this scholar.[3]

Recent history provides lots of examples of the hazards that abound when international law extends itself further than the limits of assured compliance within the community of nations. The most striking instance of such overextension may be the attempts to outlaw war, notably through the Kellogg-Briand pact.[4] In spite of the majority consensus which may be presumed to exist on the undesirability of war, it is not within the power of international law to enforce a prohibition of war.

More successful, perhaps, have been efforts within the international community to restrict certain highly undesirable practices during times of war. This was partially accomplished by putting together "rules of conduct" for times of war. Conventions about the treatment of prisoners-of-war and innocent civilian personnel, as well as some involving prohibitions of certain methods of warfare and weapons of war have been more effective, in terms of compliance, that the ill-judged and altruistic Kellogg-Brand pact.

This success in creating laws to deal with specific aspects of generally undesirable behavior has important implications in terms of understanding the attempts by the international community to deal with the sensitive issue of terrorism. Attempts by the international community to construct general treaties dealing with terrorism have been largely unsuccessful. But on treaties or conventions which deal instead with specific aspects of terrorism, greater progress has been made. A quick review of the provisions and "success" record in preventing or punishing terrorism could make it easier to decide on the most effective ways for handling the problem of current and future terrorism.

First, let us examine portions of international law that do not deal specifically with terrorism, but from which laws and regulations on terrorism have evolved. Three areas of international law come immediately to mind in this regard: laws of war, laws on piracy, and laws concerning the protection of diplomatic personnel and heads of state.

LAWS OF WAR

International law has been divided by some scholars into laws of war and laws of peace. This can be a somewhat confusing dichotomy, since some peacetime laws continue to apply even during times of war. However, it is true that the rules of behavior change in many respects during wartime. This change is usually in the direction of allowing greater latitude for suppressing or eliminating ordinary protections and courtesies. It is fair to say that, during times of war, more types of violence may be employed against a wider range of targets with far fewer safeguards for human rights than are permissible during times of peace.

This is not a tautological statement. It is instead an important point when one considers that it is the laws of war that are most often invoked by terrorists in justification of their acts. If, even under the rules which permit a broader range of acceptable actions, there are certain significant prohibited actions, then those actions could be said to be always prohibited, regardless of the provocation. If the laxity of safeguards which exists during times of war still does not allow certain actions the semblance of legality, then those actions could be regarded as unacceptable to the international community, both in times of war and in times of peace.

While the mass of rules and laws which govern warfare today has grown to immense proportions, it is possible to find a number of fundamental rules which meet the criteria described above, in that they involve the establishment of minimum standards of behavior, even for parties engaged in hostilities. Of these rules of war, perhaps the most significant for this study are those which affect the treatment of **innocent persons**.

This category of persons is an extremely important one to students of terrorism. It is crucial to establish a clear understanding of what is meant by the term *innocent*. Terrorists have claimed that "there is no such thing as an innocent person,"[5] yet the Geneva Conventions extend special protections to *"persons taking no active part in the hostilities."*[6]

Innocence, as it is used by the laws of war, has much the same meaning as that found in any expanded international dictionary definition of the term. In both cases, **innocence** signifies *freedom from guilt for a particular act*, even when the total character may be evil. It is in one sense a negative term, implying as it does something less than righteous, upright, or virtuous. Legally, it is used to specify *a lack of guilt for a particular act/crime, denoting a nonculpability.*[7]

Innocence is thus imputed to a thief found innocent of the crime of murder. By this logic, a government official guilty of only indifference, can still be said to be "innocent" of any crime committed by his government. That official, in other words, has been guilty of nothing which would justify his summary execution or injury by terrorists who have a grievance against his government.

This concept of a lack of guilt for a specific act is particularly appropriate in examining the random selection of "any Englishman, any Israeli" by terrorists as acceptable targets.[8] If innocent person status can only be removed by guilt of a specific act or crime committed by the person (not by others of the same age group, nationality, race, religion, or other similar categories), then there can be no legal justification for such a random selection of targets.

International law, like that of most civilized nations, neither recognizes nor punishes guilt by association. The Nuremberg trial records give credence to this point, in terms of the efforts made to establish personal guilt for specific criminal acts (such as murder or torture), instead of prosecuting simply on the basis of membership in the Nazi Party or Hitler's SS troops.[9] In refusing to punish all Germans or even all Nazi Party members for crimes against humanity and crimes of war, the precedent was established for differentiating between a person guilty of committing a crime during times of war, and those who were innocent of actual wrongdoing.

The importance of this legal concept of innocence as an absence of guilt for a particular act cannot be overstated. The reason for its significance lies in the justification set forth by modern terrorists for their selection of victims. Many organizations which commit terrorist acts today do so on the premise that they are legitimately engaged in seeking to overthrow an existing government or to radically change existing conditions, and are thus engaged in warfare.

Accepting, for the moment, this claim to revolutionary action, it is logical to assume that the actions of these groups should still conform to the rules of warfare. Terrorists have rejected the laws of peace as too restrictive to their revolutionary efforts. Let us instead test the legality of their actions according to the laws of war.

The Geneva Convention on the treatment of **civilians** demands special protections for *"persons taking no active part in the hostilities."* Nonactive status, like innocence, does not imply that the person is good, virtuous, or even disinterested in the outcome of the conflict. A person need only be innocent of participation in the hostilities to be protected by the Convention.

This means that membership in the civilian population of a nation against which a group is waging war is *insufficient reason for according a guilty* status to a person, thereby removing those special protections. Thus, the waging of war against "any Israeli" or "any Englishman" is not acceptable behavior under the laws of war.

What are, then, the **special provisions in the Geneva Convention** relating to the treatment of civilians? First of all, this Convention states that such persons *"shall in all circumstances be treated humanely."* Article 3 of this document lists various actions which are prohibited *"at any time and in any place whatsoever with respect to such persons.* These prohibited acts include *"violence to life and person, in particular murder of all kinds, mutilations, cruel treatment and torture; tak-*

ing of hostages; and outrages upon the personal dignity, in particular humiliating and degrading treatment."[10]

Furthermore, in Article 27, the Geneva Convention on Civilians, emphasizes the degree of legal protection afforded to these noncombatants, stating that "they are entitled, in all circumstances, to respect for their persons, their honor, their family rights, their religious convictions and practices, and their manners and customs . . . and shall at all times be treated humanely, and shall be protected especially against all acts of violence or threats thereof."[11]

Article 33 of the Geneva Convention for the Protection of Civilian Persons (1949) provides that

> No protected person may be punished for an offense he or she has not personally committed. Collective penalties and likewise all measures of intimidation or terrorism are prohibited.
> Pillage is prohibited.
> Reprisals against protected persons and their property are prohibited.

Protected persons in this Convention are *civilians who have the misfortune to be living in a combat zone or occupied territory.* Not only does this Convention specifically prohibit the use of terrorism"against this civilian population, but it also, in Article 34, *prohibits the taking of hostages of any sort.* Such rules make it clear that the kidnapping or murder of any civilian, even during times of war, to exact punishment for an injustice real or imagined, is not legal, unless the victim was directly responsible for the injustice.

This prohibition against collective punishment applies to states as well as to revolutionary organizations. Control Council Law No. 10, used in the trials of war criminals before the Nuremberg Tribunals, makes this clear.[12] Neither side in an armed conflict, whether involved in the "liberation" of a country or in the efforts of the state to maintain itself while under attack, may engage in warfare against the civilian population.

Terrorist acts against innocent persons by the state, as well as acts of terrorism by nonstate groups, are as illegal in times of war as they are in times of peace. The laws of war offer neither justification nor protection for the willful and wanton taking of innocent life. If terrorism by its very nature involves victimizing an innocent third party, in order to achieve a political goal and to evoke a particular emotional response in an audience, then it seems reasonable to say that terrorism is illegal under the laws of war.

While the Geneva Convention was drafted with the protection of civilians in occupied territories in mind, Protocols I and II to the Convention, drafted in 1976, extend these protections to civilians in nonoccupied territories. Article 46 of Protocol I codifies the customary international law doctrine that the civilian population as such, as well as individual citizens, may not be made the object of direct military attack. One significant provision in Article 46 states that *"Acts or threats of violence which have the primary object of spreading terror among the civilian population are prohibited."*

This Article goes on to prohibit indiscriminate attacks which are "of a nature to strike military objectives and civilians or civilian objectives without distinction." This Article further states that a *bombardment that treats as a single military objective a number of clearly separated and distinct military objectives located within a city, town or village, or other area which has a concentration of civilians is considered to be indiscriminate and is therefore prohibited.*

What does this mean, in terms of legal restraints on terrorism? It means, for one thing, that a state may not commit an attack on a city or town as a whole, just on the basis of the information that insurgents or combatants may be making a base in that area. To do so would be to commit an act of terrorism under international law. The Convention, in other words, make it clear that states as well as groups are prohibited from punishing the innocent in efforts to stop the insurgents in guerrilla warfare. To do so would be to commit acts of terrorism.

Article 50 of Protocol I attempts to make clear the precautions which a state or a revolutionary army must make in conducting an attack. This Article also codifies customary international law concerning what is called the **rule of proportionality**. Generally speaking, this refers to *the need for the loss of civilian life to be minimal compare with the military advantage gained.* It states specifically that those who plan or decide upon an attack must:

> . . . refrain from deciding to launch any attack which may be expected to cause incidental loss of civilian life . . . which would be excessive in relation to the concrete and direct military advantage anticipated.

In simple terms, this provision, along with other provisions in the article, means that those launching or planning to launch an attack, are legally responsible for making sure that the military objectives which they expect to gain justify the minimal loss of civilian life which may occur. This provision is extremely practical. It recognizes a basic fact of life during war: There are inevitably civilians on and around military targets who will no doubt be injured or killed during an attack on those targets.

There are two important points here. One is that the objective is assumed to be a military, never a civilian, target. The law makes it clear that, whereas legitimate attacks may be expected against military targets, there is no legal expectation or right to launch attacks against civilian targets. On the contrary, the civilians within the target zone are to be protected against the effects of that attack, as far as it is militarily possible.

The other point is that, while military reality makes note of the fact that some civilian injury may occur during an attack, the injury or deaths of civilians should be incidental to the operations, on a scale proportionate to the military objective sought. If civilian casualties are expected to be high, then the attack cannot be justified under international law.

Two thoughts come to mind with respect to these provisions. One is that guerrilla or revolutionary groups which select predominantly civilian targets are in violation of international law, even if there is a military target which may also be hit. Thus, the fact that a cafe is frequented by members of an enemy military does not make it a legitimate target, since there would be a great likelihood of many civilian casualties in such an attack. If the target area is populated predominantly with civilians, then it cannot be a justifiable military target.

The other thought which this provision evokes is that states may not strike civilian settlements, even if there are guerrilla soldiers taking refuge or making their headquarters in such settlements. To attack such places would mean inflicting unacceptably high levels of civilian casualties in proportion to the military objective sought. Thus, those who seek to destroy Palestinian revolutionaries may not, under international law, drop bombs on Palestinian refugee camps, since such camps have large civilian populations, including women and children, the sick and the infirm.

It is true that those revolutionaries who make their headquarters in the midst of civilian encampments are deliberately placing those civilians at risk in the ensuing war. But this does not justify the attacking of such settlements by the enemy. The civilians have, for the most part, no choice but to be there, in their own homes or shelters. The state seeking to destroy the revolutionaries cannot take advantage of their vulnerable state to make war on the insurgents at a cost of countless civilian lives. Even when seeking to destroy an enemy who takes refuge among protected persons, a state may not deliberately wage war on those protected persons.

PIRACY—OF AIR AND SEA

If, during times of war, terrorist acts against innocent persons are illegal, then it seem logical to assume that such acts are also illegal during times of peace. Indeed, the term "crimes against humanity," which was used to describe war crimes at Nuremberg, did not originate with laws of war, but with laws of peace. The term was used in international legal writings to describe acts of piracy. The famous English jurist Sir Edward Coke, in the time of James I, described pirates as *"hostis humanis generis,"* meaning *"common enemies of mankind."*[13]

National case law confirms this view of piracy as an international crime. The U.S. Supreme Court, in the case of *United States* v. *Smith* (1820), went on record through Mr. Justice Joseph Story as declaring piracy to be "an offense against the law of nations" and a pirate to be "an enemy of the human race."[14] Judge John Bassett Moore of the World Court reaffirmed this assessment in his opinion in the famous *Lotus* case (1927).[15]

In fact, from the Paris Declaration of 1856 to the Geneva Convention of 1958, the proliferation of treaties dealing with aspects of terror-violence on the high seas has helped to codify international law with regard to piracy.[16] Piracy—of the sea, at least—is one of the first and most universally recognized "international crimes."

Nations have not been so willing to deal, through international law, with modern **skyjacking**, which some legal experts have termed *air piracy*. One legal expert has suggested the "the legal status of aerial hijackers could become the same as sea pirates through the process of novation wherein the former would be presumed to stand in the shoes of the latter."[17] Theoretically, this would provide a way to bring perpetrators of the modern crime of skyjacking under the existing legal restrictions and penalties imposed on crimes of a similar nature, that is, of sea piracy, which were more common at an earlier date.

Novation is not a complicated process. Legally, it refers to *the substitution of a new indebtedness or obligation, creditor or debtor, for an existing one.* In other words, aerial hijackers would assume the legal "indebtedness" of sea pirates under international law. Thus, it would not be necessary to create new international law to deal with what is, in many respects, a very old form of criminal activity.

But modern nations have not seen such a process as an adequate or acceptable solution. Instead, three major agreements on aircraft hijacking have evolved in recent years, as well as a number of smaller agreements between nations concerned with this crime. A short review of these agreements sheds some light on the state of the law with regard to this modern form of piracy.

One of the more successful antihijacking agreements in recent years has been the Memorandum of Understanding on Hijacking of Aircraft and Vessels and Other Offenses, signed between the United States and Cuba on February 15, 1973.[18] In spite of a denunciation of the agreement by Cuba in October 1976, there has been a rather impressive record of interstate cooperation in combating aerial hijacking between the two countries. Many of the hijacking attempts which have occurred between the United States and Cuba since 1978 have resulted in the prompt return of the hijacked aircraft and the somewhat less prompt seizure for prosecution of the hijackers.

But treaties of a broader nature have met with less success. Three issues which need to be addressed in any successful hijacking convention have not been adequately resolved. These are the problems of determining who has jurisdiction, of establishing of a prosecutable offense, and of providing for the prompt processing of extradition requests.

The Convention on Offenses and Certain Other Acts Committed on Board Aircraft, signed in Tokyo on September 14, 1963, provided a general basis for the establishment of **jurisdiction**, that is, *legal authority to exercise control*. The hijacking of an aircraft is an act which often takes place in flight en route between countries. Such planes are often registered to yet another country, and carry citizens of many countries. So a decision as to who has the right to bring a hijacker to justice is often a difficult one.

Article 3 of the Tokyo Convention provides that the state of registration is the one which has the first and primary right to exercise jurisdiction.[19] But this Convention does not place on any signatory nation the responsibility to ensure that all alleged offenders will be prosecuted. Thus, a nation may accept jurisdiction, and then refuse or neglect to bring the offenders to justice.

The subsequent Convention for the Suppression of Unlawful Seizure of Aircraft, signed at The Hague on December 16, 1970, deals more specifically with the issues of extradition and prosecution. This Convention obliges contracting states to make the offense of unlawful seizure of aircraft punishable by severe penalties.

This Convention offers a definition for the actions which may constitute the offense of skyjacking, in Article 1. This article states that any person commits an offense who, on board an aircraft in flight:

> 1. Unlawfully, by force or threat thereof, or by any other means of intimidation, seizes, or exercises control of, that aircraft, or attempts to perform any such act; or,
> 2. Is an accomplice of a person who performs or attempts to perform any such act.

Although not as explicit as the later convention drawn up at Montreal, this Convention does provide an important legal framework for prosecution of an offense, reasonably and clearly defined in legal terms which are directly applicable in the legal systems of many states (meaning that the states are thus not given the sticky political task of creating laws to make such acts a legal offense).

Under this Convention, too, **provisions for jurisdiction** were extended. Three States were legally given the responsibility for jurisdiction, in the following order of precedence: *(1) the State of registration; (2) the State of first landing; and, (3) the State in which the lessee has its principal place of business or permanent residence.* Moreover, this Convention requires each contracting State to take measures to establish jurisdiction, if the offender is within its territory and is not to be extradited.

This Convention also addresses the issue of prosecution, obligating each contracting state to either **extradite**, that is, *to send the person to another state seeking to prosecute* an alleged offender, or to submit the case "without exception whatsoever to its competent authorities for the purpose of prosecution." While it does not create an absolute obligation to extradite, the Convention states that the offense referred to is deemed to be included as an extraditable offense in any existing extradition treaties between contracting states, and is to be included in every future extradition treaty concluded between such states.

The Convention for the Suppression of Unlawful Acts Against the Safety of Civil Aviation, signed in Montreal on September 23, 1971, adds more detail to the description of the offenses affecting aircraft and air navigation. It includes:

1. Acts of violence against a person on board an aircraft in flight if that act is likely to endanger the safety of that aircraft; or
2. Destruction of an aircraft in service or damage to such an aircraft which renders it incapable of flight, or which is likely to endanger its safety in flight; or,
3. Placing or causing to be placed on an aircraft in service, by any means whatsoever, a device or substance which is likely to destroy that aircraft, or to cause damage to it which is likely to endanger its safety in flight; or,
4. Destruction or damage of air navigation facilities or interference with their operation, if any such act is likely to endanger the safety of the aircraft in flight; or,
5. Communication of information which is known to be false, thereby endangering the safety of the aircraft in flight.[20]

In spite of these efforts to specify the crime, and to establish procedures for deciding who has jurisdiction over the crime, there remain large gaps in international legal efforts to deal with skyjacking today. There is little to compel a contracting state to honor its paper commitment to extradite or punish a terrorist who has hijacked a plane. This has become painfully evident in recent years, as the pressure and threats from powerful terrorist organizations have forced several Western nations to evade their responsibilities under these conventions.

There are no sanctions or enforcement procedures in any of these conventions; they are, in effect, "**gentlemen's agreements**," *dependent for their enforcement on the integrity of the contracting states.*

Efforts to achieve an independent enforcement convention during the ICAO Extraordinary Assembly in September 1973 ended in failure. Several proposals were made at that assembly with the aim of broadening the effectiveness of international control over interference with aircraft. A new multilateral convention was proposed, establishing an international commission with the power to investigate alleged violations of the enforcement provisions of the Tokyo, Hague, and Montreal conventions. It provided for sanctions against states that refused to comply with the Commission's recommendations. (One of the contemplated sanctions was the collective suspension of flights to and from such a state.) None of the proposals were passed by the assembly.

PROTECTION OF DIPLOMATIC PERSONNEL AND HEADS OF STATE

Similar difficulties have hindered efforts to create effective protections against attacks on diplomatic personnel and heads of state. In light of the seizure of American diplomatic personnel in Iran, which was never formally "punished" as a crime under international law, it could be argued that there still exists no effective international law concerning such acts. However, laws do exist (in spite of the fact that they are broken without punishment) on this politically sensitive subject. Since these laws concern terrorism of a specific sort, they deserve consideration here.

Perhaps the unwillingness to punish, or even to condemn, those guilty of attacks on these "protected persons" has its roots in the venerable Western tradition of granting political asylum to offenders who have committed "political" crimes. Although concern for the preserving of societal order influenced some Western European governments to modify their positions on granting asylum for "political" crimes, political asylum remains the primary focus in extradition questions in many modern states.

In 1833, Belgium enacted a law providing for nonextradition of political offenders, a principle incorporated into a Franco-Belgium treaty in 1834.[21] Following attempts, both successful and unsuccessful, on the lives of heads of state in subsequent years, however, an **attentat clause** began to be incorporated into successive treaties. *This clause made the murder or attempted murder of any head of state or his immediate family a common (not political) crime.* These clauses stated essentially that such attempts "shall not be considered a political offense or an act connected with such an offense."[22]

In 1957, the European Convention on Extradition invoked the principle of the attentat clause by making assaults on heads of state and their immediate families nonpolitical offenses.[23] The Vienna Convention on Diplomatic Relations gave evidence of a broadening concern for diplomats as well as heads of state. Under this Convention, it is made "the responsibility of the states" to prevent attacks on a diplomatic agent's person, freedom, or dignity."[24]

This broadly stated concern and general delegation of authority, however, has failed to secure significant enforceable protections for diplomats. As one expert expressed it, "what was needed, beyond the incidental tightening of police measures, is a constant vigilance on the part of states, acting individually and collectively in an organized way, to prevent the occurrence of incidents."[25]

But while subsequent treaties on this subject have attempted to make clear the specific acts which are prohibited, and the states which have a right to claim jurisdiction over the crime, there remain serious flaws in the protection afforded to diplomatic agents today. No "collective, organized" approach to the problem has evolved.

Furthermore, the delegation of responsibility for protecting diplomats and for punishing in the event of attacks on diplomats creates serious problems, when the government of a state is itself a party to, or a tacit accessory to, the taking of diplomatic hostages. It is clearly useless to expect a government which actively or tacitly approves of such a crime to prosecute the perpetrators of the crime. Such a requirement could mean that the government must at some point prosecute itself for committing what it obviously did not regard as an illegal act—a most unlikely scenario!

One further development in the law regarding the protection of diplomatic personnel should be noted. The Venice Statement on Taking of Diplomatic Hostages, issued by the Heads of State and Government of the Seven Summit Countries during their meeting in Venice in 1980, not only expressed grave concern about the Iranian hostage situation, but also called on nations to ratify the recently completed Convention Against the Taking of Hostages, adopted by the U.N. General Assembly on December 17, 1979.

Completed shortly after the seizure of the American embassy in Teheran, this Convention effectively makes it a crime to take *any* person as a hostage. Through this Convention, the protection of international law is extended to every individual, regardless of his or her position (or lack of one), with the exception of those in armed forces engaged in armed conflict.

This broadening of the law in this respect suggests that nations consider certain actions unacceptable to the community of nations. Just as in the laws of war, we noted that certain actions were prohibited at all times, whether at war or at peace, so we note that there are some actions which the international community has come to believe are unacceptable, regardless of the cause.

SUMMARY: PROTECTION OF THE INNOCENT AGAINST SPECIFIC CRIMES

Although there are limitations on the extent of the protection provided by the conventions reviewed thus far, there are several significant points which illustrate the strengths—and weaknesses—of international law on terrorism as contained in these examples of international law. Certainly, the two international crimes already reviewed—air piracy and hostage-taking—offer several interesting points which could be briefly recapitulated and summarized to good effect at this point.

Innocence, as noted earlier, connotes not virtue but an absence of guilt for a particular act. The international laws governing piracy protect those considered innocent in the most common meaning of the word, those whose only "crime" was to be in the wrong place at the wrong time. Similarly, the expanded law on hostage-taking propounded by the 1979 Convention offers legal protection to a similarly innocent person.

However, the laws on the protection of diplomatic personnel, including the 1979 Convention, offer a broader concept of the innocent person and of his right to the protection of the law. Diplomats, consular agents, and similar governmental agents are precisely that: agents who carry out the policies of a government. As the Nuremberg trials demonstrated, it is possible to hold such persons legally responsible if their actions transgress the laws of nations.

That is the crucial point, though: It must be their *own* actions, not merely any of a variety of actions of the government which they represent, which transgress the law. It is not enough that their government adheres to unacceptable or illegal policies. If the agent is to be punished for those policies, then personal guilt (in terms perhaps of the carrying out of illegal policies, such as genocide) must be established before the agent can be punished. Thus, although such persons are perhaps less "innocent" than, for example, the tourist who boards an airplane which is subsequently hijacked, government agents cannot legally be "punished" (taken hostage or executed) unless they can be proven guilty of a specific illegal action.

By the same token, the representative of a multinational corporation (MNC) must be considered legally "innocent" unless proven guilty of a specific crime. Thus, the kidnapping of a multinational corporation employee for ransom, in order to redress perceived exploitation by the company of a nation's resources, would be without legal justification.

International law, it appears, extends its protection to those truly innocent of any crime as well as those who could only be considered guilty of association with a government or corporation whose actions may be unjust. Both types of persons are regarded under the law as being sufficiently innocent to merit protection. Indeed, as the Nuremberg tribunals demonstrated, even individual governmental agents thought to be guilty of heinous "crimes against humanity" were nevertheless given a trial by law rather than a summary execution.

This presumption of innocence, which precludes summary judgment, is a major stumbling block to the justification of terrorism. The taking of any innocent life, however meritorious the cause to which the act is designed to call attention, cannot be justified under international law. No wrong can justify, or require, the commission of another wrong to rectify it. To accept such a premise would be to agree that the end for which one strives can serve to justify the means which one employs to attain it.

This does not leave revolutionary groups with no legitimate targets. While the range of innocent persons protected by international law is fairly broad, it is not absolutely inclusive. Military and police officials, for example, are far less clearly "innocent," in any sense of the term, particularly in regimes which practice forms of state terrorism. International law prohibits the summary taking of innocent life. The extent to which terrorism violates this prohibition is a measure of its transgression of the law.

TERRORISM: A POLITICAL CRIME?

The definition of what constitutes a "political" crime has become a crucial part of the modern legal debate concerning terrorism. The crux of the problem appears to be in deciding how one determines what is and what is not a "political" crime. It is a problem which is far from solved, and one whose political ramifications may well make it, for the present, insoluble.

For centuries, the nature of a **"political"crime** *rested largely upon the intended victim of the crime.* That is, the assassination of a head of state or of a diplomat was regarded as being "political" in nature, and therefore to be handled differently—more leniently or more severely, depending upon the state's system of laws—than an ordinary, nonpolitical offense, the murder of an ordinary citizen.

If such a criteria were applied to many terrorist acts today, such as the hijacking of an airplane or the bombing of a cafe, then such acts would not, on the surface, qualify as being political. The argument could be (and indeed has been) made that the real intended "victims" of such crimes are the governments who are forced to helplessly watch and perhaps ultimately capitulate as events unfold.

But in order to make the assumption that there is a victim involved beyond the obvious captives or casualties, one is forced to rely upon knowledge or inference about the motives of the perpetrators. In other words, *the action would be described as a "political" crime, not specifically by its intended victim but by the motives which prompted the commission of the crime.*

There are at least two problems with this reasoning. The first is that, in order to make such a determination concerning a motive for an action, the person rendering the judgment would have to have a knowledge of why the terrorists committed the crime. How is such knowledge to be obtained? Does it come from propaganda put out by the terrorists, which is designed to persuade but is not necessarily truthful? Does it come from interviews with the perpetrators or their allies, assuming such interviews could be arranged?

Is there any way, indeed, to discover the facts concerning the motive for a crime? To search for a factual basis is not useless by any means, but the attribution of a motive for any crime, political or common, is essentially a judgment call. In the courts of most civilized nations, assessment of motivation may affect the degree of severity with regard to the prosecution or sentencing, but has little effect on the decision as to whether or not a crime has been committed.

Yet if one allows motivation to be the determinant for delineating political from common crimes, there is reason to suspect that, for crimes judged to be "political" in motivation, there will in fact be neither prosecution nor sentencing. This is the second problem in allowing motivation to be the guiding factor in determining what constitutes a political crime. *For under the laws of many nations,* **"political offenders"** *are accorded special status. Those believed guilty of "political" offenses are eligible for the granting of political asylum by friendly states.* States granting such asylum are under no legal obligation to prosecute the perpetrator for the crime.

Even those who are prosecuted are afforded special treatment. Seldom are political criminals jailed with those who have committed common crimes. To be a political prisoner confers, in many nations, a unique status on the offender. There is nothing wrong with this: political crimes are not the same as common crimes. Their perpetrators are often regarded as being motivated by high ideals for political change for which they are willing to pay a high personal price, often imprisonment or even death.

That is another important point, however. Just like the perpetrator of any other crime, the political offender does so with the knowledge of, even the acceptance of, the penalty which must be paid for the crime. Perpetrators of political crimes in earlier centuries committed their offenses in the full expectation of being required to pay the legal penalty for their crimes. Those who would classify terrorism as a political crime today do so in order to enable the perpetrators to evade the payment of those penalties. The concept of "political offense" has become a loophole through which terrorists try to avoid having to pay the just penalty for their crimes.

This **loophole in the law**, *which allows "political offenders" to escape extradition or even punishment*, has worried international legal experts for years. Attempts have been made to advocate the creation of an international criminal code, and an international criminal court. Under these innovations, terrorism could be specified as an international crime, punishable in international courts. But thus far, the efforts to create such a system have been unable to resolve both the practical legal and political problems relating to its function. So the loophole of "political offender" still allows terrorists to commit heinous crimes for "political" purposes, and then to escape the hand of justice.

EVALUATION

International law is perhaps most useful as a measure of international concern and opinion on an issue such as terrorism. Lacking methods and mechanisms for enforcement, it cannot be said to be an effective deterrent to terrorism, either on the national or the international level. Since its formulation is so ad hoc, relying on loose associations of states, rather than any legislative body, to draft conventions, it is somewhat less than coherent, and often indecisive. Political considerations often weaken the resolve of nations to deal with politically sensitive subjects.

In the absence of a judiciary empowered to adjudicate, without the consent of all parties, and lacking an executive or police force to enforce the laws, international law on terrorism has evolved as a patchwork of treaties. Among the most successful have been those relating to specific types of terrorism. Even these treaties, however, have been seriously hampered by political concerns relating to issues of jurisdiction, prosecution, extradition, and political asylum.

As a means for combating terrorism, then, international law appears to be a somewhat dubious tool. When agreements are entered into which have enforcement capabilities, then such laws can be used to curb terrorism. But to date, few such agreements are in force within the international community.

There are, however, two other types of international legal agreements on terrorism that have been attempted. Consider each of the following descriptions of international legal efforts to deal with terrorism. Decide which, if any, have a reasonable chance of success, given what you now know about the problems of enforcement and adjudication.

1. From July 16 to August 11, 1973, three ad hoc committees of the United Nations met to define international terrorism, its underlying causes and the measures to be taken for its prevention. Virtually every participant in the general debate in the plenary session of the General Assembly before the issue was sent to the Legal Committee had found it necessary to issue a detailed separate position statement on the issue. The Legal Committee found the issue "too politically hot to handle." Will it be possible for a body, such as the United Nations to create general international law on an issue such as terrorism?

2. A Convention on the Suppression of Terrorism was adopted November 10, 1976, by the Committee of Foreign Ministers of the Council of Europe. Modeled after Europe's fairly successful Convention on Human Rights, which has both an active administrative and judicial arm, this convention seeks to outlaw certain types of terrorist acts. The problems regarding jurisdiction and prosecution appear to be somewhat resolved, but the issue of extradition was too politically sensitive to be handled effectively. Can a general treaty on terrorism, undertaken by states with a common legal and political heritage, succeed where similar ones by the entire community of nations have failed?

3. The creation of an international criminal court might well offer a solution to the "politicization" of the crime of terrorism. Some who have advocated such a system suggest that it should include such things as an international prison, in order to allow states to rid themselves of terrorist prisoners whom the states may be under pressure by other terrorists to release. Who would serve on such a court, and on whose territory should this international prison be located? Who would supply the maintenance of such a prison? Who would have the right to release a prisoner from that prison on parole? Would anyone have the right to grant clemency to a prisoner? Would, in fact, such an international criminal court system create as many problems as it would solve, even with respect to the crime of terrorism?

SUGGESTED READINGS

Bremer, L. Paul III. "Terrorism and the Rule of Law." U.S. State Department, Bureau of Public Affairs, Current Policy No. 847 (April 23, 1987).

Clough, Patricia. "Proposed West German Law to Tackle Terrorism Sparks Dissent." *Christian Science Monitor,* November 10, 1986.

Friedlander, Robert A. *Terrorism: Documents of International and Local Control.* Dobbs Ferry, NJ: Oceana, 1979.

Howe, Irving. "The Ultimate Price of Random Terror." *Skeptic: The Forum for Contemporary History,* January-February 1986.

Joyner, Nancy D. *Aerial Hijacking as an International Crime.* Dobbs Ferry, NJ: Oceana, 1974.

Levi, Werner. *Contemporary International Law: A Concise Introduction.* Boulder, CO: Westview Press, 1989.

Rozakis, Christos L. "Terrorism and the Internationally Protected Person in Light of the ILC's Draft Articles." *The International and Comparative Law Quarterly,* vol. 23 (January 1974).

Sofaer, Abraham D. "The Political Offense Exception and Terrorism." U.S. Department of State, Bureau of Public Affairs, Current Policy No. 762 (August 1, 1985).

Tokyo Convention on Offenses and Certain Other Acts Committed Onboard Aircraft. September 14, 1963. Tokyo, Japan.

ENDNOTES

1. As Werner Levi points out in his text, *Contemporary International Law: A Concise Introduction* (Boulder, CO: Westview Press, 1979) pp. 265–268, a degree of political cooperation is only implied, not stated, in the U.N. Charter. Considerable difference of opinion as to a legal obligation for political cooperation by member states continues to exist today.

2. See the Statute of the International Court of Justice, 6 U.S.T. 3517, T.I.A.S. No. 3043, 74 U.N.T.S. 244 (1944).

3. Stanley Hoffman, in his article, "International Law and the Control of Force," p. 22, suggests, for example, that "peace" as a common goal is a weak tool. He asserts that many states embrace doctrines which have stated goals of protracted confrontation and ultimate conquest—goals which are incompatible with this "common" goal of peace.

4. See the Treaty for the Renunciation of War, 46 Stat. 2343, 94 L.N.T.S., (Paris: August 27, 1928) p. 57.

5. Statement credited to Emile Henry, a nineteenth-century French anarchist who bombed a crowded Paris cafe, killing one customer and wounding twenty others. At his trial Henry is reported to have said that his only regret was that more people had not been killed. Henry's reply to the judge's exclamations that "those were innocent victims that you struck" has formed the dogma of "collective guilt" that is often invoked to justify indiscriminate acts of terror.

6. Convention Relative to the Protection of Civilian Persons in Time of War, U.S.T. 3516, T.I.A.S. No. 3365, 75, U.N.T.S. 287 (1949).

7. See Funk and Wagnall's *Standard Comprehensive International Dictionary,* International edition, vol. 1 (New York: J. Ferguson, 1977) p. 653.

8. Irving Howe, "The Ultimate Price of Random Terror," in *Skeptic: Forum for Contemporary History,* no. 11 (January–February 1976) p. 58.

9. See the Judgment of the International Military Tribunal, Nuremberg, September 30, 1946. 22, Trial of the Major War Criminals before the International Military Tribunal Proceedings, pp. 411, 427, 459, 461, and 463 (1948).

10. Marjorie M. Whiteman, *Digest of International Law,* vol. 11 (Washington, DC: Department of State, 1968) Chapter XXXV, Article 2, pp. 3518-3520.

11. Whiteman, *Digest of International Law,* Article 32, pp. 3528.

12. This law defines as criminal: "atrocities and offenses, including but not limited to murder, extermination, enslavement, deportation, imprisonment, torture, rape, or other inhuman acts committed against any civilian population . . . whether or not in violation of the domestic laws of the country where perpetrated."

13. Quoted by Robert Friedlander, *Terrorism Documents,* p. 18.

14. *United States* v. *Smith,* (1820)18 U.S. (5 Wheat.) pp. 71, 73–75.

15. The case of the *S.S. Lotus* (1927) P.C.I.J., Series A, No. 10 , 2 Hudson, World Court Rep., p. 20.

16. See "Harvard Research in International Law: Piracy," *American Journal of International Law,* vol. 26 (1932) pp. 739, 754, 759-760. See also text of Geneva Convention on the High Seas, 13 U.S.T., 2312, T.I.A.S. No. 5200, 450 U.N.T.S. 82, and Article 100 of the Third United Nations Conference on the Law of the Sea, A/Conf. 62/WP. 10/Rev. 1 (April 28, 1979).

17. Friedlander, *Terrorism Documents,* p. 13. For further insights on this subject, see Nancy Joyner, *Aerial Hijacking as and International Crime* (Dobbs Ferry, NJ: Oceana, 1974).

18. 24 U.S.T. 737, T.I.A.S. No. 7579 (1973); *International Legal Materials,* vol. 12 (1973) p. 370.

19. Tokyo Convention on Offenses and Certain Other Acts Committed on Board Aircraft, signed September 14, 1963.

20. Convention for the Suppression of Unlawful Acts Against the Safety of Civil Aviation, signed in Montreal on September 23, 1971.

21. Extradition Treaty, November 22, 1834, France-Belgium, Articles 5 and 6, *Recueil des Traites* (France) 278, 84 Perry's T.S. p. 456.

22. See for example the Treaty of Extradition between the United States and Venezuela, January 19, 1922, Article 3, 43 Stat. 1698, T.S. 675, 49 L.N.T.S. 435.

23. Convention of Extradition, December 13, 1957, 24 Europe T.S., pp. 173-175.

24. Signed April 18, 1961. 500 U.N.T.S. 95.

25. See comments by Christos L Rozakis in "Terrorism and the Internationally Protected Person in Light of the ILC's Draft Articles," *International and Comparative Law Quarterly,* vol. 23 (January 1974) p. 72.

CHAPTER NINE

COUNTERTERRORISM
The Use of Special Forces

As soon as men decide that all means are permitted to fight an evil, then their good becomes indistinguishable from the evil that they set out to destroy.

—Christopher Dawson,
The Judgment of the Nations (1942)

KEY CONCEPTS

Munich massacre
strike force
Sarayat Matkal
Special Night Squads
Irgun
King David Hotel
Entebbe raid
secrecy and surprise
Operation Nimrod

killer course
GSG9
Mogadishu
Joint Operations Command
Delta Force
Seal Team Six
Special Operations Wing
Operation Eagle's Claw

Although international laws of war and peace make it clear that terrorist acts have begun to be regarded as illegal, there does not yet exist a cohesive framework capable of guiding the actions of nations confronted with, or perpetrating, terrorism. In the absence of such a framework, the burden of regulating the acts has fallen upon individual nation-states.

Recent history abounds with examples of individual state efforts to combat the problem of international terrorism, revealing both the dangers and the degrees of success they have experienced. The success or failure of these efforts, and an assessment of the price paid for both success and failure, provide interesting insights into the strengths and limitations of nations engaged in waging single-handed war on terrorism.

Moreover, if international law truly grows or evolves from international norms, then it may be that the strategy for dealing with international terrorism internationally will strongly resemble those strategies found to be successful among nations individually. Thus a review of the responses of nations to terrorism today may provide some clues as to the shape of international responses in the future.

NATIONS WITHOUT DEFENSES

It has been said that the **Munich massacre** *of Israeli athletes by the Black September terrorists at the Olympic games in 1972* marked the turning point in the Western world's indifference toward terrorism.[1] Up to then, few if any of the nations most frequently the victims of terrorist attacks had made any coherent policy for combatting terrorism. Although CIA analysts have concluded that "terrorists continue to prefer operations in the industrialized democracies of Western Europe and North America,"[2] the very characteristics that cause nations to be included in this category also make it difficult for them to organize defenses against terrorist attacks.

In liberal democracies, dissent is part of the very fabric of the social and political milieu. This adherence to an almost absolute right to disagree sometimes creates conditions which allow radical dissent to become violent opposition before governments are able to prepare for this transformation. In West Germany, for example, before the publicized exploits of the Baader-Meinhof gang, any hint of the formation of an elite army or police unit to combat terrorism would have provoked a storm of protest inside (and outside) of the country.

Similarly, the United States, both the armed forces and the public, bearing scars from the traumas of the Vietnam War and Watergate, were in no condition to prepare for terrorist threats. This was partly due to the demoralizing effect of the Vietnam War on the army's special units, and partly to the perceived need to curtail (rather than expand) domestic surveillance operations.

Nor were these nations alone in their lack of preparedness. France (in the wake of their protracted Algerian war), shared Germany's abhorrence of secret or special armies, while the British, with their problems in Northern Ireland, were perhaps too confident in their assumption that their anti-IRA network would also deal effectively with any international terrorist. Italy, at this time, was oblivious to the growing potential for terrorism within its borders, misled by a belief that most contemporary terrorism was confined to participants in the Arab-Israeli conflict. In fact, virtually every Western nation, except Israel, lacked either the equipment or the staff to combat the growing terrorist threat, and they located the realization of the impending danger.

At Munich, this complacency and the inattention was effectively shattered. When a group of Black September terrorists, with logistical support from German and French sympathizers, captured the Israeli athlete's dormitory in the Olympic village in Munich in 1972, West Germany's response was firm—but it failed to prevent disaster. As the world watched transfixed in helpless terror, an ambush was set up by the Germans at Furstenfeldbruck Airport. Five sharpshooters succeeded in killing five of the terrorists, but not before the terrorists had killed all nine hostages.[3]

STRIKE FORCES: A FIRST LINE OF DEFENSE?

This spectacular attack and the equally spectacular failure of the government troops to secure the hostages' safety prompted several Western governments to reevaluate the quality of their counterterrorism strike forces. Since 1972, the creation of effective **strike forces,** *military or police units specially trained, equipped, and organized to combat terrorism*, has become a fairly common practice—with varying degrees of success and divergent degrees of legality. A review of the strike forces which have been created by a few nations, their methods of operation, and their patterns of success and failure, may help us understand the problems and pitfalls of the use of such forces.

Israel's Sarayat Matkal

Israel has been engaged in antiterrorism warfare for perhaps longer than any other nation. It has, as a result, a more extensive history in the use of strike teams. As such, it serves as an interesting case to determine the strengths and weaknesses of this tactic for combatting terrorism.

In Israel, the Talmudic injunction, "If someone comes to kill you, rise and kill him first," has become the slogan of the **Sarayat Matkal**. This *specialized Israeli antiterrorist strike force* is so secretive that the Israelis rarely even mention it by name. It is this unit which has been responsible for raids into Beirut to assassinate Palestinian leaders, and for the Entebbe rescue operation in 1972.

It is this unit which has both successfully thwarted terrorist attacks, and, in its zeal to "strike before being struck" and to punish terrorists, has also been guilty of the murder of innocent persons. When Prime Minister Golda Meir unleashed "hit teams" the day after the Munich massacre, with orders to roam the world seeking out and summarily executing those responsible for the attack, the results were neither entirely legal nor wholly desirable.

One of these hit teams assassinated the wrong man. At Lillehammer, Norway, in 1973, an innocent Morrocan waiter was gunned down by a hit team in front of his pregnant Norwegian wife. The team had mistaken the waiter for the architect of the Munich massacre, Ali Hassan Salameh. International indignation forced Israel to temporarily restrain the hit teams.

This was, however, only a brief setback in Israel's use of strike forces in its war on terrorism. In January 1979, one of Israel's hit teams succeeded in blowing up Salameh with a radio-controlled car bomb in Beirut. This bomb also killed his four bodyguards and five innocent people who happened to be passing by at the time. The Israeli hit team may also have been responsible for the assassination in Tunis on April 16, 1988 of Khalil al-Wazir, the PLO's mastermind of terrorist strategy against Israel.

One of the ironies of Israel's response to this incident is that, as an excusatory footnote to their (unofficial) admission of regret at the loss of innocent lives, the Israeli's suggested that these people were just "in the wrong place at the wrong time."[4] This has unfortunate echoes of the "justification" offered by terrorists of harm to innocent people caused by their bombs.

The innocent persons killed, like Susan Wareham, a British woman working as a secretary for a construction company in Beirut, committed only the mistake ("crime"?) of being too near Salameh's car when it exploded. While counterterrorist attacks like this may not deliberately take innocent life, they are undoubtedly culpable of a wanton disregard for the safety of innocent persons. Callous uncaring or deliberate disregard for the safety of innocent persons—the difference may be in the degree of disregard for the sanctity of human life. The net result for the innocent bystander is unhappily the same.

Not all of Israel's counterattacks on terrorism have been so counterproductive. Indeed, the Sarayet Matkal is one of the best trained and equipped special forces unit in operation today, with an impressive record of successful missions as well.

This unit is not part of the regular army, and reports only to the chief of intelligence. Its members do, however, wear uniforms. This unit does not rely on trained volunteers, but instead draws on raw recruits from the Kelet (the recruit depot). Usually an officer of the Sarayat Matkal will go the the Kelet to select about 15 to 20 recruits to form a team.

This team does much of its training in enemy territory, where the bullets are as real as the enemy. Recruits who survive this basic training become permanent members of a squad. Such squads are trained in the use of the .22 Baretta pistol, the Uzzi (the Israeli-invented machine pistol), and the Kalishnikov (the Russian assault rifle).

The willingness of such teams to commit acts of terrorism in order to counter terrorism may perhaps lie in the very roots of Israel's history. The joint British-Jewish **Special Night Squads**, of which Moshe Dayan was a member, operated during the 1930s. These squads *were trained by their leader, Orde Wingate, to kill rather than wait to be killed.*

The **Irgun**, *a successor to these squads in the increasing spiral of violence in the region of Palestine,* boasted Menachim Begin as a member. It is this organization which was responsible for *the bombing at* the **King David Hotel** *on July 22, 1946, which took 91 lives—British, Jewish, and Arab.* The terrorists of the Irgun who perpetrated this violence still meet annually to observe the anniversary of this bombing. Thurston Clarke's account, *By Blood and Fire: The Attack on the King David Hotel,* is detailed and well-documented in a publication by G.P. Putnam's Sons (1981), for those interested in a further review of this incident.

Given this concept that it is better to kill than to wait to be killed, which seems to have pervaded Israel's brief and bloody history, it is perhaps easier to understand both the brilliant successes, which reflect the intense training and dedication of these strike forces, and the disasters which have occasionally resulted because of the ruthless determination of these special strike force teams.

The Sarayat Matkal conducted a raid inside Lebanon, in December of 1968, which was described as an attempt to force the Lebanese to prevent Palestinian terrorists from mounting their attacks from Lebanon. Earlier that year, the Palestinians had carried out a successful hijacking, taking over an El Al aircraft en route from Rome to Tel Aviv. They had also attacked another El Al plane at Athens airport in Greece, damaging it with automatic fire and grenades. Israeli intelligence reports showed that both terrorist incidents origniated in Beirut.

So a commando raid, carried out by the Sarayat Matkal, was launched against Beirut International Airport. Thirteen Arab aircraft, including nine jetliners, were destroyed. There were no casualties, since all of the airplanes were cleared of passengers and crew first.

While the raid was a tactical success, its long-term effects were less rewarding. President De Gaulle condemned the raid as a violation of the sovereignty of a nation-state, and used it as a reason for cutting off all arms shipments to Israel. This cutoff came at a time when the Israeli Defense Forces were relying heavily on French equipment. Moreover, the other major supplier of Israeli arms, the United States, expressed its displeasure over the raid, but stopped short of cutting off arms shipments.

Furthermore, the Palestinians acquired both publicity, and a certain amount of public sympathy, for their cause. Finally, the airline company which owned and operated the planes, Middle East Airlines, was able to purchase a whole new fleet of jetliners—with the insurance money from the destroyed planes!

Other assault operations were equally "successful" but had perhaps less negative impacts. It was the Sarayat Matkal that in 1972 successfully ended the hijacking of a Sabena Boeing 707 jetliner, Flight 517 from Brussels to Tel Aviv. When four members of the Black September Palestinian group hijacked the plane and forced it to land at Lod Airport in Tel Aviv, they announced that they intended to blow up the plane, with its 90 passengers and ten crew members, unless the Israeli government met their demands for the release of over 300 Arab prisoners.

The Sarayat Matkal assault force succeeded in storming the plane and freeing the passengers and crew members. While one passenger was killed, and two of the hijackers, this minimal loss of life became the pattern for similar feats, such as that carried out by Germany's GSG9 at Mogadishu.

When the Palestinians struck again, it was at the Olympic Games in Munich, only months after the Lod Airport rescue. Israeli atheletes were the target, and the Sarayat Matkal was excluded from the attempts to free those hostages.

This unit also was responsible, however, for the successful **Entebbe raid** in June 1977. When an Air France Airbus, Flight 139 en route from Tel Aviv to Paris was hijacked after a stop at Athens ariport, Israel responded by organizing a brilliant and successful military rescue operation. The plane, which landed at Entebbe airport in Uganda, carried 248 passengers and crew members. All but 106 of these hostages were released by the terrorists before the Israeli raid. Only the Israeli citizens and Jews of other nationalities were kept hostage, to increase pressure on Israel to agree to the release of fifty-three "freedom fighters" imprisoned in Israeli prisons.

The military incursion mounted by Israel succeeded in freeing all of the hostages held at the airport, with the exception of three who either misunderstood or did not hear orders by the commandos to lie down as they opened fire on the terrorists. All seven of the terrorists (two of whom were German and five of whom were Palestinian members of the PFLP) were killed, along with a number of Ugandan soldiers, who tried to prevent the Israeli commandos from escaping with the hostages.[5]

International opinion, for the most part, supported Israel, in spite of the fact that Israel militarily invaded Uganda. Part of this approbation derives, no doubt, from a common love for a "winner." But part is due to the perceived legal right of a nation to intervene for "humanitarian" purposes in another country. While this right of "humanitarian intervention" is limited, it seemed to most of the community of nations to be acceptable in this case.[6]

Thus, Israel had the first, and arguably the most highly trained of the strike forces. Their greatest liability may lie in the fervor with which they pursue their enemies. This zeal has caused them to cross not only national boundaries in their quest for vengeance, but also international law.

The British SAS

On May 5, 1980, a clear, crisp Monday morning, Britain's 22nd SAS, the Special Air Service Regiment, supported by special police units, carried out **Operation Nimrod,** *an assault on the Iranian embassy in the heart of downtown London.* As thousands watched, black-clad SAS members swung down from ropes and burst into the building through windows. Wearing gas masks, the assault force moved from room to room throwing stun grenades mixed with CS gas. As they moved through the building, they identified the terrorists, shot them with their Heckler and Koch MP5s or Browning automaic pistols, and bundled the hostages out of the burning building.

This was not the only successful counterterrorist attack carried out by Britain's SAS, but it was unique in at least one way. Most nations do not have the opportunity to see their special strike forces in operation on their home soil. Most operations of such forces take place on foreign soil, far from home and the attention of citizens.

Even in Operation Nimrod, however, Britain worked very hard to preserve the speed and secrecy which have become the hallmark of SAS operations. The assault team wore hoods, which served to hide their identities as well as to frighten the terrorists. When the incident was over, the unit handed authority back to the police and quietly made their way to the St. John's Wood barracks for a small celebration, before returning to their permanent station at Bradbury Lines in Hereford.

Secrecy and surprise have been *the watchwords of this regiment* ever since it was formed over forty years ago. Lieutenant David Stirling, of the Scots Guard, is credited with creating this special unit. Under his plan, the SAS was designed to operate in units of five (later reduced to four) men, which continues to be the standard SAS stick.

The units have tended to be made up of a high percentage of Scottish Roman Catholics, perhaps because its founder Stirling was himself a Scot Catholic, and perhaps because the Catholics of Scotland have had a history for generations of guerrilla warfare and traditions of secrecy. All of its members are volunteers, mostly from the Parachute Regiment. It is not a "young" regiment; the average age is about 27.

Each recruit is required to give up his rank and pay (most have already reached the rank of corporal or sergeant before attempting to join), and go back to the rank of trooper. Training in the Welsh countryside is rigorous, literally a killer. Three men died on Brecon Beacons during solo treks in 1979 and 1980, in terrible weather through the Welsh mountains.

Recruits are trained in combat survival, surviving in Arctic conditions, and swimming fully clothed. They also receive special parachute training, including night jumps from extraordinary heights. Emphasis is also placed on weapons training, using the SAS weapons: the Heckler and Koch submachine gun, the Browning .45 caliber automatic pistol, the pump-action shotgun, and the Sterling submachine gun fitted with a silencer. In addition, they are given training in foreign weapons, so that they can use captured weapons and be familiar with weapons which their enemies may use on them.

Out of every 100 men who apply, only about 19 will meet the physical and mental requirements. The initial tests include a series of treks across the Welsh hills, carrying weighted packs. *The final trek covers 37 miles, carrying a 55-pound pack, over some of the toughest country in the Brecon Beacons. It must be covered in 20 hours, and it is literally a* **killer course**. As noted earlier, men have died trying to complete it.

Once they have passed these initial courses, they continue to receive specialized training in such subjects as explosives, battlefield medicine, and the operation of communication equipment of various sorts. They train in the use of various personal weapons, such as knives and crossbows for "silent" killing and submachine guns fitted with silencers. They learn about desert and jungle warfare and wilderness survival.

After this, they continue to specialize. Their specialities may be in such fields as medicine, languages, skiing, mountaineering, or underwater warfare. Individual skill development is encouraged at all times.

The SAS finds itself operating more often than most other national strike forces, with the possible exception of the Sarayat Matkal. This is due to the continuing violence in Northern Ireland. While the SAS rarely figures in press reports on antiterrorist activities in that region, it is true that many operations are carried out by this unit in cooperation with the British occupying forces. The SAS has also seen overseas service in Aden, Oman, and Borneo. Indeed, much of its training for the guerrilla warfare which it faces in Northern Ireland finds its origins in the SAS experience in Aden in the mid-1960s.

In Northern Ireland, the SAS has served as a back up for the regular army units and the Royal Ulster Constabulary. It has been a largely thankless and often a very dangerous job. As members have somewhat cynically noted, if the "Sassmen" (as the Irish have called them) are killed or injured in an ambush, little public mention is made of the incident. But if the SAS is responsible, even indirectly, for the injury or death of any civilians, then public indignation is quite vocal.

Britain, unlike Israel, has indeed been willing to criticize its own strike forces when their actions have resulted in needless injury or loss of life. As one judge noted,when two Sassmen were on trial for responsibility in the death of a civilian in a stakeout of an arms cache, *while terrorists might consider themselves outside the rule of law, the army could not.*

Forty years of experience has made the SAS into one of the best counterterrorist strike forces in the world today. Many nations today benefit from training and assistance offered by this unit to their own strike forces. Relations between the SAS and Germany's GSG9 are quite cordial, and have resulted in considerable mutual training and assistance efforts.

Relations between the SAS and Israel's Sarayat Matkal, however, are far less amiable. Both units can remember a time when the British, under the Palestine Mandate, formed Q Squads to hunt down Jewish terrorists, particularly those of the infamous Stern Gang. In one particularly nasty incident, Roy Farran, who was responsible for the formation of the Q Squads on SAS principles, was acquitted in a court martial of the murder of a suspected member of the Stern Gang. Israeli terrorists, not satisfied with the verdict, sent a book bomb to Farran's home in England. Roy's brother, Rex, opened the package, and was killed as the bomb exploded in his face. The memory of such tragedies, and the vindictiveness which caused them, make the relations between these two special forces units strained.

Moreover, the Sassmen are frequently called upon by their government to protect the leaders of various Arab states. Since many of these states, and their leaders, are regarded by some as the natural enemies of Israel, the SAS and the Sarayat Matkal often find themselves on the opposite side of these security situations.

Germany's GSG9

Grenzschutzgrupps 9, called **GSG9**, makes no claim to be a "killer troop" or "hit squad." This group, *formed when the Bavarian State police were unable to deal adequately with the Munich situation in 1972,* has made a point of being less dependent upon weapons than upon the talents, discipline, and training of its men.

The Federal Border Guard became the parent unit for this special unit, which works out well since *it is the only force in Germany which is directly under the control of the central government.* GSG9 became the ninth unit of the Border Guard, making its headquarters at St. Augustin just outside of Bonn. It was formed along very much the same lines as the SAS, operating with five-man sticks.

Within GSG9 there is a headquarters unit, a communications and documentation unit, and three fighting units. Its three technical units deal with weapons, research, equipment, backup supply, and maintenance services. Each of its three strike forces has 30 men, comprising a Command Section and five Special Tactical Sections (composed of four men and an officer)—the five-man stick.[7]

This group differs from the Sarayat Matkal and the SAS in that it is a *civilian police force.* Although much of the training given to its members is similar to that of the SAS, *it is unique in its training in the law*, particularly as that law applies to counterterrorism operations. Members of this forces are more conscious of the law, and of their need to stay within its bounds as far as possible, than are other similar strike forces.

This does not mean that GSG9 does not train its personnel in active counterterrorism techniques. In fact, Germany's elite force has one of the most sophisticated arsenals in the world. Since the deplorable shooting at Furstenfeldbruck Airport demonstrated the need for marksmanship training, every man of GSG9 is taught to be an expert marksman, using the Mausser 66 sniper's rifle, equipped with infrared sights and light intensifiers for night shooting. Like the SAS, they favor the Heckler and Koch MP5s for their routine work, but they are also armed with .357 Magnum revolvers.

Since they are required to be able to reach any part of Germany within two hours, ready for action, units are supplied with Mercedes-Benz autos of special design, and BO 105-type helicopters. They are trained to descend from hovering copters, via special ropes.

But these units are trained in more than just combat. They spend a great deal of time studying the origins and tactics of known terrorists, in order to determine how best to defeat them. Every member of a team learns such useful tricks as how to pick locks, and how to handle airport equipment, in order to facilitate efforts to mount successful attacks against terrorists who have hijacked an airplane.

GSG9 practices simulated assaults on hijacked airliners, training on mock-ups of aircraft and sometimes on aircraft on loan from Lufthansa. Such training stood them in good stead in **Mogadishu** in 1977. In October of that year, *Zohair Akache's terrorist team hijacked a Lufthansa Boeing 737 with 82 passengers, in support of the Baader-Meinhof gang.* After touring the Middle East in search of an airport willing to let them land, they finally landed at Mogadishu in Somalia.

Unlike the situation in Uganda faced by the Israelis, the Germans found Somalia more than willing to cooperate with them in their efforts to end the hostage situation. Twenty-eight hand-picked men stormed the jetliner, rescuing all hostages without harm. It was, if not a perfect raid of its kind (the original assault ladders were too short), a very good example of careful planning and execution. No laws were broken, no unnecessary injuries to innocent persons were allowed, and both the hostages and plane recovered.

Delta Force: One U.S. Option

American counterterrorist forces are based in the United States, far from the Middle East, where many terrorist attacks against Americans have occurred. The Joint Special Operations Agency, headed by a two-star general, is charged with preparing guidelines and plans to guide counterterrorist forces during their formation, training, and operations. But this agency has no command authority over the forces.

The **Joint Operations Command** is *a secret unit stationed at Fort Bragg, North Carolina.* It is reported to have control over units that might be used to repel terrorists or to rescue Americans held hostage. Such units include the U.S. Army's **Delta Force**, *comprised of specially selected soldiers stationed at Fort Bragg,* and Task Force 100, which is composed of high speed helicopters at Fort Campbell, Kentucky.

The U.S. Navy also has a counterterrorism force, **Seal Team Six**, *made up of frogmen and stationed at Little Creek, near Norfolk, Virginia.* Similarly, the U.S. Air Force boasts its own strike force as well, the **Special Operations Wing** *at Eglin Air Force Base* in Florida. This latter unit *is trained to fly specially equipped C-130 transports in counterterrorist operations.*

The problems with U.S. counterterrorism forces are obvious, and are brought on by the lack of cohesive command, as illustrated by *the abortive attempt to send a strike team into Iran to free Americans held hostage in the U.S. embassy in Teheran.* **Operation Eagle's Claw**, as this mission was called, was characterized by a confusion of command, insufficient training, and critical equipment failure.

Cloaked in so much secrecy that even some of the military officers involved were not told the aim of the mission for which they were preparing, this operation became a model for what can go wrong in a strike force manuever. In addition to too much secrecy, there were too many chiefs and not enough cooperation between military units. An army officer, Major General James Vaught, was in overall command; Colonel James Kyle of the U.S. Air Force had responsibility for fixed-wing aircraft. Colonel Charles Pitman of the U.S. Marines also had command responsibility and Colonel Beckwith controlled the Delta Force squad.

The Delta Force squad lacked sufficient training and experience for such an operation. It had been created less than five years earlier by Colonel Beckwith, and its training program was incomplete and not designed for the type of situation which evolved. It was underfunded and ill equipped to handle the hostage raid, having trained primarily for guerrilla warfare and low-intensity conflict.

Even today, the United States lacks the will to create a single unit in which to vest this specialized training and command. Within the armed services there remain strong rivalries, that make it difficult for one branch to create and recieve support for such a specialized unit. Although in the wake of the Operation Eagle's Claw disaster there was a call for the establishment of a new special counterterrorism unit, with personnel drawn from all of the armed services, there has been little success in creating such a unit. Interservice rivalries make its creation very unlikely in the near future.

The Delta Force has, according to government reports, been deployed several times, other than the highly publicized "Operation Eagle's Claw" fiasco and the *Achille Lauro* incident. It has, for instance, been sent to Venezuela to advise the armed forces there on the ways to retake a hijacked aircraft. It was sent on a similar mission to Oman to prepare to retake a hijacked plane in nearby Kuwait. At the time of the TWA hijacking, Delta Force was deployed to the

Mediterranean. But in each of these cases, its activities stopped short of assault; it simply made preparations for, or advised in preparations for, the assault.

This has, some have argued, had a detrimental effect on the morale of the individuals in Delta Force. To be always preparing but never doing counterterrorist activities is infinitely frustrating, as the men in GSG9 and SAS could attest. But the United States has been singularly reluctant to field a strike force against the terrorists which have struck at it so often.

Delta Force remains the best that the United States has to offer in terms of a strike force. It has, since the Iranian fiasco, proved itself to be capable of successful missions. The "skyjacking" of the *Achille Lauro* hijackers was an outstandingly successful operation, whose questionable legality has been overshadowed by its brilliant execution, giving a much-needed boost to Delta Force's morale.

Having, unlike Germany and Great Britain, few if any violent indigenous terrorists, the United States has focused its attentions on training its special forces to operate overseas. Emphasis seems to be placed less on secrecy than on rapid-response capabilities and combat training. If coordination of command problems can be surmounted, these forces may develop into units as efficient and respected as the SAS and GSG9.

In the wake of the Operation Eagle's Claw debacle, the Pentagon began to establish the closest thing this nation has ever had to a secret army. Small, specially trained units were developed, which were designed to operate much more covertly than some of the older paramilitary units, such as the Navy Seals. In addition to being given rather exotic code names, such as Yellow Fruit and Seaspray, these units were armed with newer, more sophisticated types of equipment. These included such items as the small, high-tech helicopters with which Task Force 160, which operates out of Fort Campbell, train.

These new units were also given more sophisticated communications gear. This includes, for example, the one-man satellite-communications radios and dishes.

More important than these new technological "toys," however, was the creation of the Intelligence Support Activity, a far-ranging intelligence organization which gave the U.S. Army, for the first time, the ability to engage in full-fledged espionage, fielding its own agents. Through this organization, for the first time, the strike forces were able to gather the information which they needed to plan their counterterrorist activities. They were no longer dependent upon the CIA or other intelligence services for vital data, which formerly was too often not available or kept classified at a critical juncture in the planning process.

Even with these innovations, however, these units have been unable to rise above the bureaucratic infighting and bungling which has for long plagued U.S. strike forces. While the units still exist, their morale, and even their preparedness, is in disarray. Seaspray, Yellow Fruit, and the ISA became involved in clandestine operations in Central America, which have seriously impaired their credibility with Congress and within the military and intelligence units of the United States. The use or misuse of counterterrorism forces in this area has jeopardized America's efforts to develop a credible and respected strike force, capable of working with such units as the SAS and GSG9.

CONCLUSIONS

The use of special forces to combat terrorism has both assets and liabilities. Too little commitment can result in an insufficiently trained and equipped force, as the U.S. forces were in the Operation Eagle's Claw disaster. Too zealous a desire to use such forces can result in the loss of innocent lives, as Israel has discovered.

Determination, unsupported by sufficient training or equipment, is also a recipe for disaster, as became evident in November of 1985. An Egyptian jetliner en route to Cairo from Athens was hijacked and diverted to Malta. Egyptian troops stormed the plane the next day, after the hijackers began to kill some of the hostages on board. As the troops rushed onto the plane, the hijackers tossed grenades at passengers. The death toll was put at 60, 57 of whom died in the rescue attempt.

It is not enough just to have such a force. Nations must train and equip them with adequate information and weaponry to meet an increasingly sophisticated terrorist threat. Nations also need to instill, as Germany has sought to do, in its strike forces, a respect for the law and its restraints on strike force activities. So equipped and so trained, such forces can operate to significantly reduce, not necessarily the number, but the success of terrorist attacks worldwide.

EVALUATION

There are many conflicting views on whether or not strike forces are a legitimate and useful tool in combatting terrorism. Some view such strike teams as potential threats to democracy, creating elite troops which could be used to quell demonstrations as well as to stop terrorist attacks. Others view them as essential to a nation's security, operating in ways not open to a large military unit to safeguard a nation's citizens, both at home and abroad.

Below are two quotations which reflect, in part, this divergence of views. Each viewpoint expressed is a bit extreme, tending toward opposite ends of the spectrum of opinion. Read each, and decide which more accurately reflects the appropriate assessment of the need and use for such forces in today's world.

1. "The danger inherent in the war against terrorism is, of course, the prospect of desperate societies willing to substitute state terror for (nonstate) terrorism, to trade individual rights and freedoms for relief from chaos and violence, reconstituting what were once relatively benign governments into coldly efficient, centralized tyrannies, whose populations are held in close check by armies of secret police and informers, widespread electronic eavesdropping, and a constant deluge of propaganda." [8]

2. "The Israeli argue the case for preemptive strikes: it is better to kill their enemies in their own bases and so prevent them mounting their operations, rather than conduct elegant sieges inside Israel. While appreciating the excellence of other forces' pieces of electronic wizardry and the skill of the talk-out experts, their aim is to prevent the need for such expertise arising. Such a policy has its attractions, especially for a beleaguered, small nation like Israel under continual attack from enemies based round its borders. When national survival is at stake all manner of actions become permissable that would not be countenanced in more secure societies."[9]

SUGGESTED READING

Dobson, Christopher, and Ronald Payne. *Counterattack: The West's Battle Against the Terrorists.* New York: Facts on File, 1982.

"International Terrorism." Issue Brief No. 1B74042. Washington, DC: Congressional Research Service, 1987.

Livingstone, N.C. "Taming Terrorism: In Search of a New U.S. Policy." *International Security Review: Terrorism Report,* vol. 7, no. 1 (Spring 1982).

"Patterns of Global Terrorism: 1994." U.S. Department of State Publication 10136 (April 1995).

Rivers, Gayle. *The Specialists: Revalations of a Counter-terrorist.* New York: Stein & Day, 1985.

Sederberg, Peter C. *Terrorist Myths: Illusion, Rhetoric, and Reality.* Englewood Cliffs, NJ: Prentice Hall, 1989.

ENDNOTES

1. Christopher Dobson and Ronald Payne, *Counterattack The West's Battle Against the Terrorists* (New York: Facts on File, 1982) p. xvi.

2. "Patterns of International Terrorism in 1980: A Research Paper" (Washington, DC: National Foreign Assessment Center, 1980) pp. iii, 1-6.

3. "International Terrorism: Issue Brief No. 1874042" (Washington, DC: Congressional Research Service, 1978) pp. 41-42.

4. Dobson and Payne, *Counterattack*, p. 84.

5. Seventy-four year old Dora Bloch was not being held with the hostages at the airport. She had been transferred to a Ugandan hospital. After the raid, she disappeared, amid reports that she was dragged screaming from her hospital bed and murdered, on Ugandan President Idi Amin's orders. She has never been seen or heard from since.

6. See the editorial by Christopher Joyner in the *Washington Post*, Friday, November 18, 1983, section A, p. 18. Dr. Joyner concludes that, except in certain carefully limited situations such as this, "armed intervention per se remains an act that contravenes sovereign rights of states that are legally inviolable."

7. Dobson and Payne, *Counterattack*, p. 96.

8. N.C. Livingstone, "Taming Terrorism: In Search of a New U.S. Policy," *International Security Review: Terrorism Report*, vol. 7, no. 1 (Spring 1982) p. 20.

9. Dobson and Payne, *Counterattack*, p. 83.

CHAPTER TEN

TERRORISM, INTELLIGENCE, AND THE LAW

The greatest threat posed by terrorists now lies in the atmos-
phere of alarm they create, which corrodes democracy and
breeds repression. . . If the government appears incompetent,
public alarm will increase and so will the clamor for draconian
measures.

—Brian Jenkins

KEY CONCEPTS

The Red Brigade	"contact ban"
FLQ (Front du Liberation du Quebec)	"propagation of violence" laws
	Virginio Rognoni
War Measures Act	Carlos Alberto Della Chiesa
Northern Ireland	"pentiti"
("Emergency Provisions) Act	INTERPOL
Prevention of Terrorism	"the Kommisar"
(Temporary Provisions) Act	PIOS
Irish Republican Army (IRA)	target searches
ETA	TREVI
Baader-Meinhof gang	phases of modern terrorist incidents
Red Army Faction	

LEGAL INITIATIVES TO COUNTERTERRORISM

Politicians and scholars have expressed grave doubts about whether any government can remain strong, but not oppressive, in the face of severe emergencies. If a government is to make a measured but effective response to the great emergencies generated by terrorist acts today, then coping strategies other than the use of strike forces must be considered.

It is not feasible to evaluate all of the options available to nations today in their efforts to deal with terrorism, both as an internal and an external threat. Various nations have experimented with a wide range of policy options in their attempts to deal with this recalcitrant problem. Some have tried to fashion a broad spectrum of legislative initiatives designed to make it clear that terrorists and groups resorting to terrorism operate outside of the law of the land, and can expect neither sanctuary nor quarter to be given them at the hands of the law.

These efforts have met with mixed success, depending in large measure on the determination of the government to enforce the laws which it creates, and also on the degree of entrenchment which the terrorists enjoy within the society. Canada's efforts to curtail the activities of the FLQ, for example, have met with considerable success. Italy's offer to pardon "penitent" terrorists, combined with its efforts to close all havens in which those engaged in terrorism might hide, also enjoyed some measure of success.

In both cases, legal initiatives were combined with efforts at social reform designed to reduce the grievances which terrorists voiced with the existing order. Italy's success in its efforts is less certain than Canada's, due in part to Italy's geographic location. Canada, with the help of a friendly nation on its only border, was able to keep terrorists from escaping across the border or from receiving help from other terrorist groups. Italy has had to contend with both indigenous and imported terrorism. Middle Eastern terrorists, as well as terrorists from several other European nations, have been able to offer support in the form of training, arms, personnel, and safe haven to Italy's indigenous terrorists. Thus, *Italy's strongest indigenous terrorist group*, **The Red Brigade**, has been able to survive several intensive police crackdowns. Its ability to revive after each such effort is perhaps due less to Italy's lack of diligence in its efforts to eradicate the group than to the inability of the Italian government to effectively shut its borders to other terrorist support groups.

The following case studies offer insights into the effectiveness—and the lack thereof—of legal initiatives in coping with terrorism. These cases were chosen to illustrate two crucial points:

1. That legal initiatives alone are insufficient to eliminate a terrorist problem.
2. That the use of extraordinary legal measures is not without risk, particularly to democracies.

CANADA'S LEGAL WAR WITH THE FLQ

Canada offers an instructive example of emergency legislation, enacted and applied on a limited scale, in terms of both scope and time. As the first North American nation to face *a vigorous and violent native terrorist campaign,* Canada from the late 1960s throughout the early 1970s was forced to create its own answer to terrorism. Faced with a series of violent attacks by the **Front du Liberation du Quebec (FLQ)** in early 1970, culminating in the kidnaping of James Cross (British Trade Commissioner for Quebec) and Pierre Laporte (Minister of Labor in the Quebec Provincial Government), Prime Minister Elliott Trudeau decided to take firm, but extraordinary, measures.[1]

In 1970, Trudeau invoked the **War Measures Act,** *which empowered him to call in the army to enforce his refusal to be coerced by terrorists.* Although Trudeau agreed to deal with the kidnappers of Mr. Cross, allowing them to be flown to Cuba in return for Cross's release, he was determined to rid Canada of the terrorists in the FLQ.

He was willing to use any means at his disposal to accomplish this aim. He was willing to subordinate civil rights to the preservation of public order. As he noted:

> When terrorists and urban guerrillas were trying to provoke the secession of Quebec, I made it clear that I wouldn't hesitate to send in the army and I did, despite the anguished cries of civil libertarians.[2]

To a large extent Trudeau succeeded in ridding Canada of its indigenous terrorist organization. In order to do so, he saturated the Montreal area with troops, which acted to pin down terrorist cells, and used the Royal Canadian Mounted Police to concentrate on locating the cells which had organized the terrorist attacks. Using broad local powers of search and arrest, more than 300 suspects were apprehended.[3]

Excesses were no doubt committed during the course of this crisis. Nevertheless, the crisis had an end point, when civil liberties were restored, the army withdrawn, and local police once again constrained by strict laws on search and seizure operations. It may be true, as David Barrett, head of the opposition New Democratic Party once stated, that

. . . the scar on Canada's record of civil liberties which occurred (at that time) is a classic illustration of how the state, in an attempt to combat terrorism, overstepped its boundaries and actually threatened its own citizens.[4]

But it is also true that after Trudeau's crackdown, Canada enjoyed a decade relatively free of terrorism, with civil rights and liberties fully restored. It is also worth noting that Trudeau was astute enough to accompany the repression of this period with political measures designed to end some of the grievances which may have contributed to the terrorism. These political initiatives included creating compulsory French courses for English-speaking persons in Quebec, and heavy government investment in the French-speaking minority areas. Such measures helped to deprive those advocating terrorist actions of the support of the moderates among the French community.

The problems, ironically, which Canada faced in the 1990s over the efforts of Quebec to secede stem at least in part to the success of the government in "co-opting" the frustrated French-speaking population which had offered some support to the FLQ. By making the option of "working with the system" to achieve their objectives more attractive, Canada diminished its terrorism problems, but may well have enhanced the probability of secession.

THE "TEMPORARY" BRITISH PROBLEM IN NORTHERN IRELAND

At what point should the general welfare of a nation take precedence over the rights of its citizens in a democratic society? How long and to what extent can those rights be reduced or taken away in order to secure that "general welfare" without doing irreparable damage to the fabric of democracy within that society?

Totalitarian and authoritarian states often justify the suspension or severe curtailment of civil and political liberties on the basis of a "need to secure the general welfare." But it is not only undemocratic states who have been guilty of repressing civil rights for this reason. This very issue is confronting the United Kingdom today, in its struggle with terrorism in Northern Ireland.

The periodic outbreaks of violence in Northern Ireland have prompted the British Parliament to enact the **Northern Ireland (Emergency Provisions) Act** in 1973. Parliament has renewed this act every year since then, retaining in its title the terms "emergency," even though it has now been in effect for more than two decades. This Draconian measure:

1. Allows suspects to be detained by the executive authority;
2. Gives police powers of arrest without warrant for up to 72 hours;
3. Gives security forces broad authority for search and seizure; and,
4. Makes it possible for those charged with terrorism to be tried by a judge, without benefit of a jury.

This extraordinary legislation was followed in 1974 by an Act called the **Prevention of Terrorism (Temporary Provisions) Act**. Under this Act, the Home Secretary was given special powers:

1. To exclude from the United Kingdom, without court proceedings, persons "concerned with the commission, preparation, or instigation of acts of terrorism; and,
2. To detain a suspect for up to seven days without bringing him to court (after his arrest by policemen without a warrant, as allowed under the Emergency Provisions Act).

The Temporary Provisions Act also allowed the prohibition in the United Kingdom of organizations considered to be concerned with terrorism.[5]

Both of these Acts have since been renewed annually by Parliament, though often with heated debates. So, although they still carry the titles of "Temporary" and "Emergency," such terms are no longer really appropriate. Emergency, by definition, refers to a "sudden condition or state of affairs calling for immediate action."[6] Used in reference to a state of affairs which has persisted for more than two decades, it is worse than meaningless.

These two legislative acts clearly demonstrate the extent to which a democratic state is willing to compromise on civil rights in order to combat terrorism within its borders. The prolonged curtailment of fundamental civil rights (such as the right to a trial by jury, the right to be charged with a crime when arrested, the right to be free to associate with organizations of one's choosing) and the granting of extraordinary powers to police (allowing them to violate certain rights in the process of search and seizure) surely diminish the democratic ideals of a state, even one which has been as committed to democracy as has the United Kingdom.

In order to create some measure of social order, Great Britain has given away some rights and freedoms of its Northern Ireland citizens. Unlike Canada, whose restriction of liberties was of relatively brief duration, the United Kingdom faces a restrictive situation which, since it shows little sign of improvement, seems likely to assume an indefinite, if not a permanent, position in the governing of this nation.

In Canada's case, the terrorists were not well organized or well armed, and they lacked substantive support from either other terrorist groups or from supporters in other nations, particularly from the nation with which it shares a border. So a determined effort by the Canadian government succeeded fairly well, in wiping out the terrorist threat. Given these conditions, the curtailment of rights and liberties was of short duration.

The situation which the United Kingdom faces is very different. The **Irish Republican Army (IRA)** *has been a well-organized, heavily armed, and well-funded resistance group in this region.* It receives both training and weapons from supporters in many places. Other terrorist organizations contribute to the arms and training of IRA operatives, while supporters and sympathizers from several nations, particularly the United States and the Republic of Ireland, have given these terrorists money, arms, and logistical support.

There are many difficulties in fighting, on one's home soil, an entrenched and heavily supported terrorist organization. As Spain has found in dealing with the **ETA**, *Spain's militant Basque separatists,* the presence of a friendly or neutral border over which terrorists can escape and find safehavens makes counterterror operations almost impossible for a nation to carry out on its own.[7] Cooperation between nations to thwart terrorists (as between Canada and the United States) can help make counterterror legislation unnecessary or at least short-term; the absence of such cooperation, particularly when linked with transnational support for the group engaged in terrorist acts, makes it very difficult for national "emergency" legislation to be effective in eliminating the terrorism.

GERMANY'S "MODERATE" LEGISLATION

Several nations have tried to deal with the need for national legislation on terrorism by enacting more "moderate" legislation. West Germany in 1978 enacted a package of antiterrorist laws which, given the scope of the terrorist problem that the nation faced (remember the excesses of the **Baader-Meinhof gang**, *the indigenous organization carrying out terrorist acts, and its successor, the anarchist* **Red Army Faction**), were regarded as fairly moderate.

Two of the most prominent of the antiterrorist laws enacted during the 1970s by West Germany were the "**contact ban**" and the "**propagation of violence**" **laws**. These laws illustrate the dangers in even such generally moderate legislation.

The curtailment of a prisoner's right of access to counsel provided for in the *"contact ban" law* was designed to restrict the flow of communication between imprisoned terrorists and their comrades still at large. German authorities believed that information was being passed between these two groups by sympathetic lawyers. But the only time that the law was invoked, information continued to flow. To many experts on German law, this made it appear that a fundamental principle of due process was being sacrificed without any appreciable benefit.[8]

The "propagation of violence" law was even more general, and possibly even more counterproductive. *This law was used against students protestors, as well as persons engaged in acts of terrorism,* with the unfortunate result that it helped to transform some nonviolent protestors into terrorists.[9]

Germany, like Canada, has been able through a combination of legislation and investigative intelligence to rid itself of many of its internal terrorist problems. The cost in Germany, though, has not been localized in one province, as it was in Canada, nor has it ended. In fact, in 1983 Germany's Minister of the Interior, under whose jurisdiction much of the counterterrorism effort has been made, steered through the cabinet several controversial amendments to the national demonstration law. These amendments were designed, for example, to make it easier for police to move into a crowd of peaceful demonstrators and arrest those who look as if they might be planning to riot or resist!

Germany has also enacted in recent years several legislative programs which have had, so far, no noticeable counterproductive effects, and have in fact been helpful in reducing the internal terrorist threat. These legal efforts have been geared toward bringing terrorists "to a sense of reality."

ITALY AND THE "PENTITI"

Italy has experimented with a similar legal strategy, with considerable success. In June 1983, Italians voted for the first time in more than a decade without an array of urban guerrilla groups holding the nation's political system at gunpoint. Long regarded as the Western European country most vulnerable during the general upsurge of terrorism in the 1970s, many of Italy's politicians and media experts hoped that their country was finally beginning to emerge from its terrorist nightmare.

The man credited with a large share in Italy's success in its war on internal terrorism was Interior Minister **Virginio Rognoni**, who assumed his office in the wake of the kidnap-murder of former Prime Minister Aldo Moro. At the time in which he took office, the Red Brigade terrorists appeared to be acting with impunity.

Statistics issued by the Interior Ministry indicated that, in 1978, there were 2,498 terrorist attacks within Italy. Between 1968 and 1982, 403 people were killed in terrorist incidents in Italy, and another 1,347 were injured. These people came from all walks of life. One out of every four was a policeman. Apart from politicians like Moro, businessmen and journalists were favorite targets. But the bulk of the dead and injured were ordinary citizens unlucky enough to be on a train or in a piazza when it was blown up.

There was, after 1980, a significant drop in Italy's internal terrorist activity. This appears to be a result of a combination of legal initiatives and coordinated police efforts. Nearly 2,000 convicted urban guerrillas, including most of the leading members of the Red Brigade, were imprisoned. The Italians gave the task of hunting down these persons to a portly *general of the Carabinieri named* **Carlo Alberto Della Chiesa**. Armed with about 150 carefully chosen men, his antiterrorist cadre, he was responsible only to the Minister of the Interior, Rognoni, and to the prime minister.

With his support, the government enacted a number of decrees: strengthening sentences for convicted terrorists; widening police powers (allowing police to hold suspects longer for questioning and to search without a warrant); and making abetting terrorism a crime. Increased powers were also given to the police in matters of detention, interrogation, and wiretapping.

Rognoni, during this period of increased police activity, began to exploit what he saw as a growing disillusionment with the efficacy of terrorism as a problem-solving instrument. He helped to have enacted in 1982 a law which promised *"repentant"* terrorists lighter sentences if they confessed. Beset by gathering doubts, large numbers of the "brigandisti" began to confess. One of the most prominent of the **"pentiti"** was Patrizio Peci, a former Red Brigade commander, from Turin. He commented that, while he had been driven to become an urban guerrilla by police harassment for bomb outrages (which were later discovered to have been committed instead by neo-fascists), he no longer believed that the Red Brigades could, using terrorism, create a better society in Italy.

Terrorism has not, in any sense, been eliminated in Italy. Both left- and right-wing terror continues to destroy individuals and property. Right-wing terrorists were responsible, in 1981, for an explosion in the Bologna train station which killed 85 people. But for a time, terrorism was significantly reduced. Consider the following facts:

- During 1980, deaths from terrorism occurred every three days on the average;
- In the first six months of 1983, in the wake of the government's police and legislative initiatives, only one terrorist-related death was reported.

The cost to Italy's democracy has been, arguably, substantial—due process was certainly impaired by the expanded police powers, for instance. But it is also possible that Italy's democracy could not have lasted much longer as a democracy under the barrage of terrorist attacks. Citizens' rights to vote, to security of person, as well as to life and liberty were under constant, serious threat of attack by terrorists. To have stabilized the situation without a civil war and without transforming Italy into an authoritarian regime is quite an accomplishment.

Much could be learned from Italy's experience. *The judicious blending of strong police investigative and arrest action, coupled with the offer of a government pardon for "penitent" transgressors, proved a potent and effective mixture.* By closing most of the "places to hide," while holding open a friendly government door to pardon, Italy has made serious efforts to resocialize a large number of its disaffected youth without unnecessary violence.

That Italy remains under attack by terrorists is due, in large measure, to the fact that its ties in the Arab world, and its position in the Mediterranean, make it a natural staging ground or pathway for terrorism from the Middle East. Most of Italy's terrorist activities in the late 1980s were conducted by foreign terrorists, mostly Middle Eastern, who were easily able to enter and exit this democratic nation.

Thus, general legislative initiatives, as well as emergency legislation, can be effective in reducing the threat of terrorism within a nation, without undue damage to democratic institutions. As one government publication noted:

> There is an almost irresistible tendency to react to terrorism by enacting laws and practices that diminish the rights of the accused or increase the authority of the state. The adverse consequences of that reaction are magnified by the equally predictable tendency to apply these specialized laws and mechanisms to an ever-increasing class of investigations. While the facts may justify certain changes, we must guard against overboard, nonproductive, or counterproductive changes.[10]

INVESTIGATION: THE INTELLIGENCE INITIATIVE

There is at least one other coping strategy which nations have used with some degree of success. Since most nations, and many terrorist groups, are currently engaged in the use of this strategy, an examination of the promises and pitfalls offered by such a strategy provides some interesting insights into the way in which nations can, and cannot, cope with the rising threat of terrorism today.

Investigation is an initial and certainly the most universal technique used by governments in their efforts to combat terrorism. Its potential as an antiterrorism tool is enormous. It has been effectively used to both prevent and punish terrorism. At the same time, its potential for abuse has been all too evident in recent years. Indeed, investigation has shown itself to be a powerful, two-edged sword, capable, when improperly applied, of resulting in serious loss of civil rights, though seldom of human life.

The successful use of investigative techniques to counter terrorism is of relatively recent vintage. While it is true that Israel has, for two decades, had an intelligence operation which accumulated vast amounts of information about Arab terrorists, even Israel has been unable to keep pace with the internationalization of terrorism, particularly of the Palestinian movement.

However, until West Germany turned its attention in the 1970s toward intelligence-gathering, Israel had the most active antiterrorist information system. Indeed, they flooded Western European governments and police forces with information about terrorists, their movements and planned actions. In fact, the French complained at one point that the mass of information gathered by Israeli agents (who had infiltrated Arab groups in France) was just too much for them to manage!

There is, of course, an international body which has been in existence for some time that would seem to be useful to national governments trying to cope with the investigation of international terrorism. *INTERPOL, the international police organization,* with its data banks on criminal activity worldwide, would appear to have many of the resources necessary for such investigations.

Under its charter, however, INTERPOL was, until very recently, restricted to investigations of ordinary crimes. Since not all of its charter members are as yet convinced that terrorism is indeed a crime, this organization has not until recently, been able to offer much substantive assistance in intelligence research. In October of 1984, changes in the rules governing this organization were made which have broadened its ability to assist nations in investigation of terrorism.

However, Germany has developed, and is sharing, what is doubtless one of the most sophisticated antiterrorist intelligence operations in existence today. In Weisbaden, a *computer nicknamed* "**The Komissar**" plays a vital role in that country's battle against terrorism. It is controlled by the Federal Criminal Investigation Department (the BKA). Over the past decade an enormous growth in federal resources has been put at the BKA's disposal.[11]

The heart of this computer system is an *index of information called* ***PIOS*** *(Personnen, Institutionen, Objekte, Sachen),* in which is stored every clue (such as addresses, contacts, and movements) about known and suspected terrorists. Every address found in a suspect's possession, every telephone number, and the name of every person who writes to him in prison is stored in this system. Information about every object found at the scene of a terrorist attack or in a place where terrorists have been becomes a part of this computer's 10 million data sheets.

This information has been effectively used by another German intelligence investigative tool—*the special unit of investigators operating in small teams on Ziefahndung*, meaning "**Target Searches.**" Target searches are instituted, according to German officials, for the apprehension of terrorists wanted under an arrest warrant, with priority given to a "hard core" of about 15 violent offenders. Every policeman in the Federal Republic carries with him at all times a set of cards bearing the photographs and identification data of all of these "targeted" persons. Each "target search" team takes one terrorist and immerses itself in his or her life, utilizing the computer at Weisbaden. All of the information about a suspect, however trivial it may seem, can be useful to the search team. If they know, for instance, that a suspect always telephones his or her mother on her birthday, the mother's phone can be wiretapped. Support for a certain soccer team indicated by the subject can lead investigators to attend that team's matches.

These intensive search methods have had documented success. Using such methods, 15 terrorists were tracked down in one six-week period in 1978. At that point, however, the success rate becomes somewhat less impressive. Having tracked the terrorists to other countries, the difficulty became one of securing their arrest and extradition for trial.

Four of the fifteen terrorists sought in 1978 were traced to Bulgaria. According to the lawyer for Till Meyer, Gabrielle Rollnick, Gudrun Sturmer, and Angelika Loder, the four suspected terrorists, four hired cars containing heavily armed German police drew up outside a cafe in Sonnenstrand, a Bulgaria resort. Meyer and the three women were overpowered, taken to a nearby bungalow, and tied up. At 2:00 A.M., they were taken to Bourgas Airport in a minibus with German Customs number plates, and put on a plane with 25 other armed German police. The cooperation of the Bulgarian authorities in this "kidnaping" of terrorists makes this a remarkable instance of cooperation between a communist and a noncommunist state in the apprehension of terrorists.[12]

Similar success was achieved in a cooperative effort with France in May 1980, when five women wanted on terrorism charges by Germany were arrested in a flat in the Rue Flatters on the Left Bank in Paris. Again, no complicated extradition procedures hampered the operation. France simply sent the five to Germany.[13]

This does not mean that cooperation on all such intelligence ventures is guaranteed. Indeed, the French, in another famous case, refused to extradite Abu Daoud, one of Black September's commanders, to either Germany or Israel. Daoud had arrived in Paris (under an assumed name) for the funeral of the Palestine Liberation Organization's representative. The French, who had photographed the funeral party, circulated the pictures to friendly governments, asking for information in their efforts to solve the murder of the representative.

When British intelligence identified Daoud from a photograph, French police promptly arrested him, much to the French government's embarrassment. Israel and West Germany immediately requested his extradition, but the French government quietly set him free—outside of their borders.

Daoud had, in fact, been formally introduced to senior government officials, and had been entertained at the Quai d'Orsay. France's decision not to extradite or punish was partly due to the embarrassment of having officially entertained Daoud, but more a result of the French government's ties to Arab states, whose sympathies lay with the PLO. Since these ties were attributable in part to France's dependency on Arab oil, the decision not to extradite was the result of both political and economic factors.[14]

Similarly, France arrested the German terrorist Wilfred Bose (whose connection with Carlos the Jackal was known to them), but released him. In this case, an extradition request was made, based on intelligence information on the crimes committed by this man. In spite of the fact that this intelligence information was made available to France, the French government decided to neither extradite nor punish this offender. Lacking a treaty or convention which could create a legal obligation to do one or the other, France was free to act, as it did, in what it perceived to be its best national interest.

Nor is France the only nation to refuse either to extradite or punish when given intelligence information about suspected terrorists. Yugoslavia, for example, refused to arrest Carlos when informed (in detail in an intelligence report) of his presence and his crimes by a German target search team. Yugoslav officials did arrest four of West Germany's most wanted terrorists (Rolf-Clemens Wagner, Brigitte Mohnhaupt, Sieglinde Hofmann, and Peter Boock) on information given by a German target search team. Subsequently, however, these suspects were released without either a trial or extradition proceedings.[15]

The point is that intelligence-gathering, as a weapon against terrorism, is often of erratic value in the absence of either a legal system with established guidelines for the treatment of terrorist suspects, or an alternative method of compelling cooperation among nations in the prosecution or extradition of such persons. Today, if a government thinks that its national interests will be best served by letting a known terrorist go free, it can (and will) usually do so. Where no overriding national interests are involved, cross-national intelligence-gathering and arrest operations are feasible; where such interest are perceived to be at stake, they are far less likely to succeed.

Today, some international police cooperation structures do exist which facilitate sharing intelligence concerning terrorism. In Europe there is a permanent, though comparatively secret, structure, code named **TREVI** for *Terrorism, Radicalism, and Violence International.* This is a formalization of the "old boy" police network, which regularly brings together police chiefs from European Union countries. It also engages in day-to-day consultations through national bureaus. At a secret meeting in April 1978, the nine Common Market countries, plus Austria and Switzerland agreed to pool resources to combat terrorism on the continent. The French have also been involved in this agreement since September of that year.

Furthermore, NATO has an antiterrorist network, which allies Canadians and Americans with Europe. This system facilitates the exchange of information on terrorists, their organizations, techniques, and weapons.

INTELLIGENCE-GATHERING AND COUNTERINTELLIGENCE BY TERRORISTS

The use of intelligence-gathering and counterintelligence is not limited to those opposing terrorism. These have long been tools of terrorists, as well. Indeed, the better organized and funded of the terrorist organizations could probably give lessons on the techniques of such operations to many governments today.

Study of the **phases of modern terrorist incidents** indicates that considerable attention is given by the terrorists to the function of intelligence-gathering. In most terrorist incidents, there is both a preincident phase and a postincident phase. Essentially, this means that before and after the incident actually occurs, the terrorists are involved in gathering and evaluating intelligence information.

In the *preincident phase*, terrorists are concerned with planning, reconnaissance, and usually a rehearsal of the event. In order to effectively carry out the planning necessary to launch an event in a country perhaps hundreds of miles from the group's home territory, considerable intelligence-gathering is clearly essential. Much of this is done, not by members of the group itself, but by members of an indigenous group sympathetic to the terrorists' cause. In incidents in which timing is crucial, intelligence information is also clearly essential—information which will allow for a realistic rehearsal according to a carefully constructed plan.

This concept of planning for a well-orchestrated terrorist event is neither new nor radical. What many observers do not realize, however, is that, today, terrorists also have an extensive *postincident phase* to most events as well. In this phase, the terrorists (the ones who survive the event), usually regroup and critique the event. They learn from their mistakes, far more rapidly, it sometimes appears, than do the police forces which are charged with combatting them. Those lessons learned from past mistakes are shared, becoming a part of the intelligence information available to terrorists in many areas of the world.

This does not mean that there exists a network of terrorists who share intelligence information on a regular basis. But information and incidents have led many observers to conclude that such sharing does in fact exist, on a regular but not an organized basis, among many terrorists. This seems to be particularly true in Europe, where anti-American and anti-NATO feelings have served to unite several diverse groups in a common cause.

Like TREVI, however, the links in intelligence-gathering and sharing among terrorists appears to be rather loosely organized, and based more on informal "contacts" than on regular channels for the dissemination of information. As long as terrorists are no more organized than the law enforcement organizations which seek to combat them, then neither side can effectively win. But that is a situation which neither side will be willing to tolerate indefinitely.

CONCLUSIONS

> For a democratic society, the issue is not merely survival, but the way in which society chooses to survive.
> —Robert Friedlander, *Terrorism Documents*

Just as terrorism is essentially a war against both the state and all of civilized society, so the struggle to eliminate, or at least to restrict, terrorism is also war of a sort. The cost of this war on terrorism, if carried by each state alone, can be quite high.

Each of the strategies used by a state to combat terrorism has potentially high costs, both politically and economically. Moreover, as noted earlier, when a state tries to pursue a strategy unilaterally, its effectiveness can be quite limited.

Furthermore, it is necessary to balance the value of a strategy for eradicating terrorism against the all-too-often concomitant loss of other democratic values and civil liberties when a nation decides to "wage war" on terrorism. Terrorists can be said to have "won" in some respects when "emergency" measures are enacted: Seeds of doubt and dissension about the government's commitment to democracy are sown; the government has been forced to take distasteful measures which could serve to reduce both its legitimacy and its stability. The first steps on a very dangerous slide toward repression and state terrorism are indeed "victories" of one sort for terrorists.

EVALUATION

Two areas of concern have been raised in recent years as governments grope for strategies with which to combat terrorism. Both concern the collection and dissemination of information—an issue of vital concern in most democratic countries today. One area involves concern about the potential for abuse by governments using intelligence services to track potential terrorists. The other area concerns the role of the media in reporting terrorist events. Consider each of these issues, as described subsequently, and decide what potential for abuse, as well as what legitimate security concerns, are involved in each.

1. The identification or "tagging" of people in order to keep track of "potential terrorists" might well be abused. If any person who participated in a peaceful demonstration or sit-in was "tagged" by intelligence services, the rights to privacy of that person could be violated without recourse to law. Indeed, would the investigative searches, conducted out of Weisbaden, Germany be constitutional in the United States today? Should they be?

2. Legal reforms which threaten the fabric of democracy are very dangerous weapons in the fight against terrorism. Are such initiatives justified by the reality of terrorism, or are they more of a danger to democratic society than the terrorism which they are designed to control? Which, if any, of the nations discussed, would be a good role model for the fashioning of national antiterrorism legal initiatives?

SUGGESTED READING

Beaton, Leonard. "Crisis in Quebec." *Round Table,* vol. 241 (1971).

Dobson, Christopher, and Ronald Payne. *Counterattack: The West's Battle Against the Terrorists.* (New York: Facts on File, 1982).

Friedlander, Robert A. *Terrorism: Documents of International and Local Control.* Dobbs Ferry, NJ: Oceana, 1979.

Jenkins, Roy. *England: Prevention of Terrorism (Temporary Provisions)—A Bill.* London: Her Majesty's Stationary Office, 1974.

Moore, Brian. *The Revolutionary Script.* New York: Holt, Rinehart & Winston, 1971.

"Report on Domestic and International Terrorism." Subcommittee on Civil and Constitutional Rights of the Committee on the Judiciary, First Session (April 1981). U.S. Government Printing Office, Washington, DC, 1981.

Weinberg, Leonard B. and Paul B. Davis. *Introduction to Political Terrorism.* New York: McGraw-Hill, 1989.

ENDNOTES

1. See Brian Moore's *The Revolution Script* (New York: Holt, Rinehart & Winston, 1971), for an account of these kidnappings; see also Leonard Beaton, "Crisis in Quebec," in *Round Table,* vol. 241 (1971) pp. 147-152.

2. Quoted by Robert Friedlander, *Terrorism: Documents of International and Local Control* (New York: Oceana, 1979) vol. 1, p. 113.

3. Christopher Dobson and Ronald Payne, *Counterattack: The West's Battle Against the Terrorists* (New York: Facts on File, 1982) p. 113. For six months, Trudeau flooded the Montreal area with troops. It took nine weeks to track down those responsible for Laporte's murder.

4. Dobson and Payne, *Counterattack,* p. 113. It was Barrett's contention that "democratic governments cannot legitimately establish consent by the use of force."

5. For information on these two Acts, see Great Britain, "Report to the Commission to Consider Legal Procedures to Deal with Terrorist Activities in Northern Ireland" (London, 1972). For analysis of the Temporary Provisions Act, see Roy Jenkins, *England: Prevention of Terrorism (Temporary Provisions)—A Bill* (London: Her Majesty's Stationery Office, 1974).

6. See Funk and Wagnall's *Standard Dictionary of the English Language,* International edition, vol. 1 (New York: J. Ferguson, 1977) p. 413.

7. There are French Basques living north of the Pyrenees, and there is little doubt that they give help to people they consider to be compatriots in Spain. ETA men on the run frequently cross the border to find refuge in "safe houses" in France. In 1979, the French government finally removed the "political refugee" status of ETA members.

8. "Report on Domestic and International Terrorism," Subcommittee on Civil and Constitutional Rights of the Committee on the Judiciary, First Session, April 1981 (Washington, DC: U.S. Government Printing Office, 1981) pp. 6-23. In spite of the concept of some lawyers as "fellow travelers of terrorism," little evidence was gathered to support this concept. In 1972, a lawyer in the Steinham trial was suspected of having transported a letter; however, after seven years of investigation and suspicion, no charges were brought.

9. "Report on Domestic and International Terrorism," p. 22. For example, one person was sentenced to eighteen months in prison for blocking the road in the anti-Springer demonstrations; he subsequently became a participant in acts of terrorism in Germany.

10. "Report on Domestic and International Terrorism," p. 4.

11. "Report on Domestic and International Terrorism," p. 18. This report includes an evaluation of German officials on the effectiveness of this intelligence system. The officials included Dr. Siegfried Froelich, State Secretary; Gerhard Siegle, Administrative Head (Head of Terrorism Office); Dieter Osterle, Deputy Head of the Director Office of the Police Superior Commission; and Captain Ulrich Grieve, Representative of GSG9.

12. Dobson and Payne, *Counterattack,* p. 101.

13. Bundeskriminalant (BKA) men stripped the apartment where the five women lived, and carried many items back to Weisbadden railway timetables, cigarette stubs, fingerprints, even even information on kitchen utensils were "fed" into the "das Komissar."

14. See *The New York Times*, January 12, 1977, Sec. 1, p. 1, for a concise recounting of this incident. This was not, of course, the only time when France refused to extradite known terrorists. However, recent French efforts to capture and prosecute "Carlos" indicate a significant change in French attitude toward the problem.

15. In this case, the reasons were both legal and political. The Yugoslavs demanded that the Germans give them in return a number of anti-Tito Croatian nationalists, some of whom were in German jails serving sentences for acts of terrorism against Yugoslav property and officials inside Germany. Germany could not, the Yugoslavian government decided, overcome the legal and moral complexities of meeting this demand.

CHAPTER ELEVEN

SECURITY MEASURES
A Frail Defense

*Power, in its most primitive sense, can be defined as the
capacity to disrupt or destroy. Terrorists through the use
of selective, yet often indiscriminate, violence have been able
to force governments to negotiate and often grant concessions
to their demands. They have been able to attract worldwide
attention to themselves and their goals. Terrorism has forced
governments to expend vast amounts of time and resources on
security.*

—M.K. Pilgrim, "Financing International Terrorism"

KEY CONCEPTS

physical security
penetration teams
operational security
personnel security
hardening the target
training programs
taggants

trace detectors
general threat indicators
local threat indicators
specific threat indicators

Confronted with a growing tide of terrorist destruction, governments
have indeed been forced to spend increasing amounts of time and

money on the problems related to security. Modern society is both fragile and complex, with much interdependence within the systems. As such, the possibilities for interference by terrorism are almost infinite.

Some aspects of security have, due to their spectacular selection as targets of terrorism, received more attention than others. It is more than possible that this focus will shift, as new technologies make current security measures obsolete, and as successful security systems "harden" certain targets against attack.

Technological developments during the past few decades have increased dramatically the potential targets and weapons available to persons committing terrorist acts. While the technology accessible to governments has also grown, governments are to some extent more hampered than helped by the technology boom. Governments are simultaneously confronted with a rapidly growing number of targets which must be secured, and constrained by democratic principles from utilizing many technological devices to secure those targets. Creating an effective security system which protects against a wide range of terrorist attacks while it continues to afford a maximum exercise of democratic freedoms and privileges is a formidable task indeed.

SECURITY HAS AT LEAST THREE FACETS

Security is not a one-dimensional issue. Instead, those confronting security problems are faced with at least three aspects to the situation which must be considered: physical security, operational security, and personnel security. Each of these aspects of security is closely related to the others and cannot be easily differentiated in an analysis of counterterrorism security efforts.

But there are certain features of each aspect which can, if explained, offer a better understanding of the security measures which nations and businesses are, even now, taking against terrorist incidents and threats. Let us briefly examine each of these aspects of security.

Physical security has, as its objective, *the hardening of the target against which an attack may be made.* While no blueprint for successful physical security measures against terrorist attack has been in any sense adopted, there are certain considerations and countermeasures which have begun to achieve acceptance in both the government and the business community.

It is slowly being recognized, for instance, in both these communities, that security measure against terrorism must go beyond the level of normal crime prevention. These terrorists are not "normal" criminals: their goals, their willingness to sacrifice innocent lives, and

their willingness to die in their attacks make them extraordinary criminals, against whom extraordinary measures must be taken if security is to be achieved and maintained.

In order to determine what, if any, extraordinary security measures are needed, to protect against a terrorist attack, government and
business have employed a number of relatively ordinary tactics. A
physical security survey, by professionals who are aware of the dangers in a particular area or to a particular business or embassy, is standard procedure. This has, in recent years, begun to include the use of
penetration teams, *whose job it is to discover holes in security systems
through which other "teams," such as terrorist attack teams, could presum-
able penetrate to sabotage or destroy the target.*

The penetration team, or the organization conducting the physical security survey may suggest, in their report, that the business
utilize certain devices which have proven to be useful in guarding
against attack or sabotage. There are, for example, a fairly wide variety of intrusion detection devices available on the market today.

Or such an evaluation may emphasize the importance of such
factors as lighting, access control, or physical security and access control codes. Organizations may be advised to inhibit surreptitious approaches by increasing lighting of entryways, fences, hallways, corri-
dors, and other points of access. Greater access control is often
recommended, usually in the form of limitations on the numbers of
individuals cleared to work in the facility as a whole, or in specific,
sensitive parts of the operation. One of the more common recommendations for improved physical security is that security and access codes
be changed fairly frequently, to make penetration of the operation
more difficult.

Some operations, where security has, until recently, been a relatively minor problem, are being urged to consider the use of personnel, such as guards, whose specific duty it is to ensure physical security. Others, who have already taken this step, have discovered from
security surveys that they have need of additional guards or specially
trained counterterrorist guards.

Physical security is clearly dependent upon other types of security—operational security and personnel security. Fortress walls,
barbed fences, and barred gates are not, in modern times, either reasonable or sufficient protection against determined terrorist fanatics.
The operation of the facility itself must be secure, and its personnel
well-trained in security procedures, in order to circumvent modern
terrorist attacks.

Operational security *has as its objective the denial of opportunity
for terrorists to collect such information on either the facility of its activities
as might enable them to predict those activities.* To be able to predict those

activities would help the terrorists to successfully penetrate the facility or activity to disrupt or destroy it. By denying that information to terrorists, the risk to terrorists carrying out an attack against the activity or facility significantly increases.

Prediction of operational activities usually relies on discerning *patterns of behavior*, so operational security analysis focuses on identifying those patterns and how they are communicated to personnel. Emphasis is placed on making such patterns less predictable, randomizing activities as far as possible without creating chaos within the organization. Too often, repeated activities create in the minds of the individuals responsible for security a numbness, a lack of alertness to small differences which may be crucial. The arrival of a particular car at the same time every morning, the use of a van of a specific color and model for delivering goods at the same place and time—these routines can deaden the alertness of personnel to such factors as the identity of the driver or the presence of an authorized person in the vehicle. Such a failure to notice, to carry out a thorough security check, can prove fatal, to the organization or some of its personnel.

The *training* of personnel in operational security measures is also important. Organizations are advised to train personnel in the recognition of intelligence-gathering activities, so that they can more readily spot individuals engaged in such activities. Screening of both employees and casual but regular contacts—such as vendors—is also a major focus of operational security efforts, as all such individuals can constitute a threat to the operation.

Moreover, the organization as a whole is often encouraged to improve its own operational security by a variety of fairly obvious, but essential, measures. These include the *maintenance of a low profile*, so that the organization does not become an attractive, publicity-provoking target; *concentrating on the improving of communications security*, so that it is less possible to penetrate the flow of commands or patterns of communications in the organization; and the *development of counterintelligence capabilities*, within both management and security-related personnel, so that the organization need not always be on the defensive in this struggle against terrorism.

Neither operational nor physical security can function effectively without the third crucial type of security: personnel security. **Personnel security** focuses on *the training of personnel to take responsibility on their own for security*, by teaching them to know how to recognize and respond to a potential terrorist threat. For many years, this type of security was directed towards "high-threat individuals," those whom the organization regarded as being at a greater risk of attack than most of the rank-and file-personnel.

Many organizations have developed individual crisis management files, which help management to decide which individuals need special security training and protection. Using those files, these at-risk individuals are often advised on how to randomize travel routes and maintain a low profile. Training is also given, to certain individuals, in special antiterrorism devices, such as bullet-proof clothing.

But today, personnel security has taken on added dimensions. Organizations routinely schedule periodic training for all personnel in counterterrorism procedures. Such training is usually designed to heighten awareness among employees of the potential for terrorist attacks, and the preincident phases—particularly intelligence-gathering—which may alert personnel to a terrorist attack in progress. The proper use of security measures at all times is stressed, so that employees are less likely to be lulled by a sense of routine into a possibly fatal breach of security procedures.

Most of all, the need to tell someone about suspicious or threatening behavior, to alert the proper authorities to potential threats has become a major focus in the training of personnel in many organizations. The alertness of personnel to security breaches may well mean the difference between a successful terrorist attack, and the failure of such an attempt.

CASE STUDY:
AIRPORT SECURITY IN THE UNITED STATES

Nations such as the United States have, at present, managed to institute some security measures at one of terrorism's favorite targets: airports. Travelers on commercial airlines in this country are routinely subjected to electronic or manual luggage inspection and to electronic or physical body searches—a practice virtually unknown only a few years ago.[1] In several major airports in the United States, too, individuals without purchased airline tickets can no longer meet arriving passengers at the arrival gates, nor can they take their friends or relatives to the departure gates.

These are potentially controversial measures, involving some invasion of privacy and some searches without a warrant of persons not accused of any crime. Yet few citizens today have serious objections to these measures. Even the presence of air marshals on randomly selected flights has been accepted with complacence by most citizens, in recognition perhaps of the fact that the threat to their lives and property created by a terrorist wielding a bomb is greater than that incurred in airline security measures.

Such security measures, of course, only offer a measure of protection, in one country, against only one type of terrorism. If such measures are not universally applied by all nations, then the potential for skyjacking or bombing remains substantial, even for citizens of countries having such security systems.[2] Moreover, even U.S. measures recently have not been completely successful in thwarting the hijacking of airplanes, partly because the measures are incomplete and poorly enforced.

Consider the results of recent investigations of airport security in several major U.S. airports. Federal auditors, testing X-ray procedures for carry-on luggage, reported recently that major airports missed, on the average, about 20 percent of the auditors' dummy weapons. One airport missed 66 percent of these weapons! This is clearly a breakdown in both physical and operational security.

Other surveys suggest that the problem does not lie exclusively with laxity in X-ray procedures. One audit, for instance, found that Los Angeles International Airport could not account for 6,000 employee identification badges. Two thousand were missing at Dulles International Airport near Washington, DC. Obviously, personnel security is also somewhat lax in this industry, contributing to a breach in operational security.

Consider the results of the informal "penetration team" of *U.S. News & World Report* reporters who recently checked several American airports:

1. At Washington National, a reporter with a suitcase walked right past a security checkpoint on the side where arriving passengers walk out of the arrival gate. The reporter pretended to make a call at a row of pay phones near the checkpoint, then slipped by when the guards backs were turned. What if his suitcase had contained a bomb?
2. At Chicago's O'Hare International Airport, a visitor found a baggage-room security door open. He walked through with his briefcase into the baggage-truck passageway, onto the tarmac where planes fuel and load, and up a Jetway staircase. He then entered the terminal as if deplaning and caught another flight—without ever going through security! He could have sabotaged either luggage or a plane, without any contact with security!
3. A reporter watched in amazement as janitors at Midway Airport in Chicago pushed large trash cans up to the passenger checkpoint. The janitors went through the metal detectors, but they pulled the cans through on the unscreened side! Guards neither inspected the trash cans—a serious security breach—nor did they check parcels brought into the same area by food vendors.
4. A reporter at Atlanta's Hartsfield Airport watched as an employee punched a code into a security door's lock. She then tried the same code on several other doors in the concourse. It opened them all! These doors led, among other things, to the planes on the tarmac.[3]

Such lapses in airport security must frighten and worry both those responsible for such security and the passengers and crew whom such security is designed to protect. The lapses are clearly in personnel and operational security. The argument is made that security personnel operate under the disadvantage of a mandate by their employers to make air travel as pleasant as possible. In other words, we want airport employees to be both unfailingly courteous and unrelentingly suspicious—of everyone. They are trained to put the comfort and convenience of the passengers first—but also to regard all individuals, including those same passengers, as potential threats to the airline's peace and security. It would appear, on the surface, to be an almost impossible task.

Moreover, physical security is still not completely effective. Weapons experts have testified before Congress as to the possibility of smuggling guns through metal detectors, by carrying them on certain spots on the body. Nor are these metal detectors, on which much airline physical security relies, effective at all heights.

There is not, at this time, a system in place to X-ray checked baggage on domestic flights, according to the FAA. The argument is made that the volume of such baggage is too high, and that many weapons which are forbidden in carry-on baggage (for which the current detectors are designed) are still permitted on checked baggage. Since an explosive "sniffer" that would detect bombs is still years away, this means that it is still quite possible to send a suitcase bomb through checked luggage in domestic flights within the United States!

So what are airports to do to "harden" themselves as targets against terrorism? They could retrain their personnel to be more security conscious, but it might well be at the cost of a loss of the "friendly" image with which airlines have sought to market their services. They could install more and better-maintenanced detection devices, but again unless the laws regarding the types of weapons which may be carried in checked luggage are changed, and the public becomes more reconciled to delays in flights due to essential security checks, then the cost of such measures to the airline industry may seem prohibitive.

THE COSTS OF SECURITY

The costs of such antiterrorism measures are great, materially as well as politically. Unfortunately, a great deal more money is required to erect defenses against terrorist attacks than to commit such acts.

If the cost of defending just one type of industry against attack is so high, then the cost of erecting coordinated international defenses against a multitude of terrorist attacks may well be prohibitive. The protection of specific targets against terrorists, including air transport facilities, would be a mammoth task. It is also one which would not in itself be sufficient to secure entire nations and persons against terrorist attacks of all kinds.

The difficulty, as Dr. Robert Kupperman has noted, is that potential targets for terrorist attacks are not limited to airports. As he has pointed out, there are numerous vulnerable targets in our sophisticated society. *Electrical power systems*, for example, are very tempting as accessible targets. A well-placed bomb or shots from a high-powered rifle could conceivably cause a blackout in an entire city. The same is true about the potential for destructive attacks on *telephone systems, gas pipelines, dams*, and *water systems*.

Dr. Kupperman has also noted that, with the extensive reliance on *computer information systems* —for banking, credit cards transactions, real estate, and so forth—which now characterizes industrial societies, the potential for economic disruption by terrorist attacks on those systems may also be substantial.[4] As any computer hacker knows, no matter how carefully a computer system's security may be designed, a blend of time, patience, knowledge, and a little bit of luck will usually suffice to break into it.

Concern has surfaced in recent years, too, over the protection of oil rigs in international waters. By the end of the next decade, there will no doubt be thousands of oil rigs in the Gulf of Mexico, and a rapidly growing number in the North Sea. All of these are quite vulnerable to terrorist attacks. Recent movies and novels depicting attacks on such rigs serve to highlight the plausibility of this potential disaster.

This industry, so vital to modern economies, is particularly open to attack, according to some experts, not only at its drilling operations, but at a variety of points. Although established petroleum and natural gas operations, their pipeline inter-ties, and associated tankage and storage facilities have been the most attractive targets to date, there is "no part of the industry that is immune to being seriously damaged by someone who has little knowledge of it, or who makes an effort to learn its frailties."[5]

The point is that the list of potential targets which could require security measures is fairly extensive, and growing with the development of modern technological interdependence. While it might be possible, although incredibly expensive, for a nation to undertake to protect its own citizens and structures, destructive attacks in another nation can have a substantial impact on the economy and lifestyle of the "protected" nation.

An attack on a North Sea oil rig, for example, would not only affect the cost of oil in Britain (and any nations which Britain supplies), but it could damage the North Sea countries' fishing industries also. A successful attack on the computerized international banking system could have serious consequences for many national economies. The poisoning of a water supply in one nation could affect all of the other nations who share that poisoned river or lake.

Just as no nation can entirely protect itself from terrorism by securing all potential terrorist targets, it is probably impossible for any nation, acting alone, to prevent or control the flow of weapons to terrorists. If targets cannot be fully protected, the next security step would logically appear to be an effort to curb the number and types of instruments of destruction available to terrorists. But again, the vast array of security measures required are staggering.

Some of the security measures in place or under consideration involve what is called **hardening the target**, which *involves efforts to make targets less accessible.* As noted earlier, these include the *installation of metal detectors and X-ray machines at points of entry, the use of sensors or closed-circuit television to monitor accessways, and other similar technical devices.* Such measures also can include the erection of fences, vision barriers, and heavy barriers around the perimeters of the installation. Related security measures can involve increased use of such items as armored cars, security guard forces, and bullet-proof vests. An increasing number of executives are enrolling employees in expensive **training programs** designed *to teach skills in such things as high-speed car chases, surviving a kidnaping, and "how not to look like a businessman traveling abroad."*

Indeed, companies offering to help make a business or a businessman more "secure" from terrorism have grown in number in recent years. One enterprising woman launched a business in 1987 which offered fake passports from nonexistent countries. Most of her clients have been military men and businessmen traveling in the Middle East, South America, and Europe. Donna Walker, president of International Documents Service, pointed out that, "When you're up against a bunch of gun-waving crazies, you should have an option"— such as a passport that does not label you as an American.

Whether such exercises in protecting the target are useful or not, they continue to generate both interest in and money for the companies providing them. What is not clear is whether they offer real protection against a terrorist attack which is commensurate with the money expended on them.

Nor is it clear whether such measures are either legal or acceptable in a democratic society. Fake passports could well be used by criminals to baffle legitimate customs officials. The erection of heavy barriers and guards around public buildings, while perhaps necessary to protect them from attack, are still unpopular with a democratic public, accustomed to easy access to, for example, their nation's capitol build-ings. It is, as the United States has found in the wake of the Oklahoma City bombing, neither popular nor practical to "harden" all buildings that have federal offices against the public which they serve.

PREVENTIVE SECURITY

Security has not been exclusively concerned with the "hardening" of targets which terrorists may—or may not—select today. Some efforts are also being directed at what has been termed "preventive security," meaning the making of terrorist attacks themselves less likely.

One such security technique in use today involves efforts to tag and trace various weapon components. There exist **taggants**—*chemically identifiable agents* —for many types of explosives today. It is also possible, although not as easy, to use **trace detectors** *for chemical agents*, which would enable security agents *to detect the presence of dangerous or hazardous chemicals in* innocuous-looking containers.

The use of tagging devices and trace elements for man-portable rocket security, in addition to more complete inventory control mea-sures, is also under advisement. The advantage in the use of taggants, in addition to an ability to detect certain trace substances, is an abil-ity to determine the country, and sometimes even the company, of origin. Although this would not necessarily be of immediate use in preventing terrorist attacks, it would be of considerable use in deter-mining *responsibility*, and perhaps thereby making similar future such attacks less likely.

However, companies and countries manufacturing such materi-als, from explosives to handguns, from nuclear to chemical and biolog-ical weapons, have resisted many attempts to institute a comprehen-sive tagging effort. Most have argued that laws requiring such security measures violate the rights of businesses engaged in lawful enterprises.

Political reality has made it clear that nations cherish their right to sell arms to whomever they please, under whatever conditions they deem advisable. Even nations which have made no secret of the fact that they sponsor, with arms and war materiel, terrorist groups, have little difficulty securing those arms on the world arms market.

CASE STUDY:
WHO ARMS IRAN?

In spite of all that is known about the active support which Iran gives to terrorism worldwide, neither this nation, nor Iraq, its adversary in a seven-year war, experienced any difficulty in securing a wide variety of lethal weapons. During the course of this war, at least 50 nations have sent arms to both Iran and Iraq.

It is Iran, with its record of support for terrorism, which is the focus of this study. Iran got small arms from the East bloc nations and North Korea, SCUD-B surface-to-surface missiles from Syria, tank parts and radar systems from Britain, and speedboats (which they have used to attack shipping in the Persian Gulf) from Sweden. It also bought from China a variety of tanks, fighter planes, artillery, rockets, and Silkworm missiles.

In the 1980s, Iran's biggest sources for arms were China and North Korea. China reportedly sold Iran more than $1.6 billion worth of military equipment, while the North Koreans were engaged in filling a $250 million order for small arms, munitions, and mines.

Arms deals make strange political bedfellows. While the Soviet Union primarily supported Iraq in the conflict, eleven of its satellite states were busy providing Iran with artillery pieces, radar equipment, heavy machine guns, and mortars. South Africa became a key supplier of armored vehicles, aircraft, and explosives for Iran, since Iran was one of the few nations which did not embargo South African goods.

Stranger still was Israel's relationship with Iran during this decade. Israel sold at least $500 million worth of arms of various sorts to Iran in just one year, in an effort to help Teheran defeat Iraq, which Israel regards as its enemy. Yet from Teheran have come terrorist teams which have struck against Israel, both at home and abroad. In the arms market jungle, it is evidently difficult to decide who is friend and who is foe.

Part of the motivation for such sales is clearly monetary. Arms merchants must export to survive, so many governments have turned a blind eye to the illegal sale of arms to belligerents due to an unspoken understanding of this need. The sale of arms, even on the legal market, is a multibillion dollar annual industry which few governments, including the U.S. government, can afford to ignore or cripple. But another part of the motivation is equally and clearly political, as Israel's sales to Iran and as the U.S.–Iran-contra deals indicate. Some arms are sold simply to make a profit, others are bartered for political advantage.

Regardless of the motivation, however, it is obvious that arms are increasingly available to anyone with the money (or a moneyed sponsor) to pay for them. This makes the efforts to limit terrorist access to weapons, as a form of preventive terrorism, largely futile. What terrorists cannot purchase legally, on the open arms market, they can surely procure illegally, on the black market. Fake end-user certificates are readily available from several countries, such as Nigeria, "like confetti."

Moreover, it is difficult, in the shadow world of illegal arms sales, to use most preventive measure effectively. Shell companies, Swiss bank accounts, and the routing of weapons from country to country, three or four times, to hide the country of origin, make the labyrinth of arms deals difficult to penetrate with regulation or preventive action.

Whereas the use of taggants might make the tracing of the country of origin feasible, (even through the maze of sale and resale), it is also highly probable that nations which wink at such sales by their industries are going to be unwilling to force those industries to institute measures which might make it easier for a finger to be pointed accurately in accusing violators of arms agreements. For monetary reasons they may have tacitly agreed to the sales; for political reasons they do not want such arms sales easily traced home. Preventing terrorism becomes, in such cases, a less crucial aim than not being held accountable for violation of arms control laws and agreements.

THREAT ASSESSMENT: HOW DO YOU KNOW WHEN YOU ARE AT RISK?

How do nations or businesses decide which of their operations or activities are likely to be victims of terrorist attacks? There are three types of indicators which nations and individuals use to assess the potential threat of terrorism. These can be described as general threat indicators, local threat indicators, and specific threat indicators. Let us look briefly at each of these indicators.

General threat indicators are used *to determine whether, within the nation or state, there exist condition which might stimulate or provoke terrorism.* Such indicators are extremely general, and are consequently of little use in predicting the likelihood of a specific terrorist attack. Instead, they are used to assess the climate—political, ideological, religious, and so forth—which might influence the willingness of a portion of the population to resort to terrorism. Politically, for example, the presence of an unpopular, repressive, or corrupt government is considered a positive indicator of the probability of terrorism. Similarly, an economic climate which includes extreme poverty and high unemployment is regarded as conducive to terrorism.

This does not mean that any nation or region possessing these political or economic conditions will necessarily have a large degree of terrorism. It simply means that the presence of such conditions makes the likelihood of terrorism greater in such places than it might be in areas which do not have similar political or economic climates. These are indicators only, not predictors of terrorism. For instance, one geopolitical indicator has been the concentration of large foreign populations within a nation. Yet, in the United States many such concentrations exist in major cities without outbreaks of terrorism. But in occupied territories, or in nations involved in border disputes, such populations have indeed been useful indicators of the probability of terrorism.

Local threat indicators are used to assess more specific and localized possibilities for terrorism. Usually, such indicators focus on the forms which dissent tends to take on the local level, and the degree of violence involved in the expression of such dissent. The formation of radical groups; reports of stolen firearms, ammunition, and explosives; violence against local property, including looting and arson; violence against individuals, including murders, beatings, threats, and abductions; and the discovery of weapon, ammunition, and explosives caches are all considered to be local threat indicators. Again, this does not mean that any radical group which forms must necessarily be a terrorist threat, nor that any demonstration against a government or a company must be the prelude to a terrorist attack. These are just some indicators of the possibility of terrorism in a particular location.

Specific threat indicators are used *to evaluate the vulnerability of a particular target to terrorism*, not the likelihood of terrorism in a nation or neighborhood. These indicators include such things as the history of attacks on similar targets, the publicity value of the target, the target's access to infiltration, its counterterror capability, its communications capability, the tactical attractiveness of the target, and the availability of the police or other security personnel.

Some of these indicators are essentially judgment calls, such as the determination as to whether or not the industry involves a "sensitive" installation, which is generally used to refer to a nuclear, chemical, or other similar facility. Others are very easily quantified, such as the population density in the immediate area.

None of the three types of indicators can be said to "predict" the probability of a terrorist attack. Nevertheless, government and industry are beginning to rely increasingly on such indicators to help them decide what, if any, terrorist threat exists, and what direction such attacks might take. With the cost of installing, staffing, and maintaining security systems spiraling upwards, no one is anxious to spend more than is warranted on protection against a threat which may never materialize. But few are willing, either, to risk remaining unsecured where strong indications exist that terrorist attacks may cripple or destroy costly facilities and irreplaceable lives.

CONCLUSIONS

The question basically is how much a company, a government, or a people are willing to sacrifice in order to achieve a greater security from terrorist attacks. For some, as long as the attack happens to "somebody else," the sacrifice of rights to prevent terrorism will always seem too high a price. To others, the prevention of terrorism will justify the loss of precious rights and freedoms. Governments, in trying to strike a delicate balance between the need for its citizens to be secure and the need to protect its citizens rights, have an increasingly difficult task.

Terrorism is fundamentally an attack on the state. Just as offshore maritime terrorism is "a crime waiting to happen," terrorism with nuclear, biological, or chemical weapons is an international disaster waiting to occur. Neither national nor international security measures have proved adequate in terms of either protecting targets or preventing the dissemination of such agents of mass destruction.

As governments and industries come to grips with the rocketing costs of securing themselves against terrorism, serious questions continue to be raised concerning the priority which security should have in the allocation of resources. However real the terrorist threat may be, few are willing as yet meet the exorbitant costs, both political and economic, of providing adequate security against that threat.

Unlike the issues raised with intelligence-gathering and investigative counterterrorism measure, security measures costs are reckoned less in terms of political ideals such as civil liberties. Instead, the costs are felt to be more in terms of convenience and, more important, money. Until terrorism is felt to be enough of a threat to the economic well-being of both nations and industries to justify the expenditure, of countless millions of dollars, security will remain a weak weapon in the arsenal of nations against terrorism. Until terrorism seriously pinches the pocketbook of nations and businesses, that pocketbook will be slow to open to defeat or prevent that "pinch."

EVALUATION

Making a decision to take on the costs, economic, political and in terms of public relations of installing and enforcing security systems is seldom easy. Seldom is there a clear indication which makes such a decision "easy" or "obvious." Governments and industries continue to wrestle with the problems, and, while their solutions seldom satisfy everyone, it is often difficult to state, unequivocally, what they should do in a given situation.

Consider the following cases, and try to formulate an appropriate response. Remember to take into account both the monetary and political costs of any decision. Could you justify your decision to a corporate board—or an irate citizen—in terms of cost-effectiveness? That is, does the security measure that you may recommend "pay" for itself in terms of the security gained, in a way that would recommend itself to a stockholder or taxpayer?

1. In spite of the gaps in airport security in the United States noted earlier, the Federal Aviation Authority and airline officials stress that U.S. aviation works pretty well. In 1987, airlines screened 1.2 billion passengers in this country, and seized 3,000 weapons. Only four persons tried to hijack planes that year; none of them were successful and none carried a gun.

   In light of this record, should the FAA require increased security training for airline employees, as well as the installation of more and better screening devices for baggage? Do the airlines and airport personnel deserve an indictment for the flaws noted earlier, or a commendation for the record of terrorism prevention which it has accumulated in recent years? In light of that record, could you justify spending large sums for increased security? As a citizen, passenger, and potential target of aircraft terrorism, do you want better security systems in place? Are you willing to pay for these systems, in higher-priced airline tickets, longer lines, and more flight delays?

2. Israel has resolved to pay the price, both monetary and political, involved in increasing airport security at Tel Aviv. Passengers boarding at this airport are warned to expect to spend several hours in security checks. Checked luggage, carryon luggage, and handbags are scrupulously examined. Detailed scrutiny is also made of the passengers themselves, their contacts, their personal histories.

   These searches are often what would, in the United States, be considered "unreasonable" in that there is no effort to establish a "probable cause" for believing that the individuals subjected to such searches and invasions of privacy are terrorists. The delays while these security measures are implemented are tedious and time-consuming. But Israel has so successfully "hardened" its airports as targets that terrorists seeking to target Israeli airlines or tourists have been forced to choose airports in other nations from which to launch their attacks.

   Are such measures justified, in terms of monetary costs, political costs, and inconvenience? Do they continue to be justified, even though Israel's airlines continue to be an accessible target through other airports in other nations? What more can Israel do to prevent its airlines from being vulnerable to terrorist attacks, if other nations do not institute similar security measures at their airports?

3. The development and public sale of plastic handguns would be a security nightmare. This deadly technological breakthrough would enable terrorists to carry handguns through checkpoints and detection devices without fear of discovery. The plastic gun existed, in 1988, only as a concept and computer model patented by a five-person company called Red Eye Arms, Inc., in Winter Park, Florida. This gun employs state-of-the-art plastics and a design which allows the gases to be vented when a shot is fired, thereby eliminating recoil. The basic design could be used, theoretically, for anything from handguns to howitzers.

Furthermore, plastic weapons are lighter, less expensive, corrosion proof, and almost completely maintenance-free. What a market breakthrough this would be, not only for military arsenals, but for terrorists, who often have to hope that their weapons will last for many years!

It is a terrorist's dream, and a security nightmare. This weapon will slip undetected through the most sophisticated detection equipment now in place in most industries. Cost-efficient, undetectable, with a potentially long service life, it would be an ideal weapon.

What kind of security, if any, would be useful against such an innovation? If it cannot be detected (since it has no metal parts) by metal detectors, would it be feasible to require that its makers build in a microchip which would set off a detection device? How could you be sure that a manufacturer would in fact build in such a chip, or that it could not be readily removed by an unscrupulous owner?

How can security measures best be developed to meet not only today's arsenal of weapons, which is quite formidable, but also the weapons of the not-very-distant future? Is there a point at which security measures become increasingly futile, as the sophistication of the terrorist threat grows to match technological development? If so, what does a nation, a business, an individual turn to deal with this growing threat?

SUGGESTED READINGS

Fenelo, Michael J. "Technical Prevention of Air Piracy." *International Conciliation.*, no. 585 (1971).

"Gaping Holes In Airport Security." *U.S. News & World Report,* April 25, 1988.

Joyner, Christopher C. "Offshore Maritime Terrorism: International Implications and the Legal Response." *Naval War College Review,* vol. 36, no. 4 (July-August 1983).

Stephens, Maynard M. "The Oil and Gas Industries: A Potential Target of Terrorists," in Robert H. Kupperman and Darrell M. Trent, eds. *Terrorism: Threat, Reality, and Response.* Stanford, CA: Hoover Institution Press, 1979.

"Who Arms Iran? Almost Everyone." *U.S. News & World Report*, August 31, 1987.

ENDNOTES

1. See Michael J. Fenelo, "Technical Prevention of Air Piracy," *International Conciliation*, no. 585 (1971) pp. 28-41.
2. One CIA official (who requested anonymity) noted that in many less-developed nations, the lack of any real security at airports constitutes "a terrorist attack waiting to happen."
3. "The Next Bomb," *Life* (March 1989) pp. 130-138.
4. In an interview on April 8, 1982, Dr. Kupperman expanded on this theme (of the potential targets of terrorism), which he has previously described in his book *Terrorism: Threat, Reality, and Response*, coauthored by Darrell M. Trent (Stanford, CA: Hoover Institution Press, 1979).
5. Maynard M. Stephens, "The Oil and Gas Industries: A Potential Target of Terrorists," in *Terrorism: Threat, Reality and Response*, p. 200.

CHAPTER TWELVE

FUTURE TRENDS

*Terrorism is becoming commonplace—ordinary, banal
and therefore somehow tolerable . . . Extraordinary security
measures no longer attract any comment. We expect
diplomats to be assassinated and states to be involved.*

—Brian Jenkins, "The Future Course of Terrorism"

KEY CONCEPTS

bureaucratic banality
institutionalized
semipermanent subculture
   of terrorism
volume of terrorist incidents
lethality
right-wing terrorism

"generational" differences
PFLP-General Command
Hamas
victims
preferred tool
unthinkable weapons

BANALITY AND TERROR

The late Hannah Arendt, in her controversial book on the trial of
Adolf Eichmann, coined the phrase "the banality of evil." She used
this phrase to describe the way in which a "terrifyingly normal" per-

son was able to help turn the murder of a people into an ordinary bureaucratic routine. Eichmann became the quintessential government bureaucrat—highly efficient and mindlessly, remorselessly, obedient to orders.

Brian Jenkins, of the Rand Corporation, suggests that terrorism has achieved a similar level of **bureaucratic banality**: *its perpetrators carry out heinous crimes with increasing efficiency, while a worldwide audience becomes increasingly "unshockable" when viewing those acts.* Statistics have replaced headlines in referring to the escalation of terrorism. Terrorism has become so much the norm that it is "commonplace," not "unthinkable," today.

Moreover, terrorism has become increasingly **institutionalized**. As several reports recently noted, *some governments today not only provide logistical support for terrorists, but actually create or designate government agencies to supervise relations with the terrorists.* "Like any bureaucracy," notes Jenkins, chief terrorism analyst for the Rand Corporation, in his paper "The Future Course of Terrorism," such an agency "competes for influence and budget, promises results and resists dismantling."[1]

In fact, this expert, in a seminar at Georgetown University's Center for Strategic and International Studies, suggested that a **"semipermanent subculture of terrorism"** may be emerging, with shared personnel and some common sources of weapons and financing. Walter Lacquer, on a similar note in his 1987 study of the subject, compared terrorism with the "anonymous character of a multinational corporation."

Recognizing what threatens to become a permanent part of the international landscape, many nations now spend billions of dollars every year trying to improve security, providing for increased protection for ordinary citizens and civilian facilities, and adopting special measures for ensuring the safety of diplomats and government officials. Several nations have established commando units trained to combat terrorists. Large corporations now often provide their top executives with instruction in protecting themselves and their families.

The cost and the personnel involved both in terrorism itself and in the fight against it have, to a great degree in recent years, become institutionalized. Expenses for overseeing relations with terrorists, or for securing against terrorism, are now more often a part of the regular budget of both government and industry.

However, the 1990s have been a decade of significant change. Organizations, such as the PLO, which until the mid-1990s engaged in and supported terrorism, are becoming a legitimate part of the international community. The PLO began achieving diplomatic recognition from several states, and initiated diplomatic dialogue with the United States government in December 1988. It acted as a major participant in the peace process with Israel, resulting in the creation of semiautonomous Palestinian systems in the Gaza Strip and in parts of the West Bank in 1994. PLO leader Yasser Arafat enjoyed, by the mid-1990s, acceptance as chief executive of a legitimate organization, not a terrorist group. Required for this transformation was a renunciation of the threat to use terrorism as a means to secure political independence. The reality of the terrorist acts committed by this group were neither denied nor apologized for; instead, the leadership declared that this would no longer be a tactic employed against its enemies.

We have, perhaps, come to accept the existence of terrorism in our daily lives. It has become routine, commonplace, ordinary. The level of violence which our society is willing to tolerate has risen in concert with the rise of terrorism in recent years. There is less talk of "eliminating" terrorism now, and more emphasis on "limiting its effectiveness."

Success in peace efforts in the Middle East and in Northern Ireland (while disrupted by bombings in London and Tel Aviv from time to time) generate optimism about the potential for eliminating terrorism by eliminating the political and social causes for which the terrorists fight. Yet in both cases, political solutions acceptable to a large faction of those who have felt alienated to the point of resorting in terrorism are not acceptable to all factions of the same people. While the PLO leadership appears willing to work with Israel toward settlement on the issue of Palestine, the Hamas faction continues to carry out violent attacks, particularly suicide bombings against Israeli targets. Similarly, the IRA in Northern Ireland was unable to prevent smaller factions from continuing to carry out acts of terrorism against civilian targets, particularly in London.

Perhaps it is true, as Jenkins suggests, that there is no cure for terrorism. He refers to it as a condition, not a specific disease, which can be treated but not cured. If this is true, then it seems likely that the prognosis for this "condition" will be a grim one. Terrorism could, in fact, grow worse, as the technology available becomes more sophisticated.

N.C. Livingstone notes:

> As the nations of the globe learn to live with routine low-level violence, it can be expected that there will be a movement by terrorists toward more dramatic and increasingly destructive acts of terrorism designed to ensure that the public does not forget about them and their causes.[2]

The explosive growth of technology which has brought with it new vulnerabilities to superindustrialized societies will continue to provide incentives for increased destruction.

So our world is, and will be for the foreseeable future, afflicted with the "condition" of terrorism, which will, in the view of most experts, probably get worse rather than better. As the world public becomes inured to low-level violence, that violence will escalate, perhaps in very undesirable ways which utilize the incredible innovations in modern technology.

TRENDS IN TERRORISM

It is a grim picture. But it is unfortunately fairly accurate, at least as accurate as any predictions of future events and trends can be. There are some specific **trends in terrorism** in recent years which may help to bring this view of the future into better focus.

The **volume of terrorist incidents,** *the number occurring annually,* has increased. Since the 1972 attack on Olympic athletes in Munich, the number of terrorist incidents has risen at an annual rate of between 12 and 15 percent. This rate of increase has not been constant throughout that time frame. In the 1980s, there was a marked acceleration, which brought the average rate up. From 1980-1983, for instance there was an approximately 30 percent annual increase. During 1990 and 1991, the escalation continued, although certain types of incidents became less common (for example, skyjacking).

Terrorism has not only increased in volume, it has also increased in **lethality,** that is, in *the number of people killed in attacks.* In the last four decades of the twentieth century, the number of incidents involving fatalities has increased by an estimated 20 percent annually over the number killed annually in the first six decades of this century. In 1983, for example, 720 people died in terrorist incidents, and another 963 were wounded. A bomb on an Air India flight in June 1986 killed 329, and 115 people died from a bomb on a Korean Airlines flight in 1987. The bombing of PanAm Flight 103 over Lockerbie, Scotland, in December 1988 resulted in the death of 270. Between 1969 and 1989, 1,128 people died as a result of bombs exploding aboard aircraft or in cargo containers on the ground.

There has been a trend toward large-scale indiscriminate terrorist attacks in mundane, everyday locations such as airports, or office buildings, or subways. The number of attacks against ordinary citizens has risen dramatically in recent years, by as much as 68 percent since the turn of the century.

There has also been a surge in **right-wing terrorism** recently, *carried out by militant, conservative, fundamentalist individuals and groups.* If the 1960s can be described in terms of left-wing terrorism, with the 1970s carrying that trend to its logical conclusion by witnessing the involvement of liberation struggles in terrorism, the 1980s and 1990s witnessed a resurgence of right-wing terrorism. This was particularly true in Europe and the United States. The activities of such organizations as the German neo-Nazi youth groups who are against refugees from Eastern Europe, and the Aryan Nations in the United States have provided grim reminders of the existence of right-wing groups which are increasingly willing to resort to violence. The bombing attack in Oklahoma City in 1995 certainly raised concern over the possibility of violence generated by right-wing domestic militia groups.

Moreover, there is what has been called a **"generational" difference**, *between young militants and older leaders,* in the terrorists operating today. Today's terrorists seem less likely to be involved in pickets and demonstrations before resorting to violence. Instead, they seem more willing to throw a bomb first, and then talk later (if at all) about their grievances.

This "do something now" mentality has caused some difficulties and even embarrassment for some of the older leaders of established movements. In the PLO, for instance, the decade of the 1990s has witnessed a number of splits, frequently between the older, more "institutionalized" members of the organization, and the younger members, who want to take violent action now against the existing situation. Certainly Yasser Arafat, in his December 1988 speech promising that the PLO will not engage in terrorism, could not be sure that he spoke for the whole of that organization's membership.

George Habash's radical faction, **the PFLP-General Command**, strongly rejected any such renunciation of terrorist tactics, as have the fundamentalist **Hamas**, supported by Iran and active in the West Bank and Gaza Strip. The difficulties experienced by Arafat in governing Gaza during the mid-1990s illustrates the deepening splits between the older leadership, willing to compromise in order to achieve a portion of that for which they fought, and the younger factions, willing to continue the struggle with violence and unwilling to settle for less than full success.

Terrorism has also contributed to changes in the mode of conflict both between nations and within nations. Conflicts today appear to be less coherent, at times exhibiting not two clear sides, but several confusing and shifting alliances. Such conflicts are also less decisive, with no clear "winner" or "loser." As states use terrorism to engage in irregular warfare against other states, the stakes in the conflict become confused, the rules less clear, and the heroes hard to find.

GRAPHIC EVIDENCE

There is ample evidence of the trends in terrorism in recent years. The U.S. Department of State issues a summary report annually, entitled "Patterns of Global Terrorism," in which it reveals not only interesting insights into terrorism during the previous year, but also describes patterns of terrorism over several previous years. A brief look at some of these collective figures on terrorist incidents, victims, locations, and modes of operation may help us to understand both the scope of the problem of terrorism and its probable course in the next century.

Figure 12.1, culled from the April 1994 edition of this report, illustrates the incidents of international terrorism in 1993 from four perspectives: the region in which the incident occurred, the type of facility against which it was directed, the type of victim, and the type of event. Some observations can be made from these graphs, and the accompanying statistics in the report.

In 1987, there were 832 international terrorist incidents reported by the Department of State. These incidents resulted in the deaths of 633 persons, and the wounding of another 2,272. Much of this injury and loss of life resulted from terrorism in the Middle East and its spillover into Western Europe, which accounted for 295 deaths and 770 injuries. Not surprisingly, the Middle East had the highest incidence of terrorism in that year, of all of the world regions, incurring 371 attacks (about 45 percent of the worldwide total).

The annual report, (released in April 1994) for 1993 indicates a substantial decrease in terrorism worldwide. Only 427 incidents of international terrorism were recorded, with 109 deaths from these attacks, and 1,393 people wounded. While these figures are considerably lower than those of 1987, it is worth noting that they represent an increase from the 1992 statistics. Only 364 total incidents were recorded during that year. This rather diminishes the "good news" in the decrease of terrorism in the 1990s when compared with the 1980s, since the 1990's seem to be experiencing another small increase.

Moreover, *the citizens and property of many nations* were the **victims** of terrorist attacks in 1987. Eighty-four nations were victims of such attacks. About 80 percent of those attacks were carried out against nonofficial, and often unprotected targets, such as businesses and tourists. Less than 20 percent of the total number of terrorist attacks were against government, diplomatic, or military targets. It ob-

FIGURE 12.1 International Terrorist Incidents, 1993

TYPE OF VICTIM

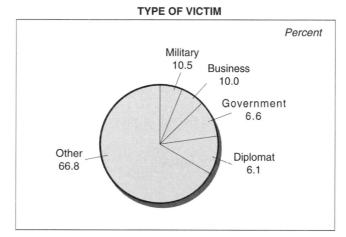

SOURCE: "Patterns of Global Terrorism: 1993." U.S. Department of State, Publication 10136, p. 68.

viously remains the case that terrorist acts are carried out predominantly against innocent, noncombattant bystanders, who are made the victims of violence in struggles of which they have no part.

Bombs remain the **preferred tool** of today's terrorists, with bombing attacks making up about 53 percent of the total number of terrorist incidents. While kidnappings still occurred, these events remain relatively infrequent in terms of the total number of terrorist incidents (approximately 8 percent of the incidents in 1993 were kidnappings).

On a positive note, there appears to be little evidence that terrorists have begun to use Armageddon-type weapons (such as chemical, biological, or nuclear weapons) in their attacks. However, there is increasing use of more sophisticated versions of their more familiar tools. The Czech-made plastic explosive Semtex, which is colorless, virtually odorless, and almost completely undetectable by most modern security systems, has apparently come into recent use in aircraft bombing attempts, including the PanAm Lockerbie explosion.

U.S. State Department records indicate that thus far, few terrorist attacks have involved the use of doomsday weapons. International concern has heightened in recent months over the use of such weapons. With the demise of the Soviet Union, the covert sale of nuclear weapons and weapons-grade materials has been of great concern to Europe and the United States. Four separate incidents, noted at the beginning of this text, involving such sales highlight the reality of nuclear options for terrorists in the twenty-first century. The lack of willingness on the part of governments, to limit nuclear proliferation, as more governments seek to enter the group of nuclear-capable states, will make it increasingly difficult for the international community to successfully prevent terrorist groups from acquiring or using nuclear weapons. The moral "high ground" of nuclear nonproliferation is rapidly eroding. The day when one small nation uses nuclear weapons against a larger opponent as a measure of "justified war" will certainly diminish any moral restraint on terrorist groups against the use of such weapons.

Terrorism, although obviously prevalent in many forms in the 1990s, has not taken on the more ominous overtones involving the use of those **"unthinkable weapons,"** the *nuclear, biological, or chemical* types, for the most part. But it is well to remember that, in labeling any such weapon use "unthinkable," one is subject to the same type of erroneous thinking which led many only a few short years ago to assume that "no one" would deliberately make war on innocent women and children. As Figure 12.1 indicates, most of the victims of terrorism in 1993 were not diplomats, government officials, or soldiers. They were "others": men and women working for corporations with interests in more than one nation; elderly people taking the tour for which they had saved all of their lives; housewives who went to the wrong supermarket at the wrong time; children. "Someone" did, in fact, make war on these people.

Terrorism, like other forms of warfare, is an act that takes or maims lives. In 1993, statistics indicate that terrorist acts were quite successful in this respect. More than 100 died and over 1,000 were wounded in terrorist attacks around the world.

Figure 12.2 illustrates the casualties caused by international terrorist incidents in 1993, by region. The first graph indicates the number of individuals killed or wounded in terrorist events, broken down according to the region in which the attack occurred. One interesting insight from this graph relates to the two areas in which the greatest number of deaths and injuries occurred: the Middle East and Asia.

In 1987, the war in Afghanistan resulted in government-directed attacks on Afghan refugees in camps along the Pakistani border. Since the defeat of the communist regime in Kabul in April 1992, many of the non-Afghan Muslims, who had fought in that war with the rebel forces, have returned home and become active in insurgent movements. The cyclical nature of violence is again painfully illustrated.

Not all incidents in this area were caused by the war in Afghanistan. Sectarian violence increased throughout the region,

FIGURE 12.2 Casualties Caused by International Terrorist Incidents

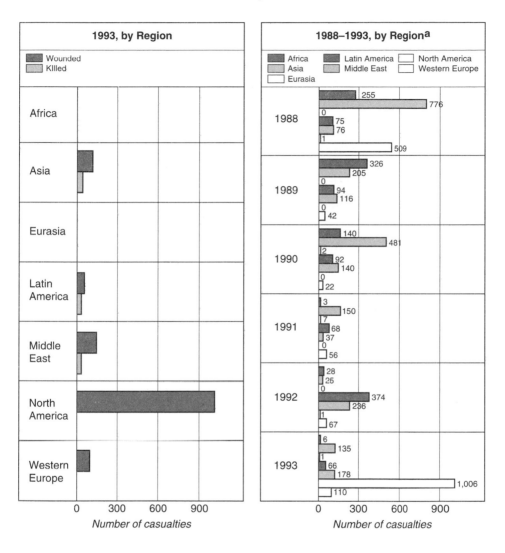

SOURCE: "Patterns of Global Terrorism: 1993," U.S. Department of State, Publication No. 10136, p. 70.

particularly in the Philippines, with bombing of churches and mosques killing some and injuring far more.

Similarly, few of the incidents occurring in the Middle East in 1993 were a result of the conflict between Israel and its Arab neighbors. The civil strife in Egypt and Algeria contributed significantly to the large number of casualties, as did the attacks against U.N. and other humanitarian efforts in northern Iraq.

It is also significant to note that North America recorded that highest number of people wounded in terrorist incidents. This anomaly was created by the results of the bombing of the World Trade Center in New York City on February 26, which resulted in over 1,000 injuries.

The second part of Figure 12.2 illustrates the trends of such deaths and injuries by region over a period of six years. It is interesting to note that, although Americans have frequently been targets for terrorism during those years, few individuals died or were injured as a result of terrorist incidents in this nation until the World Trade Center bombing.

Eurasia (which according to the U.S. State Department report includes all of the former Soviet Union and Eastern Europe) has also had a marginal history of deaths or injuries taking place on its soil as a result of terrorist incidents. Casualties appear to have decreased in Africa; the other regions have experienced a decline from 1988 through 1990, but then witnessed an increase in casualties from 1991-1993. This is insufficient data to substantiate a "trend," but it does look as though the last decade of the twentieth century may be indicative of increasing levels of casualties from terrorism in the twenty-first century.

Figures 12.3 and 12.4 continue this examination of international terrorist incidents over time. Study of these graphs illuminates some interesting trends. About these trends certain generalizations can safely be made:

1. The number of terrorist incidents, while having increased at an alarming rate during the 1980s, was in 1992 approximately at the same level as that recorded for 1975. From a "low" of less that 400 incidents reported in 1975, terrorism reached a peak of almost 700 such incidents in 1987, a staggering increase in just over a decade.

2. The greatest increase in terrorism has occurred in Latin America and Western Europe. Both of these regions experienced some decline in incidents from 1988 through 1990, but reported significant increases in 1991. Political compromises in the 1990s between both the PLO and Israel, and between the Hashamite Kingdom of Jordan and Israel, have removed at least some of the actors and sponsors of terrorism from the scene, leaving room for some optimism in that region.

FIGURE 12.3 International Terrorist Incidents Over Time

1975–1993

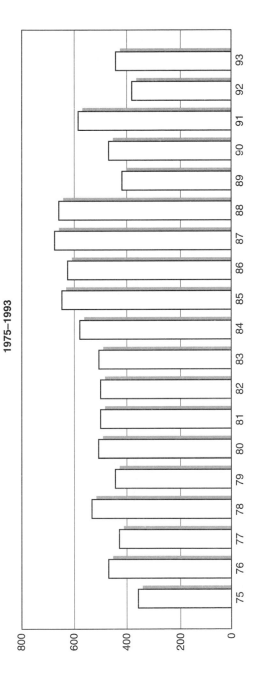

In past years, serious violence by Palestinians against other Palestinians in the occupied territories was included in the data base of worldwide international terrorist incidents because Palestinians are considered stateless people. This resulted in such incidents being treated differently from intraethnic violence in other parts of the world. In 1989, as a result of further review of the nature of intra-Palestinian violence, such violence stopped being included in the US Government's statistical data base on international terrorism. The figures shown above for the years 1984 through 1988 have been revised to exclude intra-Palestinian violence, thus making the data base consistent.

Investigations into terrorist incidents sometimes yield evidence that necessitates a change in the information previously held true (such as whether the incident fits the definition of international terrorism, which group or state sponsor was responsible, or the number of victims killed or injured). As a result of these adjustments, the statistics given in this report may vary slightly from numbers cited in previous reports.

SOURCE: "Patterns of Global Terrorism: 1993." U.S. Department of State, Publication No. 10136, p. 69.

FIGURE 12.4 International Terrorist Incidents Over Time (continued)

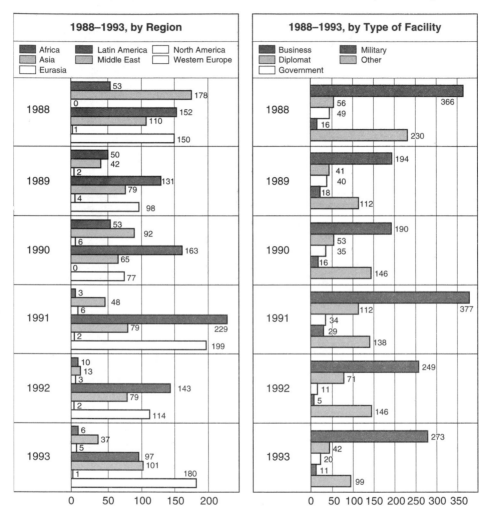

SOURCE: "Patterns of Global Terrorism: 1993." U.S. Department
of State, Publication No. 10136, April 1994, p. 70.

FIGURE 12.5 International Terrorist Incidents, 1993

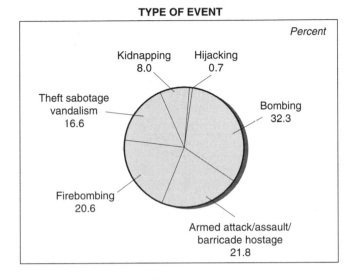

TYPE OF EVENT

Percent

Kidnapping 8.0

Hijacking 0.7

Theft sabotage vandalism 16.6

Bombing 32.3

Firebombing 20.6

Armed attack/assault/ barricade hostage 21.8

SOURCE: "Patterns of Global Terrorism: 1993." U.S. Department of State, Publication No. 10136, p. 69.

3. In terms of both the type of facility targeted, and the type of victim there has been in recent years a continuous dominance of "business" as the target of choice for most terrorist attacks. From the year 1988 forward, terrorists have apparently chosen targets other than the military, government, or diplomatic personnel, who had in earlier years been their prime targets. The only other category which indicates a strong position as "favorite" for terrorist attacks is "other," which according the U.S. State Department includes grocery stores, restaurants, and other such "dangerous" places.

The final observation, to be drawn from the last graph in this series, Figure 12.5, is that, as noted in an earlier chapter, bombing has indeed become the preferred, if not the exclusive method of modern terrorists. Bombs have, of course, several advantages. They are impersonal. As terrorist attacks shift more and more toward what had been regarded in many societies as proscribed targets, it is psychologically less of a strain to bomb a victim whom the attacker may never see than to deliberately kill at close range one of those "proscribed" targets.

Bombs are also easy to make, relatively inexpensive, and increasingly effective, thanks to modern technological advances. They can be detonated remotely, thus reducing the danger to the attacker. Their method of delivery can vary quite widely, in order to counter security measures. They can be sent by mail, wired under a car, dropped from a plane, driven into a compound on a truck, concealed in a briefcase, or carried aboard an airplane in luggage. Bombing is limited only by the attacker's imagination and the security counter-measures in the target area.

As the graph indicates, bombs have long been the favorite weapon of terrorists. But this love affair between terrorists and bombs has become increasingly evident in recent years, as bombs easily outstripped all other forms of attack in international terrorist incidents. In 1993, for example, only one other terrorist event accounts for a comparable number of incidents. Bombing and fire-bombing account for more than 50 percent of the total events recorded for that year.

These graphs, then, reinforce the trends noted earlier: Terrorism is becoming increasingly lethal (bombs are designed usually to kill masses of people, not individuals) and random, as the victimization of "others" becomes the rule rather than the exception in terrorist events. Terrorist incidents increased in number at an alarming rate during the 1980s, and have begun to reflect a pattern of increase in the mid-1990s, after declining for three years.

One other group of statistics may be of interest in evaluating trends in terrorism. It has been stated repeatedly that terrorism has become "internationalized." One facet of such an "international-ization" has been discussed: the evolving of a "network" linking ter-rorist groups and their supporters worldwide. Another facet of this internationalization can be seen in the following: the spillover of terrorist violence whose roots or causes lie in one region, but whose attacks are carried out in a variety of different regions. The "Pat-terns of Global Terrorism" the U.S. State Department for 1987 details this spillover of Middle East terrorism into other nations in 1986. The U.S. State Department records indicate that 50 such "spillover" events occurred in that year. Of these, 43 took place in Western Eu-rope. Altogether, spillover events occurred in 16 different countries. Sixteen nations became victims, in many different ways, of one or more terrorist event whose real target was far away. Such nations are compelled to watch their cities and their citizens become en-meshed in violent struggles over which they may have little direct control.

It is worth noting, then, that the increased movement toward peace in the Middle East may contribute to a corresponding decline in terrorism in Europe, since there will be less terrorism to "spillover." It is also possible that individuals and groups dissatisfied with the peace process, and not willing to make attacks which might cause the deaths of their own people, may seek to export terrorism to other regions. The World Trade Center bombing in New York could be an incident giving credence to this trend's potential, as could the hijacking of the French plane by individuals dissatisfied with the efforts to end the Algerian conflict. At this time, there is too little data to conclude that this will be true in the twenty-first century, but these are at least disturbing indications of this potential trend.

CONCLUSIONS

> The world community is now required to deal with unprecedented problems arising from acts of international terrorism. . . which raise many issues of a humanitarian, moral, legal, and political character for which, at the present time, no commonly agreed rules or solutions exist.[3]

The world community must meet the challenge of terrorism. If it is indeed a condition for which there is no known cure, then let us at least seek to understand the phenomenon in order to better cope with its presence in our midst.

To recognize the existence of terrorism is not to recognize its right to exist, or its inevitability. A doctor, faced with an epidemic, must first recognize the problem, and then take steps to deal with it, at least in terms of containment and perhaps prevention. Similarly, students of world social, legal, political, and security issues today must study the phenomenon of terrorism in order to better cope with its presence in the world today.

Just as that hypothetical doctor facing that epidemic has restraints on what he may do to handle the problem, so nations searching for ways to cope with modern terrorism must exercise restraint in their responses. Nations must weigh the cost, in terms of the loss of liberties and freedoms, against the gains achieved in subduing terrorism, recognizing that to sacrifice too many liberties may well be to give terrorists the victory they seek: the destruction of democratic systems. The cost of winning some battles against terrorism may be too great.

But to concede that there are some ways in which a nation or a people may not combat terrorism is not to concede that terrorism cannot be fought, or is in any way acceptable. Regardless of the cause, terrorism is not an acceptable mode of behavior and cannot be permitted to prevail unchecked. The end does not, and can never, justify the means. To attempt to remedy perceived acts of injustice by committing even greater acts of injustice neither solves anything nor excuses anything. As Robert Friedlander notes: "Human atrocity is not an excusing condition, but rather a moral wrong which affects all humankind."[4]

EVALUATION

Consider the following statement concerning the danger of terrorism in the modern world. Is this an accurate assessment of the situation, or are there other "overriding" concerns which should be taken into consideration?

> The greatest threat posed by terrorists now lies in the atmosphere of alarm they create, which corrodes democracy and breeds repression . . . If the government appears incompetent, public alarm will increase and so will the clamor for Draconian measures.
> —Brian Jenkins, "Upgrading the Fight Against Terrorism"

> So in the Libyan fable it is told
> That once an eagle, stricken with a dart,
> Said when he saw the fashion of the shaft,
> "With our own feathers, not by other' hands
> Are we now smitten"
> —Aeschylus, *Wisdom of the Ages*

SUGGESTED READINGS

Friedlander, Robert A. "Terrorism and National Liberation Movements: Can Rights Derive From Wrongs?" *Case Western Reserve Journal of International Law,* vol. 13, no. 2 (Spring 1981).

Livingstone, N.C. "Taming Terrorism: In Search of a New U.S. Policy." *International Security Review*, vol. 7, no. 1 (Spring 1992).

Nanes, Allan S. "The Changing Nature of International Terrorism." Congressional Research Service, Library of Congress (March 1, 1985).

"Patterns of Global Terrorism: 1987 and 1993." U.S. Department of State, Publication No. 9661 (August 1988) and Publication No. 10136 (April 1994).

Schultz, G.P. "Terrorism and the Modern World." *Terrorism* (1985) pp. 431-447.

Wright, Robin, and Norman Kempster. "Experts Fear New Bombings: Terrorist Attacks May Be Increasing." *Miami Herald*, January 1, 1989.

ENDNOTES

1. See Brian Jenkins' paper on "The Future Course of Terrorism" (Santa Monica, CA: Rand, 1989).
2. N.C. Livingstone, "Taming Terrorism: In Search of a New U.S. Policy," *International Security Review*, vol. VII, no. 1 (Spring 1992) p. 17.
3. Statement by Kurt Waldheim, made July 9, 1976, before the U.N. Security Council at the beginning of the Council debate over the Israeli Entebbe raid. See the *New York Times,* July 10, 1976, reprinted in the *Wall Street Journal*, July 29, 1976, p. 10, col. 4.
4. Robert A. Friedlander, "Terrorism and National Liberation Movements: Can Rights Derive From Wrongs?" *Case Western Reserve Journal of International Law*, vol. 13, no. 2 (Spring 1981) p. 310.

INDEX

A

Abbu Abbas, 33, 90
Abortion issue, 49
Abu Daoud, 196
Abu Nidal, 4, 70, 71, 105
   case study, 73–74
Abu Nidal Organization, 87, 90
Achille Lauro hijacking, 4, 6, 32, 140, 180, 182
Action Direct (France), 3, 100
Adams, James, 102, 106, 109
Aerial hijacking. See Skyjacking
Africa, state terrorism in, 78, 79
African National Congress (ANC), 49, 101
Age, of modern terrorists, 68–69
Air piracy, 32
Airport security, U.S., 206–8, 216
Akache, Zohair, 179
Al-Assad, Hafez, 91–94, 95
Al-Banna, Sabri, 4, 70, 71
Alexander, Yonah, 88
Alexander II, Tzar, 28, 29, 30, 63
Algeria, terrorist training in, 121
Al-Ghussein, Jawaeed, 103
Al-Hassan ibn Sabbah, 106–7
Allende, Salvador, 86
Al-Wazir, Khalil, 172
Ambushes, as terrorist tactic, 139–40
Amin, Idi, 79
Amnesty International, 83, 85
Amplification effect, 143
Anarchism, 38–39
Anthrax, 132
Arafat, Yassir, 33, 60, 134, 135, 221, 223
Arendt, Hannah, 82, 219
Argentina, state terrorism in, 77, 79, 80
Armenian genocide, terrorism and, 25–26
Arm of the Lord, 48
Arms sales, 89–91
Arsenal of weapons, increase in, 33

Arson
   as terrorist tactic, 137–38
   terrorist training in, 124–25
Aryan Nations, 48
Asia, casualties of terrorism in, 226–28
Assad, Rifat, 114
Assassinations, 20–22
   diversity of targets, 139–40
   political, 12, 22–24, 31
   terrorist training in, 125
Assets of terrorism, 96
Athens, international arms trade and, 90
Attentat clause, 160–61
Audience, as terrorism component, 8, 9
Austria, international arms trade and, 89–90
Authorized terror, 14
Automatic weapons, 127, 129–30

B

Baader-Meinhoff gang, 64, 70, 101, 104, 106, 111, 190
Bakunin, Mikhail, 28
Balkan states, revolutionary terrorism in, 26
Ballesteros, Juan Mata, 114
Banality, terrorism and, 219–22
Barrett, David, 187–88
Beckwith, Col. Charles, 180
Begin, Menachim, 46, 63, 173
Belief system, terrorist, 44–47
Bell, J. Boyer, 14
Biological agents of destruction, 131–33
Biological attacks, as terrorist tactic, 141
Black Hand, 26
Black September, 104, 171, 174
Blanqui, Louis August, 38
Bolivia, state terrorism in, 79
Bombing
   as terrorist tactic, 136–37
   terrorist training in, 124–25